# Learn ...k

*by*

## MARY FOSTER

(*formerly Head of Housecraft Department, Bromsgrove High School and Sir James Smith's School, Camelford*)

SECOND EDITION

HEINEMANN EDUCATIONAL BOOKS
LONDON

Heinemann Educational Books Ltd
LONDON   EDINBURGH   MELBOURNE   AUCKLAND   TORONTO
HONG KONG   SINGAPORE   KUALA LUMPUR   NEW DELHI
NAIROBI   JOHANNESBURG   LUSAKA   IBADAN
KINGSTON

ISBN 0 435 42501 3

© Mary Foster 1966, 1971
First published 1966
Reprinted with corrections 1967
Reprinted 1968, 1969
Second (metric) Edition 1971
Reprinted 1972, 1973, 1974, 1976, 1978

Published by
Heinemann Educational Books Ltd
48 Charles Street, London W1X 8AH
Made in Great Britain at
The Pitman Press, Bath

# Contents

| Chapter | | Page |
|---|---|---|
| 1. | Food Values | 1 |
| 2. | Meal Planning<br>Serving and Presentation of Meals<br>Table Laying | 10 |
| 3. | Food Requirements for Different Age Groups and Occupations | 16 |
| 4. | Marketing | 19 |
| 5. | Storage of Food at Home | 20 |
| 6. | Cooking Food | 23 |
| 7. | Common Cookery Terms | 28 |
| 8. | Handy Measures | 30 |
| 9. | Simple Hors d'Œuvres | 31 |
| 10. | Stocks and Soups | 33 |
| 11. | Fish | 41 |
| 12. | Meat | 56 |
| 13. | Vegetables | 80 |
| 14. | Sauces | 96 |
| 15. | Cheese | 105 |
| 16. | Eggs | 113 |
| 17. | Puddings and Sweets | 120 |
| 18. | Pastries | 139 |
| 19. | Scones | 144 |
| 20. | Cakes | 147 |
| 21. | Biscuits | 165 |
| 22. | Fillings and Icings | 169 |
| 23. | Bread and Yeast Mixtures | 174 |
| 24. | Reheated Dishes | 180 |
| 25. | Beverages | 183 |
| 26. | Invalid Cookery | 187 |
| 27. | Vegetarian Cookery | 190 |
| 28. | Preserving | 194 |
| 29. | Use of Convenience Foods | 206 |
| 30. | Time and Labour Saving Devices | 208 |
| INDEX I | | 211 |
| INDEX II | | 219 |

# Preface

This book is designed to cater for the needs of the Secondary School pupil. The step-by-step recipes it contains eliminate the need for the pupil to record all her basic work. It is hoped that it will prove valuable from the first stages in Cookery up to 5th form standard, and also as a basic recipe book for use at home. All theory has been made as concise as possible; it covers the scope of the Cookery section of the C.S.E. examination and will also be useful as quick revision for the G.C.E. 'O' Level Examination in Cookery.

The author wishes to thank Miss Heald for allowing her to use the diagrams of cuts of meat which appear in 'Better Cookery' by Mrs Aileen King; also Miss Margaret Dale for her help in preparing the manuscript.

**Conversion to Metric Measurement**
This book has been converted to metric measurement in preparation for the scheduled change-over to metric system planned for 1975.

In working out recipes, 25 grammes has been used as the basic unit in order to give ease of calculation, and recipes have been balanced according to standard proportions.

In some recipes, reference is made to a 'standard' egg (which weighs approx. 25 g) and this is in order to keep the proportions for a particular recipe correct. This is especially important in the creaming method of cake making. Where really large eggs are used, some slight variation in proportion may be necessary.

E.g. for a Victoria Sandwich, calculate on

'2 eggs and their weight in fat, sugar and flour.'

Where tin sizes are given, existing and commonly used tins have simply been measured and expressed in centimetres.

# 1. Food Values

If a housewife is to feed her family wisely and keep them in good health, it is helpful if she has some knowledge of the nutritive value of foodstuffs.

## THE NUTRITIVE VALUE OF FOODS

Most of the food we eat is in a very complex form; it is made up of basic substances which can be divided into the following main groups:

1. Proteins
2. Fats
3. Carbohydrates
4. Vitamins
5. Mineral elements
6. Water
7. Roughage

The basic substances are known as 'nutrients' and each one has a specific part to play in the diet and in the proper nutrition of the body. Human beings usually take in a 'mixed diet' in which all the above nutrients are represented.

## FUNCTIONS AND SOURCES OF THE MAIN FOOD CONSTITUENTS

### 1. Proteins

The word 'protein' is derived from a Greek word meaning 'taking first place'.

*Function:* Proteins are essential to life being necessary for the building up of new tissue during growth of the body, and the repair of damaged and broken down cells.

Proteins also provide a source of energy for the body, though this is only a secondary function.

*Composition:* Proteins are very complex chemical substances and are made up of simpler units known as 'amino acids'. There are many different amino acids but ten of these are essential for growth and repair of body tissues.

If a food contains the ten essential amino acids it is known as a '1st Class' or 'complete' protein. (These are mainly the animal protein foods.)

If a food is lacking in one or more of the essential amino acids it is known as a '2nd Class' or 'incomplete' protein. These include the vegetable protein foods.

*Sources:* 1st Class Protein: meat, fish, eggs, milk, cheese.
2nd Class Protein: nuts, cereals (wheat, barley, oats, etc.), pulses (peas, beans, lentils).

## 2. Fats

*Function:* Fats form a highly concentrated source of fuel and energy for the body. Fats can be stored in the body, particularly under the skin where it forms an insulation helping to keep the body warm; also around delicate internal organs, e.g. kidneys, helping to protect them. Stored fats provide a reserve of fuel for the body. A meal containing fat is more satisfying than one prepared without it.

*Sources:* Fats can be of either animal or vegetable origin. Some fats are in the form of oils, i.e. they are liquid at room temperature.

ANIMAL FATS: From meat—dripping, suet, lard, bacon fat.
From fish—fish liver oils, flesh of oily fish.
From milk—cream, butter, cheese.
From eggs—fat is contained in the yolk.
Some margarine.
Also used in cakes, pastry, general cooking.

VEGETABLE FATS: Some margarine is made purely from vegetable oils.
Olive oil.
Frying oils—cottonseed oil, sunflower oil, maize oil.
Nut oils, e.g. ground nut oil.
Peanut butter.
Trex; Spry; compound cooking fats.

(N.B. Fat is sometimes found hard to digest. It should always be taken with some carbohydrate food which will make digestion easier, e.g. bread and butter, fried bread.)

## 3. Carbohydrates

All carbohydrates, with the exception of glycogen* are of vegetable origin. They can be divided into three main groups—sugars, starches and cellulose.

*Function:* Carbohydrates are necessary as the chief (and most immediate) source of energy in the body.

They also act as 'protein sparers'. Without carbohydrates the body would derive much of its energy from proteins, depriving proteins of their main function of 'body building'. For this reason, protein foods should always be eaten with some carbohydrate food—e.g. bread and cheese, fish and chips, etc.

*Sources:*

(a) SUGARS: Glucose—in ripe fruits, sweets, honey, some vegetables, etc. (Glucose can be absorbed very rapidly in to the blood stream and so can be given as a quick source of energy for invalids, athletes.)

* *Glycogen:* Excess carbohydrate taken in by the body may be converted to fat and stored; or it may be stored in the liver in the form of 'glycogen'. It is sometimes known as 'animal starch'.

Cane and beet sugar (sucrose), added to cooking, cakes, biscuits, drinks, etc.
Syrup; treacle; jam
In milk (lactose or milk sugar)
In malted foods (maltose or malt sugar)

(b) STARCHES: All cereals—wheat, oats, barley, rice, maize, etc.
All cereal products—flour, cornflour, semolina, etc.
Foods made from cereal products—bread, cakes, puddings, pastries, biscuits, etc.
Potatoes
Bananas

(c) CELLULOSE: This is a complex carbohydrate. It forms the fibrous structure of plants, fruits and seeds. Cellulose does not form available food. See 'Roughage'.

## 4. Vitamins

Vitamins are chemical substances which are found in minute quantities in foodstuffs, the absence of any one of which will cause a corresponding 'deficiency disease'. (Severe deficiency diseases due to the lack of vitamins are almost unknown in this country today but still occur in poorer countries and where food is scarce, particularly in the Middle and Far East.)

Vitamins are of two types:

(a) Fat Soluble—Vitamins A, D, E, K
(b) Water Soluble—Vitamins B complex, C

**Fat Soluble Vitamins**

VITAMIN A

This vitamin is also known as the 'anti-infective vitamin' and 'axerophthol'.

*Functions:* Vitamin A is necessary for:
 (i) normal growth and development in children;
 (ii) the health and protection from disease of the mucous membranes such as those found in the linings of the throat and respiratory tract and the digestive tract; it also protects the skin;
 (iii) the health of the eyes and the adaptability of the eyes to dim light.

*Sources:* Vitamin A is found in animal foods. Carotene is known as the 'vegetable precursor' of Vitamin A. It is obtained from the orange colouring found in carrots and most orange, yellow and green vegetables and fruits. During digestion, the body can convert carotene to Vitamin A; after conversion, only one unit of Vitamin A is obtained from three units of carotene.

| Vitamin A | Carotene |
|---|---|
| Meat, liver, kidney | Orange and yellow vegetables and fruits |
| Oily fish | |
| Fish liver oils | Carrots, turnips |
| Milk cream | Peaches, apricots |
| Egg yolk | Oranges |
| Cheese | Tomatoes |
| Butter | Green vegetables—cabbage, spinach, watercress |
| Vitaminized margarine | |

*Deficiency:* Lack of Vitamin A in the diet can cause:
   (i) retarded growth in children, especially of bones and teeth;
   (ii) an unhealthy condition of the mucous membranes of the respiratory and digestive tracts, so that mucus is not secreted properly. In this condition, the membranes can quickly become infected;
   (iii) nightblindness, when the eye is unable to adapt itself to dim light. In extreme cases, an eye disease known as xeropthalmia and finally total blindness can result.

## Vitamin D

This vitamin is also known as the 'anti-rachitic vitamin' and 'calciferol'.

*Functions*
   (i) It is necessary (together with calcium and phosphorus) for the formation of sound bones and teeth.
   (ii) It is necessary for the absorption of calcium and phosphorus from the intestine.

*Sources:* There are two main sources from which Vitamin D can be obtained: (i) from food; (ii) by the action of sunlight on the body.
   (i) *Food sources:* Vitamin D is found in foods similar to those containing Vitamin A—animal fats, oily fish, fish liver oils, egg yolk, milk, cheese, butter, vitaminized margarine.
   (ii) *Action of sunlight:* Vitamin D can be produced in the body itself by the action of sunlight (or ultra-violet light) or ergosterol, a substance present in the layer of fat under the skin.

*Deficiency:* Lack of Vitamin D in the diet can cause:
   (i) disturbances in the absorption of calcium and phosphorus from the intestine;
   (ii) rickets in children; osteomalacia or bone softening in adults.

## Vitamin E

*Function:* Not a great deal is known about this vitamin. It is thought to have an effect on fertility.

*Sources:* Wheat germ, milk, green vegetables, watercress. There is usually a good supply of the vitamin in a mixed diet.

*Deficiency:* May be a cause of sterility.

## Vitamin K

*Function:* This vitamin is one of the factors necessary in the clotting of blood.

*Sources:* Green vegetables.

## Water Soluble Vitamins

### Vitamin B Complex

At least eleven different substances form the group known as the 'Vitamin B Complex'. Of these, the three most important in the diet are:

Vitamin $B_1$ (also known as thiamine and aneurine);
Vitamin $B_2$ (also known as riboflavine);
Nicotinic acid (also known as niacine).

### Vitamin $B_1$

*Functions:* Vitamin $B_1$ is necessary for:
  (i) the release of energy from carbohydrate foods;
  (ii) proper growth in children;
  (iii) general good health;
  (iv) the health of the nervous system.

*Sources*

| | |
|---|---|
| Whole grain cereals | Lean meat; bacon |
| Wholemeal flour; National flour | Pulses |
| Bemax (wheat germ) | Eggs |
| Yeast; Marmite | Fish |
| Liver, kidneys, heart | Small amount in milk |

*Deficiency:* Lack of Vitamin $B_1$ in the diet can cause:
  (i) a check in the growth of children;
  (ii) general depression and fatigue;
  (iii) nervous irritability and inflammation of the nerves. A prolonged lack of Vitamin $B_1$ can lead to beri-beri, a disease of the nervous system causing paralysis. This disease is found in the Far East where many of the poorer people live on a diet of polished rice. (In polished rice, the outer skin which contains thiamine has been removed.)

## Vitamin B₂

*Functions:* Similar to those of Vitamin B₁.

*Sources:* Similar to those for Vitamin B₁.

| | |
|---|---|
| Whole grain cereals | Milk, cheese, eggs |
| Wholemeal and National flour | Yeast, Marmite |
| Bemax | Green, vegetables, pulses, nuts |
| Meat, liver | |

*Deficiency:* Lack of Vitamin B₂ in the diet can cause:
(i) retarded growth in children;
(ii) general depression;
(iii) unhealthy skin and digestive disorders;
(iv) soreness of the mouth and tongue;
(v) mistiness of the eyes and blurred vision.

## Nicotinic Acid

*Functions:* It is necessary for:
(i) the release of energy from carbohydrate foods;
(ii) normal growth in children;
(iii) general good health, especially of the nervous system and skin;
(iv) proper digestion.

*Sources:* Similar to those for Vitamin B₁.

| | |
|---|---|
| Whole grain cereals | Lean meat, liver, kidney |
| National and wholemeal flour | Fish |
| Bemax | Vegetables |
| Yeast, Marmite | |

*Deficiency:* Lack of nicotinic acid in the diet causes:
(i) retarded growth in children;
(ii) rough sore skin;
(iii) digestive upsets and diarrhoea;
(iv) mental disorders.

Prolonged lack of nicotinic acid can cause the disease pellagra.

## Vitamin C

This Vitamin is also known as 'Ascorbic acid'.

*Functions:* Vitamin C is necessary for:
(i) the general health of the body and skin;
(ii) the healing of wounds and fractures;
(iii) the health of gums and teeth;
(iv) prevention of the disease 'scurvy'.

*Sources:*   Citrus fruits                         Tomatoes
             Rosehips (rosehip syrup)              Fresh green vegetables
             Blackcurrants (blackcurrant           Small amount in milk
               syrup and purée)

*Deficiency:* Lack of Vitamin C can cause:
  (i) unhealthy skin;
  (ii) slow healing of wounds and fractures;
  (iii) unhealthy condition of gums and teeth;
  (iv) tiredness and depression;
  (v) retarded growth in children.

In severe cases, a lack of Vitamin C can cause the disease scurvy, characterized by swollen and painful gums and joints and internal haemorrhages.

*Loss of Vitamin C:* Vitamin C is easily lost during the preparation and cooking of food. It is soluble in water and is mainly lost by soaking green vegetables instead of washing them quickly, and by careless and prolonged cooking in large quantities of water.

Vitamin C is destroyed by heat and for this reason, green vegetables and fruit should be eaten raw whenever possible. It is destroyed by oxidation; chopping and grating uncooked vegetables allows more oxygen to attack and render the vitamin useless.

There is some Vitamin C in fresh milk though this is largely destroyed if the milk is left exposed to the sun, or if it is heated.

## 5. Mineral Elements

About one twentieth of the total body weight is made up from inorganic material obtained from the mineral elements present in our food. There are nineteen different mineral elements present in the body; some (e.g. calcium, phosphorus, iron, sulphur) are necessary in relatively large amounts; others (e.g. iodine, copper, zinc) only in very small amounts and these are known as 'trace elements'. Mineral elements are necessary to form the skeletal structure of the body, are present in every body cell and in all body fluids. Each element is specific in its action. As with vitamins, the lack of any particular mineral element can cause a corresponding deficiency disease. The most important mineral elements in the diet are calcium, phosphorus, iron, iodine, sulphur and sodium chloride.

CALCIUM

*Functions:* It is necessary for:
  (i) the normal formation and hardening of bones and teeth;
  (ii) the clotting of blood;
  (iii) the proper functioning of muscles.

*Sources:* Milk, cheese; bread and flour (calcium fortified); green vegetables; hard water.

*Deficiency:* Lack of calcium causes:
  (i) poorly developed bones and teeth in children; in severe cases, rickets can occur;
  (ii) soft and brittle bones in old people;
  (iii) failure of blood to clot properly;
  (iv) muscular cramp.

## Phosphorus

*Functions:* It is necessary for:
  (i) the normal hardening of bones and teeth, together with calcium;
  (ii) forms an essential part of nerve and brain tissue and is present in every body cell.

*Sources:* It is found widely distributed in foods—meat and meat products; milk; dairy products; green vegetables; fish, etc.

## Iron

*Functions:* Iron is necessary for the formation of haemoglobin, the pigment present in red blood corpuscles. Haemoglobin is essential for the transport of oxygen in the blood.

*Sources:* Lean beef, corned beef; liver, kidney; egg yolk; dried fruit; green vegetables; spinach, watercress, parsley; plain chocolate. The iron content of foods can be increased by the use of iron knives and cooking utensils.

*Deficiency:* Lack of iron in the diet can cause anaemia.

## Iodine

*Functions:* Iodine is necessary for the proper functioning of the thyroid gland.

*Sources:* Fish; sea food; vegetables (if the soil has an iodine content); water; iodized table salt.

Iodine is derived from soil and water. It is frequently found that soil in mountainous areas is deficient in this mineral element.

*Deficiency:* In an adult, a deficiency of iodine can cause a disease of the thyroid gland known as goitre. If a child is born to a mother suffering from a severe lack of iodine it is possible that the child may be a cretin.

## Sulphur

*Function:* Necessary for the health of the skin.
*Sources:* Protein foods, green vegetables, onions.

SODIUM CHLORIDE (or common salt)

Sodium chloride is present in all body fluids and is necessary for the correct functioning of muscles. A lack of salt in the body can cause muscular cramp. Salt is continually lost in sweat and in urine and must be replaced in foodstuffs, or added to cooking.

## 6. Water

About three-quarters of the total body-weight is made up by water.

*Functions:* Water is necessary for:
  (i) the formation of all body fluids;
  (ii) the excretion of waste material from the kidneys and in sweat;
  (iii) maintaining body temperature by perspiration;
  (iv) aiding the digestion and absorption of food.

Water is continually lost from the body by excretion, perspiration and from the lungs and must be replaced.

*Sources:* Water, drinks and beverages, fruit and vegetables. Present in varying amounts in most foods.

## 7. Roughage

Roughage is composed of cellulose, a complex carbohydrate. It cannot be digested but adds bulk to the diet, helping the elimination and excretion of waste material from the digestive tract.

*Sources:* Cell walls of all fruit and vegetables; skins and seeds of fruits; stalks and ribs of leaves in vegetables; cereals, etc.

# 2. Meal Planning

## SERVING AND PRESENTATION OF MEALS

Several factors affect the pattern of meals taken during the day in any household. Family circumstances, the working hours of different members of the family, and to some extent the part of the country lived in, can all make a difference.

A substantial breakfast should always be eaten to give a good start to the day; allow enough time to eat it without hurrying!

Dinner is the main meal of the day. If dinner is eaten in the evening, lunch should be a lighter meal. If dinner is eaten at midday, it may be followed by either Afternoon Tea or Supper, or by High Tea and then a Bedtime Snack.

Afternoon Tea consists of small sandwiches, often scones, and small cakes with tea to drink.

With dinner in the middle of the day, supper should be a fairly substantial meal, though one which can be easily and quickly prepared. Often supper dishes can be made while cooking during the morning.

High Tea usually consists of a hot or cold savoury dish often eaten with bread or rolls and butter; there may or may not be a sweet; scones or bread and butter with jam; cakes; tea to drink.

The snack at bedtime usually consists of a drink, often a milky one, and something small to eat—a sandwich or biscuits, or biscuits and cheese if this is not found indigestible at night.

The housewife must plan meal times which are best suited to the needs of her family. Frequently it is only at mealtimes that the family are together and this should be a pleasant occasion with a happy and relaxed atmosphere. This can only be achieved with careful planning. In planning meals, the following points should be taken into consideration:

(*a*) **Food Value:** Meals should be well balanced nutritionally; foods from each group of nutrients should be included in all meals. In planning any meal, it is easiest to decide first on the main protein content (e.g. meat, fish, cheese, etc.) and afterwards plan the accompaniments and other dishes.

(*b*) **The Needs of Different Members of the Family:** Age is important. There may be a baby or a toddler to cater for; grandparents or elderly relatives may live with the family and have special food requirements. Remember that, in general, a boy eats more than a girl and a man more than a woman. In any family, it may be necessary to prepare food for an invalid or convalescent. Food requirements also vary according to the occupations of different people. A manual worker, say a farm worker or a miner, will use more energy than a sedentary worker, and therefore the amount of energy giving food (carbohydrates and fats) should be increased for the manual worker. At the same time, a good intake of body building and protective foods (proteins, mineral elements and vitamins) must be maintained. For example:

*Lunch for a Manual Worker:*
Brown Stew and Dumplings
Brussels Sprouts
Boiled Potatoes

Jam Cap Pudding
Custard

*Lunch for a Sedentary Worker:*
Grilled Lamb Chop and Tomato
Gravy
Brussels Sprouts
Creamed Potatoes

Fresh Fruit Salad and Cream

(*c*) **Money Available for Food:** Food is probably the biggest single item in the housewife's budget. It is false economy to cut down on money for food; unless properly fed, the health of the family can suffer. Remember that it is not always the dearest foods which have the highest food value. Cheaper cuts of meat, such as shin of beef, breast and neck of mutton, are just as nutritious as dearer joints; herrings and mackerel are cheap and have high food value; cheese provides an economical and excellent source of protein. For example:

*A Cheap Meal:*
Irish Stew
Carrots


Fruit Crumble
Custard

*An Expensive Meal:*
Mixed Grill with Mushrooms
and Tomatoes
Maître d'Hotel Butter
Green Salad
Chipped Potatoes
Fresh Fruit

Fruit and vegetables in season are at their cheapest and best, and full use should be made of garden produce if it is available. Always try to buy the right quantities of foods to avoid waste, and make good use of any 'left overs'.

(*d*) **Fuel Economy:** As far as possible, take care to plan meals which will make economical use of the cooker. Cooking facilities may be limited in some cases so that the housewife can only prepare simple meals.

*A Meal using the Stove Top only:*  *Using the Oven only:*
   Fried Liver and Bacon        Braised Stuffed Breast of Mutton
      Gravy                      Mirepoix of Vegetables
   Runner Beans              Jacket Potatoes
   Creamed Potatoes

                                 Queen of Puddings
   Stewed Fruit
   Custard

(*e*) **Time:** The type of meal prepared must partly depend on how much time the housewife has available; she may have small children to look after, or she may be out at work all day. Where time is limited, use can often be made of convenience foods and automatic timing on cookers. Careful shopping and the wise use of a refrigerator can also save a lot of time.

(*f*) **Choice of Food:** Careful selection of dishes and foods for different meals is important. Any meal should be suitable for the occasion whether it is a family meal or a special occasion. Whatever dishes are chosen, they should be within the housewife's capabilities—it is better to make something simple very well than an elaborate dish badly.

Try to give variation and interest in meals by introducing new recipes with old favourite ones. Even though some recipes may be great favourites, do not repeat them too often. Look for fresh recipes and new ideas which you can often find in magazines and newspapers; cut out and keep the best of these and start your own recipe book.

Likes and dislikes of certain foods may have to be considered. It is not always wise to give way to dislikes with children—their dislike of a food is sometimes only imaginary!

Meals prepared should be suitable for the time of year, making use of fresh fruit and vegetables and cold meals in summer, and hot stimulating meals in winter. For example,

*A Summer Meal:*                *A Winter Meal:*

   Scotch Eggs                Mixed Vegetable Soup
   Summer Salad
   Creamed Potatoes        Steak and Kidney Pie
     or Rolls and Butter     Carrots
                                   Potatoes
   Lemon Meringue Pie

                                   Baked Stuffed Apples
                                   Custard

In any meal there should be variety in flavour and texture. Try not to repeat flavours—for example, tomato soup followed by **tomatoes** as a vegetable. There should be crispness or 'bite' in any meal to contrast with softer food. Always try to make meals as colourful and attractive as possible.

## Preparation of the Meal

When planning a meal, consider how long each dish will take to cook and make sure that all dishes are finally ready at the same time and in the correct order. For example, if a casserole is being prepared for the first course (cooking time 2½—3 hours) and a pudding which will bake in ¾ hour is being made, the pudding should be put into the oven when the casserole has been in for about 2 hours. It is of no use to put the two dishes in at the same time and then have to 'keep the pudding warm' until it is needed.

In preparing a meal, allow time at the end for serving the dishes, preparing sauces and garnishing. With careful timing, meals can be served punctually.

## Presentation of Meals

One's enjoyment of even a well cooked meal can be spoiled if it is not well presented. As food is being prepared, the cook should check flavourings and make sure that everything is properly seasoned. Poorly flavoured food is insipid and unappetizing. Consistencies should also be corrected where necessary.

The choice of serving dishes for the food is also important. Food crowded into a small dish can never be shown to advantage; equally, a dish which is far too large should not be selected. Try not to choose a dish of a colour which will clash with the food. Food should be attractively garnished, and garnishes should be colourful and neat. Take care not to over-garnish—a small piece of parsley in the centre of the dish looks far better than several large pieces. Try to serve suitable sauces or accompaniments with meals whenever possible. Hot food should be served hot, in heated dishes and on heated plates. Cold food should be really cold. A table neatly set with a crisp cloth, well polished cutlery, china and glass, and in a tidy dining room, are all important.

## TABLE LAYING

Table laying plays an important part in the serving of any meal and an attractive table can add greatly to one's enjoyment. When laying the table, the housewife should consider the food to be eaten and make sure that all the necessary dishes and cutlery are available. The table setting will largely depend on the type of meal and the occasion: for any meal, china, glass and cutlery should be well polished and the cloth clean. Nowadays, family snack meals are sometimes eaten in a dining kitchen, or on a plain formica top table.

## Choice of Cloth
Breakfast: check or seersucker cloth
Lunch or Dinner: plain linen cloth (usually white) or linen mats
Afternoon Tea: small embroidered or lace-edged cloth
High Tea or Supper: embroidered or bordered linen cloth.

**Place Setting:** Each person's place setting is called a 'cover'.

Cutlery is placed in order of courses working from the outside and should be 2 cm in from the edge of the table. A tumbler (or wine

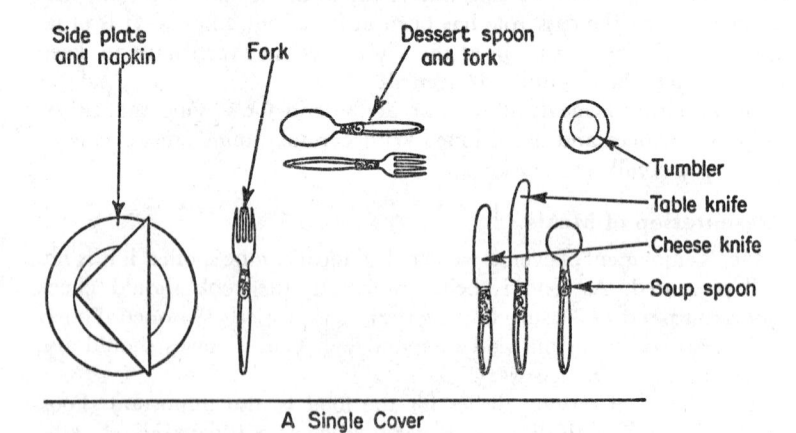

*A Single Cover*

glass) is placed on the right above the knives. The side plate is placed on the left hand side. The table napkin can be put on the side plate or in the centre of the cover; it should be neatly folded or, for a family meal, rolled in a serviette ring.

**Laying the Complete Table:** Each person's place should be set. Heat resistant mats should be placed on the table where necessary.

Meat should be carved, or the main dish served by the host or hostess; the carving knife and fork are placed at the side of the meat dish. Vegetable dishes should be handed to guests so that they can help themselves. Serving cutlery should be conveniently placed on the table. Where space is limited, meat can be carved or vegetables served from a side table.

The cruet should be placed where it can be easily reached or passed. Where the table is large, or there are many guests, there should be a cruet between four people.

Any flower decoration on the table should be low so that people can see over it.

Tea or coffee can be poured on a side table and handed to guests.

Where cups are set on the table, they should be placed near the person who will pour.

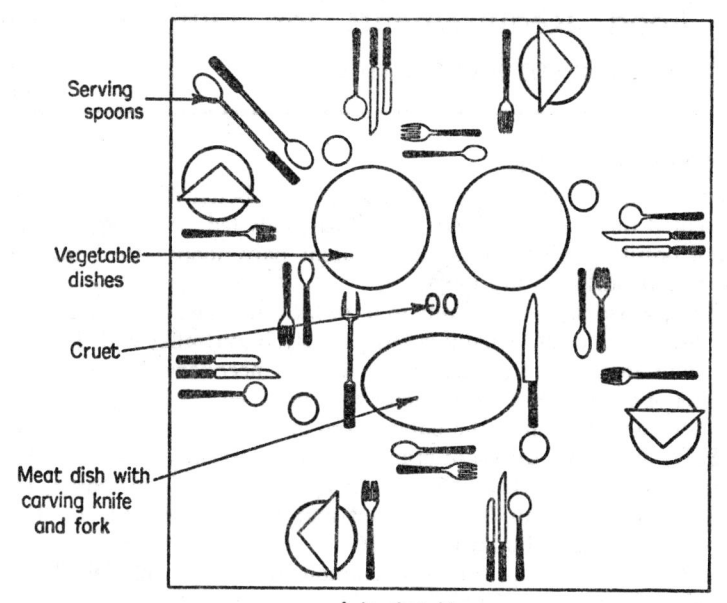

*A lunch table*
(Labels: Serving spoons; Vegetable dishes; Cruet; Meat dish with carving knife and fork)

**Setting a Trolley:** Afternoon Tea is frequently served on a trolley. The shelves should be layed with embroidered or lace-edged trolley cloths or large traycloths.

The teapot and hot water jug, milk jug and sugar basin, teacups and saucers and teaplates should be placed on the top shelf. Teacups should be neatly placed with handles pointing in the same direction and teaspoons at the same angles. Small napkins should be folded and placed between each plate, and tea knives on top of the plates if necessary.

Plates with food should be placed on the lower shelves of the trolley.

# 3. Food Requirements for Different Age Groups and Occupations

**The Baby** (0-1 years)

A baby which can be breast fed often has a better start and is more contented than one which has to be artificially fed; if natural feeding is not possible, substitutes such as patent baby foods, dried milk or cows' milk (diluted) are used.

A baby's stomach is very tiny so feeds have to be small and frequent. For the first month, a baby is fed exclusively on milk, with feeds at 3-4 hour intervals, and during the night if necessary. Between feeds a drink of boiled water with glucose may be given.

After about a month, the baby is also given cod liver oil (Vitamins A & D) and small drinks of orange or blackcurrant juice or rose-hip syrup (Vitamin C) Gradually the quantity of food is increased, the period between meals is lengthened and the baby is able to sleep through the night without food.

From 3 months onwards, small amounts of more solid foods are introduced—powdered cereals may be included in the mid-day feed; by 4-6 months, small quantities of raw egg yolk and cereal can be given at breakfast time, and puréed vegetables and fruit such as carrots, spinach, apples, prunes at lunch time. New flavours should be introduced gradually and given at the beginning of the feed, with milk at the end.

Between 6-9 months the first teeth appear and the baby should be given something to chew on such as rusks or baked crusts. Gradually the amount of solid food given should be increased and milk feeds decreased, and by 9 months to 1 year, the baby should be eating a mixed diet. Foods should be puréed, mashed or cut up finely to eliminate most of the roughage, though as more teeth appear the child will be able to chew food.

As soon as possible, the baby should be encouraged to drink from a cup and later to feed itself with a teaspoon, though help must be given when needed.

**The Toddler** (1-5 years)

Throughout this stage the child is growing rapidly and should have a plentiful supply of body building and protective foods (proteins, vitamins and mineral elements). Often the appetite is small so it is wise to see that the essential foods are eaten first and extra energy giving foods are only given at the end of the meal, if needed.

Food should be attractive and colourful. It should be prepared in a way which is easy for a small child to manage: meat should be cut into small pieces, bones removed from fish, surplus fat and other uneatable parts taken away. Food should not be all soft but there should be something to give 'bite' in each meal.

Drinks should include milk and fruit drinks; often small children want tea to copy grown-ups—if given, this should be very weak and milky. Strong tea and coffee should not be allowed.

Different foods and new flavours should be introduced gradually into the child's diet; food fads should be carefully discouraged.

Food should be served in suitable dishes—a straight sided baby plate and a spoon at the earliest stage, and later a plate and a small knife and fork. At this age, children can be taught good table manners and to enjoy properly balanced meals.

Very rich foods such as fried foods, cream cakes, pastries and highly seasoned foods should be avoided. Children should not be allowed to develop the habit of eating between meals.

### The Child of Junior School Age (5–11 years)

During this period the child grows rapidly and uses up a great deal of energy. A good mixed diet should be given. More carbohydrates and fats will be required because of the increased energy of the child, but at the same time care must be taken to provide adequate protein and protective foods.

Throughout this stage new foods should be introduced whenever possible; adults should continue to cultivate good table manners in children of this age when their manners frequently deteriorate, particularly if they have dinner at school.

### The Adolescent (12–17 years)

During this period, the child is very active and uses up much energy. The body grows rapidly and becomes fully developed. Appetites, particularly with boys, tend to be very large.

The adolescent should have well balanced meals; there should be plenty of protein for body building and a good supply of mineral elements, especially calcium and iron. Plenty of fresh fruit and vegetables should be eaten to ensure a good supply of Vitamin C.

### The Sedentary Worker

All meals must be well balanced nutritionally. As the sedentary worker is sitting or standing fairly still for most of the day and not using up a great deal of energy, too much carbohydrate food and fat should not be included in meals. Adequate protein foods, vitamins and mineral elements and fresh fruit and vegetables must be taken.

If packed mid-day meals are eaten, care must be taken that these too are well balanced; it is very easy to include too much carbohydrate food in a packed meal in the form of bread, pastry, cake and biscuits. Adequate protein and fresh fruit should be included.

The sedentary worker should take care to get sufficient fresh air and exercise.

### The Manual Worker

The manual worker has a large output of energy and so the amount of carbohydrate and fat in his diet must be increased. At the same time, meals must supply adequate protein and protective foods.

In general meals will need to be large, and there should be three full scale meals a day; it may also be necessary to provide snacks between meals.

Extra water and drinks will be needed to replace that lost by sweating. Salt will also be lost in sweat. In hot climates, workers are often provided with salt tablets.

### The Old Person

If an old person is fit and well cared for, there may be no need to change the pattern of meals to which he has become accustomed. Generally, however, the appetite becomes smaller and digestion of certain foods—particularly fatty and fried foods—is often found difficult.

Food should be light and easily digestible. There should be a good supply of protein for the repair of worn tissues. Frequently the bones of an old person become soft and brittle; to combat this, foods rich in calcium and Vitamin D should be given. A good supply of iron should also be given to avoid anaemia. Often an old person's sense of taste is impaired so that foods have to be more highly seasoned if they are to be enjoyed.

Social problems often account for cases of poor nutrition and under feeding in old people; distance from the shops, lack of money where the person is living only on an old age pension, poor cooking facilities, and loneliness are all important. There are also physical problems which may include rheumatism and a weak heart (making shopping difficult), poor sight; also poor teeth and digestion.

# 4. Marketing

'Marketing' or 'shopping' needs to be carefully planned so that it can be done as quickly and economically as possible. Is is helpful if the housewife thinks out the main meals she intends to have for a few days ahead. This not only ensures that there is variety in the meals, but also helps her to budget carefully. When shopping for food, it is always wise to buy the best quality which can be afforded; remember though, that it is not always the dearest food which has the highest food value.

Before shopping, look in the larder; see what food there is to be used up; also check to see if any replacements are necessary, either in dry stores, convenience foods, fats, etc. Make a shopping list and try to plan your route so that shopping is done methodically.

Whether you shop at a village store or a big supermarket, try to choose a shop where there is a quick turnover so that goods are always fresh. Take advantage of 'special offers', but do not buy them for the sake of doing so; such goods are only bargains if you really need them! Often, because of their big and fast sales, large stores and supermarkets can offer branded goods at lower prices than the small shop can afford. But supermarkets, by their easy shopping methods and usually good displays, often tend to make customers buy more than they really need.

Only order food by telephone if it is really necessary; it is far more satisfactory to visit the shops so that you can compare values. Make sure you know the appearance of really fresh foods, meat, fish, fruit and vegetables. Take full advantage of foods 'in season' (particularly fresh fruit and vegetables) as then they are at their cheapest and best.

It is both interesting and helpful to keep an account of how housekeeping money is spent.

**Hygiene in Shops:** Wherever you shop, try always to choose the cleanest shops. Carelessly handled food prepared in unclean conditions can be the cause of digestive upsets or even severe food poisoning. The shop itself should be scrupulously clean. Assistants serving food should wear clean protective overalls. They should not handle food, but use tongs or paper for lifting it whenever possible. Food and money should not be handled at the same time.

Unwrapped food (e.g. cakes and bread) set out on display should be protected by glass, so that customers cannot breathe over it. Cooked meats and meat products should be stored in a refrigerated cabinet if possible. It is essential with these that they are sold quickly and that supplies are always very fresh. Neither smoking nor animals should be allowed in food shops. Precautions should be taken to keep flies off all food.

# 5. Storage of Food at Home

Many foods have to be purchased in fairly large quantities, or perishable foods may have to be bought before they are needed, and careful storage is necessary if they are to be kept in good condition.

For most foods, a cool, well ventilated larder is the best storage place, and a refrigerator for perishable goods. Whatever the food being stored, it should be protected from dust and flies, both of which can carry harmful bacteria.

## STORAGE OF INDIVIDUAL FOODS

**Milk:** Ideally, store milk in the refrigerator. If this is not possible, it should be kept in a cool dark place, such as on a tiled slab, or stone floor in the larder. Milk is best kept in the bottle with the cap on. Any milk put in a jug should not be tipped back into the bottle, and the milk jug should be covered to keep out dust and flies. After use, wash the milk jug thoroughly, scald it and allow to drain. Care should be taken not to mix one day's milk with a previous day's supply. If the milk is in a jug in the refrigerator, keep it away from cheese, fruit or other strong smelling foods, so that their flavour is not absorbed into the milk.

**Cheese:** Do not buy very large quantities as cheese goes dry if stored too long. Keep cheese in a polythene box or container in a refrigerator. Alternatively, keep it loosely wrapped in greaseproof paper in a cool larder.

**Meat:** Whenever possible, buy meat on the day it is to be used. If it has to be kept, put the meat on a clean plate, cover lightly with greaseproof paper and place in a refrigerator. Where no refrigerator is available, put the meat on a small wire tray standing on a plate, cover with a linen meat cover to protect it from flies, and stand it in a very cool well ventilated place. Meat should not be stored longer than a day in hot weather and two days in cold weather.

**Fish:** Unless a refrigerator is available, fish should be bought and cooked on the same day. To store fish in a refrigerator, remove wrapping paper and place the fish in the tray directly underneath the freezing compartment. Do not store for more than 48 hours.

**Bread:** Bread should be kept in a cool airy place, in a ventilated bread bin or 'crock'. All crumbs should be tipped out of the bread bin every few days, and the bin washed and thoroughly dried once a week.

**Cakes and Biscuits:** Keep in airtight tins, lined with greaseproof paper. Crumbs, also stale cakes or biscuits, should be removed and the tins washed frequently. Cakes and biscuits must not be stored in the same tin or the biscuits will soften and spoil.

'**Dry Stores**': When buying groceries, do not buy too large a stock, as most dry ingredients are better when used fairly fresh.
Keep dry stores in a cool dry place. When packets or paper containers have been opened, it is best to put the remaining ingredients in clearly labelled store jars. For this purpose, screw top jars, plastic containers, special storage jars or tins can be used. These should be emptied, washed and thoroughly dried whenever necessary.

**Frozen Foods**: Where no refrigerator is available, frozen foods should be used within 24 hours of purchase. They may be kept up to 48 hours in the freezing compartment of a domestic refrigerator, or longer in 'deep freeze' compartments. Most new domestic refrigerators now have a 'star grading' on the freezing compartment to show the length of time that frozen foods can be safely stored. Great care must be taken that frozen food which has been allowed to thaw is not refrozen. Some frozen foods, such as vegetables, are usually cooked while still frozen; other foods, such as meat and poultry, are usually allowed to thaw before cooking. In all cases, the makers' instructions should be followed.

**Root and Green Vegetables**: See pp. 80–1.

## FOOD HYGIENE IN THE HOME

If food is to be safe to eat, it is essential that all precautions should be taken to handle, prepare and serve it in the cleanest possible conditions. Food can easily become infected with bacteria which are always present in the air, in water, on all surfaces, on food, and also on and inside our bodies. Not all bacteria are harmful, but many can cause food poisoning which may in some cases be severe or even fatal.

Harmful bacteria can cause food poisoning in two different ways: if infected food is eaten, bacteria can mulitply inside the body and cause illness; alternatively, bacteria may produce toxins or poisons inside the food, and these toxins will cause food poisoning. Most bacteria flourish at ordinary room temperatures though their growth is retarded in very cold conditions, such as those of a refrigerator or deep freeze, and they are usually destroyed by heating to the boiling point of water. For this reason, it is dangerous to merely 'warm up' left-over foods, and great care must be taken to reheat food properly.

Bacteria flourish on protein foods; foods most susceptible to bacterial infection include cooked and uncooked meat, fish, soups, stock, gravy, 'prepared' meat dishes (such as pies, sausages, etc.), duck eggs, ice-cream, synthetic cream, milk, and occasionally tinned food and vegetables.

When preparing food at home, both the cook, and her kitchen, should be scrupulously clean.

**Kitchen Hygiene**: All cooking utensils, cutlery and crockery must be perfectly clean. Wash up in water as hot as possible, using a good detergent. Dishcloths and teatowels must be very clean. They should be washed through in soapy water, rinsed and hung to dry after use, and the dishcloth especially should be boiled at least once a week. Dirty cloths in contact with food or utensils can be a source of infection. At the end of each meal, all food scraps should be disposed of, spare food put away, and all used crockery and cutlery washed straight away. Nothing which can attract flies or mice should be left out in the kitchen.

All working surfaces in the kitchen should be washed each day. The floor must be kept clean; sweep it each day and wash it at least once a week. Any food spilt on the floor must be wiped up straight away. If a waste bin is used in the kitchen, make sure it is covered, so that flies are not attracted. It must be emptied and washed out each day.

**Personal Hygiene for the Cook:** The cook must always wash her hands and scrub her nails well in hot water and with soap before handling food. Similarly, hands must be washed after going to the lavatory, using a handkerchief, or touching anything which may be a source of infection. Any cuts or open wounds on the hands must be covered with clean dressings. The cook should wear a clean protective overall or apron when handling food; hair should be well out of the way. Coughing and sneezing can spread infection. No one suffering from a severe cold, or from any gastric disorder, should handle food.

# 6. Cooking Food

Although some foods, especially fresh fruit and vegetables can be eaten raw, most foods are cooked before they are eaten. Cooking is necessary for several reasons:

(a) Cooked foods are more easily digested and absorbed than raw ones; e.g. in starchy food, such as potatoes and flour the cooking process breaks down the starch grains.

(b) Cooking helps to sterilize food, killing bacteria which may be present.

(c) Cooked food is usually more attractive, both to look at, and to eat. This is particularly true of meat and fish. During cooking, new flavours develop, and these are stimulating to the digestive system.

(d) Many foods can be cooked in several ways and this helps to give variety to meals.

## METHODS OF COOKING

There are two main classes of cooking:
1. Moist methods, including boiling, steaming, stewing and braising.
2. Dry methods, including baking roasting, grilling and frying.

### MOIST METHODS

**Boiling:** In boiling, the food to be cooked is placed in a saucepan and either partly or completely covered with water. Depending on the type of food being cooked, the water may be boiling or cold (e.g. green vegetables have boiling water added; old potatoes are covered in cold water). Salt is usually added to the water.

The pan is brought to boiling point, the heat reduced and the water allowed to boil gently or simmer until the food is soft. The saucepan should have a well fitting lid to prevent undue evaporation of the water.

The liquid left after boiling can usually be used in soup, gravies or sauces to accompany the boiled food.

*Food Suitable for Boiling:* Root and green vegetables (see pp. 82–5); some cuts of meat (see p. 65).

**Steaming:** In steaming, the food is cooked in the steam which rises from boiling water. The food may or may not come in contact with the steam. Foods can be steamed in several ways:

(a) In a steamer with a perforated base, standing over a saucepan of boiling water. The steamer must have a well fitting lid.

This method is suitable for root vegetables, potatoes, steamed puddings, joints of ham or bacon, chicken and some types of fish which should first be wrapped in aluminium foil.

(It is possible to pile up two or more perforated base steamers and cook several foods at once. The base of the steamer, containing the boiling water, can also be used at the same time for cooking potatoes or other root vegetables.)

(*b*) The food to be cooked may be placed in a basin and covered with greaseproof paper or aluminium foil. The basin is then placed in a large saucepan containing enough boiling water to come half way up the basin, and the pan covered with a well-fitting lid. This method is suitable for steamed puddings, especially suet puddings.

(*c*) Small pieces of fish are often steamed by placing between two plates over a saucepan of boiling water.

In steaming, care must be taken to see that the steamer does not 'boil dry'. It should be refilled from time to time with boiling water. Any seasoning added to food being steamed must be sprinkled directly on to the food (e.g. salt sprinkled lightly over vegetables to be steamed). It is useless to add seasoning to the water below a steamer.

Steaming is a slow method of cooking; foods steamed are usually easily digestible. If carefully planned, it can be a very economical method of cooking.

Less of the soluble nutrients are lost from root vegetables and meat which are steamed compared with those which are boiled.

**Stewing:** Stewing is a very long slow and gentle method of cooking. Usually the amount of liquid added to food to be stewed is fairly small; as the food cooks, soluble nutrients pass into the liquid and excellent flavours are developed.

As the stewed food is served in the liquid in which it was cooked, no food value is lost.

Stews can be made in a saucepan on top of the stove, or in a casserole in the oven. In either case, the pot must have a well fitting lid.

Once prepared, stews (and especially casseroles) need very little attention. To make a casserole helps to cut down washing-up, since both meat and vegetables are cooked and served in the same dish.

*Foods Suitable for Stewing:* Tough, and tender, cuts of meat (the meat must be lean); root vegetables are usually added to stews for flavour, (also tomatoes and mushrooms are valuable for flavouring); fruit can be stewed.

**Braising:** Braising is a method of cooking combining both stewing and roasting. It is suitable for some vegetables, such as whole root vegetables and celery; also for cuts of meat which tend to be 'firm' if roasted (see pp. 57, 58).

A strong metal casserole or stewpan with a well fitting lid is used. Cooking on top of the stove, dripping is heated in the pan and the root vegetables are thoroughly browned. Stock is added to cover the vegetables and often additional flavourings of herbs and bacon are added.

The browned meat is placed on top of the mixed vegetables and simmered very gently until tender on top of the cooker or in the oven.

For the final 20–30 minutes of cooking time, the lid is removed from the pan and the braise cooked in a hot oven to brown the meat.

## DRY METHODS

**Roasting, Baking:** The term 'roasting' should really only be applied to the method of cooking meat on a rotating spit in front of an open fire (or other source of radiant heat). Nowadays, most meat is really baked in an oven.

Food to be baked is placed in a preheated oven. In the case of meat and dishes which require long cooking time, it is usual to put them in a hot oven to seal the outer surface, then reduce the heat and cook more gently until the inside is also cooked. (The more intense heat used for the first few minutes of baking seals in meat juices and helps set the shape of bread, cakes and pastries.)

*Foods Suitable for Baking:* Many tender cuts of meat (see p. 60); some fruits and vegetables; cakes, pastries, bread, etc.

**Grilling:** Grilling is a very quick method of cooking. The food is placed directly underneath the intense heat of the grill, and food surfaces are quickly sealed retaining juices and flavour. The heat is then reduced and the food cooked through more gently.

Grilling is only suitable for small and fairly thin foods. (In the case of meat, it must be very tender.) During grilling, it is necessary to turn food frequently to prevent burning and drying.

*Foods Suitable for Grilling:* Chops, steak; liver and kidney (not from ox); bacon, sausages; mushrooms, tomatoes.

**Frying:** Frying, like grilling, is a very quick method of cooking. The intense heat of the fat in frying seals the outer surface of the food so that juices and flavour are retained.

There are three main types of frying:
(*a*)  Deep fat frying
(*b*)  Shallow fat frying
(*c*)  Dry frying.

*Choice of Fat for Frying:* The fat used must be free from water, or it will 'spit' during frying. Choose a fat which has a high decomposition temperature or smoking point. Olive oil, frying oils and white cooking fats made from vegetable oils have a high decomposition temperature and are good for frying, especially deep fat frying. Margarine and most dripping contain a fairly large amount of water and are only suitable for dry and shallow frying. Butter has a relatively low decomposition point and burns quickly.

*Testing the Temperature of Fat for Frying:* Melt and heat the fat. Drop in a 1 cm cube of dry bread. It should turn pale golden in 30–40 seconds. When hot enough for frying, most fats are still and have a very faint haze rising from the surface. A thick haze, or worse still smoke, shows that the fat is burning and is far too hot for adding food. Burnt fat has a bitter flavour and an acrid smell. Food put into fat which is too cool will absorb fat and be greasy. The food may also break up.

*Coating Food to be Fried:* Most foods need to be coated before they are fried. Coating helps to dry the surface of the food (wet foods must never be put into hot fat). Coating also seals in flavour and moisture, and prevents fat entering the food. Coatings include:

Seasoned flour (used for fish, liver, etc.);
Beaten egg, and breadcrumbs or raspings (used for fish, fishcakes, Scotch eggs, etc.);
Batter (used for fish, etc.).

(*a*) DEEP FAT FRYING: Suitable for pieces of fish, reheated foods (Scotch eggs, chips, doughnuts, etc.). The food must be completely coated in either egg and raspings, or batter. Chips must be thoroughly dried before frying. Heat the fat in a deep fat pan (or saucepan) so that the fat does not come more than half way up the pan. As food is lowered into pan, the fat will bubble and rise up. Because of this, the foods must be lowered in gently and carefully. Foods coated in egg and raspings, also chips, can be placed in a basket for cooking; those coated in batter must not be cooked in a basket. The food must be completely covered by the hot fat. The food should be fried gently until crisp and golden and thoroughly heated through, and in the case of chips, soft in the centre.

(*b*) SHALLOW FAT FRYING: Suitable for steak, liver, onions, fish, fishcakes, eggs, etc. The most suitable coatings are egg and raspings, and seasoned flour. Use an ordinary frying pan. Heat sufficient fat to come half way up the food. Lower the food into the hot fat. Cook gently until the first side is golden. Turn carefully taking care not to prick the coating or break the food. Fry until the second side is golden. Make sure the food is thoroughly cooked. In the case of eggs where it is not possible to turn the food, baste with the hot fat during cooking.

(*c*) DRY FRYING: In dry frying, the frying fat is gently extracted from the actual food being cooked—e.g. bacon, sausages. Extra fat is not usually necessary. The very small quantity of fat used in frying pancakes can be regarded as 'dry frying'. Most fried foods need to be drained on absorbent paper. They must be served really hot and freshly cooked. After frying, leave the fat pan to cool down slightly. Strain fat into a clean bowl and allow to go cold. This can be used again for frying.

**CARE WITH FRYING:** Frying can be a dangerous method of cooking unless great care is taken. Boiling fat reaches a temperature of 180°C–215°C and can give a very severe burn; also fat is highly inflammable. When frying, take the precaution of keeping a large flat baking tin, big enough to cover the pan, near the stove. In the event of the fat pan catching fire, this should be placed over the pan immediately to exclude air, and the hotplate should be turned off.

NEVER throw water on burning fat.

NEVER move a pan of burning fat unless absolutely essential.

# 7. Common Cookery Terms

**Au Gratin:** The term is applied to dishes coated with sauce, the surface sprinkled with breadcrumbs and often cheese, and the dish then browned under the grill or in a hot oven. e.g. Cauliflower au Gratin (see p. 109).
**Bake blind, to:** To bake a pastry case without any filling. Greaseproof paper and baking beans are usually put into the prepared pastry case before baking in order to hold the base down.
**Baste, to:** To spoon hot liquid over the surface of foods during cooking, to keep them moist, e.g. basting meat with hot fat during roasting.
**Blanch, to:** To put food into cold water and bring just to boiling point, then to remove the food and plunge it immediately into cold water. This is used to remove skins from almonds and tomatoes, to whiten some foods, or remove strong flavours.
**Bouquet Garni:** A small bunch of mixed herbs, including a piece of thyme, marjoram, parsley and a bay leaf, tied together (or tied in muslin) and used to flavour stews and soups.
**Croûtes:** Slices of bread, 5 mm thick, toasted or fried, cut into small triangles or circles and used to garnish some savoury dishes (e.g. Macaroni Cheese) or for dishing individual portions of some foods (e.g. Scotch eggs).
**Croûtons:** Small 7 mm dice of fried or toasted bread, used as a garnish to accompany purée soups (see p. 40).
**Glaze, to:** A shiny coating given to pastries before baking, by brushing with beaten egg and water, or egg white, or sugar and water syrup.
**Mirepoix:** A mixture of root vegetables, herbs and bacon used as a bed on which to braise meat (see p. 69).
**Panada:** A very thick sauce, usually made by the roux method, used for binding together ingredients for fish cakes, rissoles, etc. (see pp. 96, 181).
**Purée:** Fruit, vegetables, (or sometimes meat) reduced to a pulp by stewing, then pressed through a sieve to give a smooth pulp.
   Purée is also the name given to a group of soups where the cooked ingredients are passed through a sieve (see p. 36).
**Raspings:** Very fine browned breadcrumbs used with beaten egg for coating food to be fried. To make raspings, see p. 182.
**Roux:** A thickening used for some sauces, stews and soups, **made** by cooking together equal quantities of fat and flour.
   A roux may be white or brown, depending on the length of time it is cooked (see pp. 96, 99).
**Simmer, to:** To cook food in liquid which is only just boiling, so that bubbles rise and break gently on the surface.

**Sweat, to:** To cook prepared vegetables gently in a small amount of fat without browning them and in a covered saucepan, until juice runs from the food (see Mushrooms, p. 88).

**Zest:** The very thin coloured outer part of the skin of citrus fruits. The zest contains essential oils which give the flavour to the skin. The white pith underneath the zest is very bitter and should not be used as flavouring.

# 8. Handy Measures

The following measures can be used as a rough guide when cooking. However, they are not completely accurate and should not be relied upon, for example, when making cakes, pastries or large mixtures.

*Flour, cornflour, custard powder*          *Sugar, rice*
  25 g = 1 heaped tablespoonful           25 g = 1 level tablesp.
  100 g = 1 small teacup

*Syrup, treacle*
  25 g = 1 tablespoonful (warmed)
  50 g = 1 tablespoonful (cold)

*Margarine, cooking fat, etc.*
It is useful when opening a new block to mark it off in suitable portions (e.g. 50 g) with the back of a knife.

*Liquids*
  1 large tumbler holds approx. 250–300 ml
  1 average size teacup holds approx. 200 ml

*N.B.*
  1000 g (gramme) = 1 kg (kilogramme)
  1000 ml (millilitres) = 1 litre

When measuring with a spoon, a 'spoonful' should contain as much of the ingredient above as below the bowl of the spoon.

Half a spoonful is a level spoonful.

Quarter of a spoonful is a level spoonful divided in half lengthways.

*Comparative Oven Temperatures.*

| Description | Gas 'Regulo' | Electric, °C | Electric, °F |
| --- | --- | --- | --- |
| Very slow | ¼ | 100° | 200° |
|  | ½ | 110° | 225° |
| Slow | 1 | 120° | 250° |
|  | 2 | 130–140° | 275° |
| Moderate | 3 | 150° | 300° |
|  | 4 | 160–180° | 325–350° |
| Moderately hot | 5 | 180–190° | 375° |
|  | 6 | 200° | 400° |
| Hot | 7 | 220° | 425° |
| Very hot | 8 | 230° | 450° |
|  | 9 | 240° | 475° |

# 9. Simple Hors d'Œuvres

Hors d'œuvres can be served as the first course of a luncheon or dinner menu. They consist of small portions of well flavoured foods, attractively served, and are intended to stimulate, and not satisfy, the appetite. As hors d'œuvres are usually served cold, they can be prepared and placed on the table before guests arrive; this can be a great help to the cook.

## SIMPLE HORS D'ŒUVRES

**Grapefruit** (serves 2)

    1 *grapefruit*         1 *cocktail or glacé cherry*
    1 *tsp. caster sugar*

1. Wipe grapefruit. Cut in half (across stalk). Remove pips.
2. Using a small pointed knife or grapefruit knife, loosen each segment of fruit from the skin.
3. Then cut round the edge of the fruit, just inside the pith, and then underneath to loosen it from the outer skin. Carefully hold the segment skins in the centre and lift them out without disarranging the fruit.
4. Sprinkle lightly with caster sugar; garnish with half a cocktail or glacé cherry.
5. Place grapefruit halves in sundae glasses; chill well before serving.

**Melon**

1. Wipe the melon skin and cut into slices. Remove seeds.
2. Cut each half in slices (cut a medium-sized melon into about six pieces). Chill the melon slices well.
3. Serve the slices on individual plates. Hand ground ginger and caster sugar separately in small dishes.

**Tomato Juice** (serves 2)

    300 *ml canned tomato juice*
    1 *tsp. Worcester sauce*

1. Add Worcester sauce to tomato juice and stir in.
2. Chill well before serving.

## MIXED HORS D'ŒUVRES

In a mixed hors d'œuvres, six or more small items should be offered. The hors d'œuvres may be arranged on a divided hors d'œuvres dish, or in separate bowls placed on a tray or, alternatively, **arranged on** individual plates.

Foods suitable for mixed hors d'œuvres include:

*Vegetables:* Lettuce, tomatoes, beetroot, spring onions, cucumber, celery, peas, cress, potato salad, gherkins, olives, etc.

*Fish:* Sardines, anchovy fillets, prawns, shrimps, etc.

*Eggs:* Sliced hard boiled egg.

*Cheese:* Small cubes of hard cheese, such as Cheddar or Gruyère.

*Meat:* Boiled ham, cold chicken, sliced salami, liver sausage, etc.

In selecting ingredients for a mixed hors d'œuvres, a good variety should be given. It is not good to choose, for instance, too much meat or fish, but ingredients should be varied.

## A Mixed Hors d'Œuvres (serves 4)

*Potato salad*     *Boiled ham*
*Tomato*           *Hard boiled egg*
*Cucumber*         *Cold chicken*
*Shrimps or Prawns*  *Gherkins*

1. *Potato Salad:* Cut 2 cold cooked potatoes in 1 cm dice. Add 1–2 tablespoons. mayonnaise and mix lightly together. Place in a dish, and sprinkle with finely chopped parsley or chives.
2. *Tomatoes:* Wash and dry 2 tomatoes. Slice thinly across the stalk and arrange neatly in a dish. Pour over French dressing. Sprinkle with finely chopped onion.
3. *Cucumber:* Peel if liked. Slice very thinly and arrange in a dish. Sprinkle with salt.
4. *Shrimps:* Peel 100 g shrimps. Arrange in a dish. Sprinkle lightly with lemon juice. Garnish with very small lettuce leaves, or cress.
5. *Boiled ham* (50 g): Slice thinly. Cut into attractive shapes (triangles or 5 cm squares) and arrange in a dish.
6. *Hard boiled eggs:* Cut 2 hard boiled eggs in thin slices. Arrange in a dish and coat thinly with mayonnaise. Garnish with parsley.
7. *Cold chicken:* Slice thinly and arrange in a dish. Sprinkle with chopped spring onion or chives.
8. *Gherkins:* Cut 8 pickled gherkins to form a 'fan', or serve whole.

Instead of arranging in separate dishes, these ingredients can be made into individual mixed hors d'œuvres. Great care must be taken in arranging them attractively.

Serve the mixed hors d'œuvres with small bread rolls and butter.

# 10. Stocks and Soups

In making soup, the liquid used may be stock or water or milk, or a mixture of these.

## STOCK

Stock forms the best basis for most soups, stews and gravies, and the use of a good quality stock greatly adds to the flavour of the finished dish. Stock is made by the prolonged simmering of bones or meat and vegetables in water.

### To Make Stock

*Bones, meat scraps, skin, giblets, etc.*     6 *peppercorns*
   *(raw or cooked)*                          1 *onion*
*Cold water to cover*                         1 *carrot*
1 *level tsp. salt*

1. If fresh bones are being used, have them chopped by the butcher. Wash any fresh meat and cut up very small so that all possible flavour will be extracted. Remove all fat from meat or bones.
2. Put bones, meat scraps and seasoning into a large saucepan, cover with water and bring to the boil. Simmer gently for 1–2 hours. (Alternatively, the stock can be made in a casserole in the oven.)
3. Wash and peel the vegetables; leave them whole. Add the raw vegetables to the stock and simmer for 1–2 hours longer.
4. Strain stock into a clean pan or jug, and allow to cool. Discard the meat and vegetables.
5. Before use, remove any fat which has hardened on the surface of the stock.

Use stock as quickly as possible after making. If the stock to be used straight away, fat can be skimmed off with a spoon or removed with absorbent paper. If it has to be kept overnight, store in a refrigerator or a very cool place, and boil up before use. There is a great danger in keeping stock for too long as it is an ideal 'breeding ground' for bacteria which can cause a severe form of food poisoning.

**Foods Suitable for Making Stock:** Bones (raw and cooked); scraps of cooked meat, skin, trimmings, etc.; cheap cuts of meat such as shin of beef, knuckle of veal, etc.; carcases of poultry; giblets; root vegetables (raw); gravy which has no added thickening.

When making stock from fresh ingredients, allow 500 g bones or meat to 1 litre water. If using left-over meat scraps, bones or carcase of

poultry, or any other cooked ingredients, they must be absolutely fresh·
**Foods Unsuitable for Stock:** Green vegetables; potatoes; bread; thickened gravy; fat.
**Types of Stock:** Brown stock is made from beef or mutton, or beef bones. White stock is made from knuckle of veal or poultry carcase. Vegetable stock is made from root vegetables or vegetable trimmings only. Fish stock can be made from fish heads, skin and bones.
**The Use of 'Stock Cubes':** Making stock takes a long time, and for a small quantity it is not always worth making it from the fresh ingredients. As a substitute, bouillon-cubes can be dissolved in water to give a well flavoured stock. Meat or yeast extracts can also be used though the flavour is much stronger and more definite, and is not always so suitable. Using bouillon-cubes for a large quantity of stock is expensive, though compared with making home-made stock it is more economical in time and fuel. Alternatively, a meaty bone can be stewed with the other ingredients when making soup and removed before serving, rather than first making stock with the bone.

## SOUPS

A good soup can form an excellent beginning to lunch or dinner in winter or summer, or it may be used 'informally' as the main course of a family meal, or for supper.

Soups can be prepared from simple ingredients and need not be expensive. They are an economical way of making a meal more substantial and satisfying.

**Classification of Soups:** Soups can be classified according to the method of making:

(a) Thickened soups, e.g. White Vegetable Soup
(b) Purée soups, e.g. Tomato Soup, Mushroom Soup
(c) Broths, e.g. Chicken Broth
(d) Clear soups or Consommés, e.g. Consommé à la Jardinière
(e) Fish soups or Bisques.

**Food Value:** The food value of soup is variable. In a thickened soup, a purée, or a broth, where all the ingredients are eaten, the food value will be fairly high; in a clear soup where there is little or no added meat or vegetable, there is little nourishment. (Stock itself has no nutritive value.) A well flavoured soup stimulates the appetite, and this is its main value.

**Amount of Soup to Serve:** As the first course in a 3 course meal, allow 150–200 ml per person; as a main course, allow 250–300 ml per person.

### THICKENED SOUPS

These can be thickened either by adding blended flour or cornflour, or by using a roux as the basis of the thickening. The consistency should be like that of thin cream.

## White Vegetable Soup (serves 3-4)

Diced vegetables to fill a 250 ml measure (carrot, turnip, onion or leek, celery, peas, etc.)
Bouquet garni: 1 bay leaf, sprig each of thyme, parsley, marjoram

15 g margarine
500 ml white stock or water (boiling)
150 ml milk
15 g plain flour
Salt and pepper

1. Wash and peel small quantities of mixed vegetables. (Avoid large quantities of strong flavoured vegetables such as turnip and onion.)
2. Cut the vegetables into neat 5 mm dice.
3. Melt the margarine in a saucepan and 'sweat the vegetables'.
4. Add the boiling stock and bouquet garni. Cover the pan. Reduce the heat and simmer for approx. 8-10 mins until vegetables are cooked. Remove the bouquet garni.
5. Blend the flour with the milk to form a smooth paste.
6. Add the blended flour to the soup. Stirring all the time, bring to the boil, and cook for 2-3 mins.
7. Season the soup with salt and pepper. Taste and correct the seasoning if necessary.
8. Serve in a heated soup tureen.

## Kidney Soup (serves 3)

2 lamb kidneys
25 g lean bacon
1 small onion
1 medium sized carrot
15 g dripping

500 ml brown stock or water
Salt and pepper
15 g plain flour blended with 100 ml of stock or water

1. Prepare the kidneys (see p. 62). Soak in cold water for 15 mins. Cut into 5 mm dice.
2. Remove the rind and dice bacon.
3. Wash and prepare vegetables. Cut into neat 5 mm dice.
4. Melt dripping in a saucepan. Fry the diced kidney and bacon until brown. Remove from pan.
5. Add onion and fry until golden brown.
6. Add carrot, stock, ½ level tsp. salt, 2 shakes pepper, also the kidney and bacon.
7. Bring to the boil; simmer gently for ½ hour.
8. Blend the flour with 100 ml of stock or water; add to the soup. Stirring all the time, bring the soup to the boil and cook for 2-3 mins.
9. Taste and correct seasoning.
   Add 2-3 drops gravy browning if necessary to give a rich brown colour.

## Mushroom Soup (serves 3)

| | |
|---|---|
| 100 g mushrooms | 250 ml white stock or water |
| ½ small onion | 250 ml milk |
| 15 g margarine | Salt and pepper |
| 15 g plain flour | |

1. Skin the mushrooms and slice very thinly or chop finely. Chop onion very finely.
2. Melt margarine in a saucepan; cook the vegetables very gently without browning until tender (approx. 5 mins.).
3. Add flour to make a roux, and cook 1–2 mins.
4. Remove pan from heat; gradually blend in the stock and milk.
5. Stirring all the time, bring soup to the boil; reduce heat and simmer gently for 1–2 mins.
6. Season soup with salt and pepper. Taste and correct seasoning if necessary.

## *PURÉE SOUPS*

In this type of soup the main ingredients are cooked in stock, water or milk until soft; then the whole is pressed through a sieve to form a purée. A small quantity of blended flour or cornflour is added to the purée to absorb fat and to bind the purée in the liquid. The finished consistency of a purée soup should be like that of thin cream.

## Celery Soup (serves 3–4)

| | |
|---|---|
| 15 g margarine | Bouquet garni |
| 500 g celery | 15 g plain flour ⎫ to 500 ml purée |
| 1 small onion | 150 ml milk ⎭ |
| 500 ml white stock or water | |
| ¼ tsp. salt; 2–3 shakes pepper | Garnish: *Croûtons*\* |

1. Clean celery. Cut up into 2 cm pieces. Prepare onion and slice thinly.
2. Melt margarine in a saucepan; sauté the vegetables until the fat has been absorbed.
3. Add stock, seasoning, bouquet garni. Cover pan, bring to the boil then reduce heat and simmer gently until vegetables are soft. (½–¾ hour).
4. Press the vegetables through a nylon or hair sieve to form a purée. Rinse saucepan.
5. Measure purée and return to the pan.
6. Blend flour with stock or milk and add to the purée. Stirring all the time bring to the boil and cook gently for 2–3 mins.
7. Taste and correct seasoning if necessary.
8. Serve with croûtons handed separately.

\* To make croûtons, see p. 40.

## STOCKS AND SOUPS

### Mixed Vegetable Soup (serves 3-4)

15 g *dripping or margarine*  
1 *onion*  
1 *carrot*  
1 *stick celery*  
*Small piece turnip*  
1-2 *tomatoes*  

500 ml *stock or water*  
¼ tsp. *salt; 2-3 shakes pepper*  
*Bouquet garni*  
15 g *plain flour* ⎫  
150 ml *stock or milk* ⎭ to 500 ml purée  
Garnish: *Croûtons*

1. Wash and prepare vegetables according to kind. Slice up thinly.
2. Continue as for Celery Soup.
3. Serve with croûtons handed separately.

### Mushroom Soup (serves 3-4)

15 g *margarine*  
100 g *mushrooms*  
½ *small onion*  
500 ml *white stock or water*  

¼ tsp. *salt; 2-3 shakes pepper*  
15 g *plain flour* ⎫  
150 ml *milk* ⎭ to 500 ml purée  
Garnish: *Croûtons*

1. Wash mushrooms; chop up roughly. Skin, then slice, onion thinly.
2. Continue as for Celery Soup.
3. Serve with croûtons handed separately.

### Onion Soup (serves 3-4)

15 g *margarine*  
250 g *onions*  
1 *small piece celery*  
500 ml *white stock or water*  

¼ tsp. *salt; 2-3 shapes pepper*  
15 g *plain flour* ⎫  
150 ml *milk* ⎭ to 500 ml purée  
Garnish: *Croûtons*  
*Grated cheese*

1. Skin onions. Slice thinly. Wash and cut up celery.
2. Continue as for Celery Soup.
3. Serve with croûtons and finely grated cheese handed separately.

### Potato Soup (serves 3-4)

15 g *margarine*  
500 g *potatoes*  
1 *small onion*  
1 *small piece celery*  

500 ml *white stock or water*  
¼ tsp. *salt; 2-3 shakes pepper*  
150 ml *milk*  
Garnish: *Chopped parsley*

1. Wash and peel potatoes. Cut up roughly. Prepare onion and celery and slice thinly.
2. Continue as for Celery Soup (Method Nos. 2-5)
3. Add milk (no thickening) and reheat soup.
4. Taste and correct seasoning if necessary.
5. Serve in a soup tureen, garnished with finely chopped parsley.

## Tomato Soup (serves 3)

| | |
|---|---|
| 15 g margarine | 500 ml white stock or water (or juice from tinned tomatoes) |
| 25 g bacon | |
| 500 g tomatoes, or a medium size tin tomatoes | ¼ tsp. salt; 2-3 shakes pepper |
| | Bouquet garni |
| 1 small carrot | 15 g pl. flour ⎫ to 500 ml purée |
| 1 small onion | 150 ml milk ⎭ |
| 1 small piece celery | Garnish: Croûtons |

1. Wash and prepare vegetables according to kind. Slice up thinly.
2. Continue as for Celery Soup.
3. Serve with croûtons handed separately.

## BROTHS

Broths may be served strained or 'clear', or they may have the meat and vegetables used in making them left in the finished soup. No extra thickening is added to bind any ingredients into the liquid.

## Chicken Broth (serves 3-4)

| | |
|---|---|
| 1 chicken carcase (after roasting) | Bouquet garni |
| 1 onion | 1 litre white stock or water |
| 1 carrot | 1 level tsp. salt; 2-3 shakes pepper |
| 1 stick celery | |
| | 25 g rice |

Garnish: *Finely chopped parsley*

1. Put chicken carcase, skin and any trimmings into a large saucepan. Cover with stock or water, add seasoning. Bring to the boil, and simmer gently for 1 hour in a covered pan.
2. Prepare vegetables. Cut up roughly. Add to the saucepan and cook for another hour.
3. Strain the broth; rinse pan.
4. Return broth to the pan; bring to the boil.
5. Add washed rice and cook for 15 mins. until rice is soft.
6. Taste broth and correct seasoning.
7. Serve in a tureen, sprinkled with parsley.

## Scotch Broth (serves 3-4)

| | |
|---|---|
| 500 g scrag end or middle neck of mutton | 1 carrot |
| | Small piece of turnip |
| 40 g pearl barley | 1 litre water |
| 1 onion | 1 level tsp. salt; 2-3 shakes pepper |
| 1 leek | |

Garnish: *2 tsp. finely chopped parsley*

## STOCKS AND SOUPS

1. Put pearl barley in a small saucepan; cover with cold water. Bring to the boil; then strain the barley.
2. Joint the meat and wash. Trim off any fat. Put meat, barley, seasoning and water in a large pan and bring to the boil. Skim well. Cover pan and simmer gently for 1 hour.
3. Prepare vegetables and cut into neat 5 mm dice. Add to the broth and simmer for a further 1 hour.
4. Remove meat from pan. Discard bones, cut meat in 1 cm dice, and return to pan.
5. Taste broth and correct seasoning if necessary.
7. Bring broth to the boil; sprinkle in the chopped parsley and serve immediately.

### CLEAR SOUPS

To make a clear soup or consommé, it is necessary to use a very fine well flavoured stock made from meat. All the flavour should be in the stock, and the vegetables added only form a garnish.

It is expensive to make stock of this quality; stock cubes can be used as a substitute.

### Consommé à la Jardinière (serves 3–4)

500 ml best white stock
150 ml mixed vegetables (carrot, cauliflower, peas)

1. Prepare vegetables according to kind. Shell peas; cut carrot into very small dice; cut cauliflower into very small sprigs about the size of the peas.
2. Cook the vegetables in boiling salted water for 5 mins. until soft.
3. Boil the stock; re-season if necessary.
4. Put cooked vegetables in a heated soup tureen.
5. Pour on the boiling stock. Serve immediately.

### Chicken and Mushroom Soup (serves 3–4)

500 ml chicken stock        1 tsp. finely chopped onion
25 g mushrooms              50 g cooked chicken

1. Peel mushrooms; slice very thinly. Peel onion; chop very finely.
2. Bring chicken stock to the boil; check seasoning.
3. Add sliced mushroom and onion and simmer gently for 20 mins.
4. Cut chicken into 1 cm dice; add to the soup and simmer for 5–10 mins.
5. Serve in a heated tureen.

## To Make Croûtons

Croûtons can be fried in deep fat, or toasted.

*To fry:* Slice bread 5 mm thick. Cut off crusts. Cut bread into neat 5 mm dice. Deep fry in fat at hazing point until golden brown. Drain well and serve on a small dish.

*To toast:* Slice bread 5 mm thick. Toast to an even golden brown on both sides. Trim off crusts. Cut into 5 mm dice.

# 11. Fish

**Classification:** For culinary purposes, fish can be classified as follows:
(a) White fish, e.g. cod, haddock, hake, halibut, plaice, sole, whiting, etc.
(b) Oily fish, e.g. herring, mackerel, salmon, trout, etc.
(c) Shell fish, e.g. crab, lobster, prawns, shrimps, cockles, mussels, etc.

**Food Value**
1st *Class Protein:* a good source.
*Fat:* White fish contains fat in the liver only—fish liver oils; oily fish has fat dispersed throughout the flesh.
*Carbohydrate:* Fish contains no carbohydrate.
*Vitamins:* A and D found in fish liver oils and in the flesh of most oily fish.
*Mineral Elements:* a good source of iodine and phosphorus; also of calcium when the bones are eaten.
*Water:* contains a large amount. In oily fish, fat replaces water in the flesh and not protein.

**Average Composition of Fish**

|  | White | Oily |
| --- | --- | --- |
| Protein | 17.5% | 18.6% |
| Fat | 0.5% | 10.9% |
| Water | 80.0% | 67.5% |
| Mineral Matter | 1.2% | 2.6% |

**Digestibility:** The flesh or muscle of fish is in the form of flakes loosely held together by connective tissue. The connective tissue is made up of collagen which is easily converted to gelatine during cooking. Because of this, fish cooks and becomes tender quickly; the lack of connective tissue makes it easily digestible and a suitable food for invalids.
White fish is more easily digested than oily fish.

**Buying Fish:** Fish should be bought from a reliable fishmonger or, wherever possible, directly from the fisherman.
It must be absolutely fresh as it deteriorates very rapidly, especially oily and shell fish. All fish should be used the day it is bought.
*Points to look for:*
1. No unpleasant smell
2. Eyes bright and not sunken; gills red
3. Flesh firm and a good colour
4. Skin moist and unbroken; plentiful scales

The price of fish is not always an indication of food value; cheaper varieties are often as nutritious, sometimes more so, as expensive fish.

**Quantities to buy per person**
(a) Fillets, cutlets, steaks from large fish, e.g. cod, haddock, hake, halibut, salmon: 150–200 g per person to allow for waste such as skin and bone.
(b) Fillets from smaller fish, e.g. plaice, sole: 2 small or 1 large per person.
(c) Whole fish, e.g. herring, mackerel, trout, dabs: 2 small or 1 medium sized fish per person.
(d) Crab, lobster: 1 medium sized serves two people; 1 large serves three or four people.
(e) Shrimps, prawns: 100 g whole or 50 g peeled, per person.

**Types of Preserved Fish**
(a) *Cured fish:* Fish can be cured by salting or smoking, or both.
Herring—as bloaters, bucklings, kippers, red herrings, salted herrings. They are also pickled to form 'Roll Mops'.
Haddock—as Finnan haddock, smoked haddock, etc.
Cod—as golden fillets when smoked; salted cod.
Salted fish will keep for long periods; smoked fish keeps longer than fresh fish.
(b) *Tinned fish:* It is usually varieties of oily fish which are canned, e.g. salmon, sardine, pilchards, etc. Depending on the variety, fish is either canned in oil or tomato. The canning process softens bones of fish making them edible; bones provide a good source of calcium.
(c) *Frozen fish:* Most varieties of fresh fish, including some shell fish, can now be bought 'deep frozen'. This fish is ready prepared, of good quality and there is no waste. Instructions on the packet should be read carefully; usually it can be cooked in any of the normal ways either while it is still frozen or after allowing the fish to thaw. Frozen fish can be kept in the freezing compartment of a domestic refrigerator for 24 to 48 hours; once thawed, it must not be refrozen.

## THE COOKING OF FISH

**Preparation of Fish before Cooking:** Many varieties of fish, particularly the larger ones such as cod, haddock, halibut, plaice, are prepared by the fishmonger; the head and gut are removed and the fish filleted or cut into steaks or cutlets. Smaller varieties such as herring, trout, mackerel, and sometimes flat fish such as plaice and sole, are bought whole and prepared as follows:

*Round Fish* (e.g. herring, mackerel)
1. Place fish on a piece of paper; trim tail and remove fins with scissors.

2. Hold fish firmly by the tail. Using the back of a knife, scrape fish from the tail towards the head to remove scales. Rinse under cold running water.
3. Cut off head just behind the gills. (If the head is to be left on, eyes and gills should be removed.)
4. Insert scissors in body cavity and cut down the underside of the fish as far as the vent. Scrape out internal parts; keep roe if any. (Roll up all waste in paper and burn.)
5. Remove any dark skin and blood from body cavity by rubbing lightly with salt.
6. Rinse fish in cold water; dry on absorbent kitchen paper if necessary.
7. To remove backbone, slit fish from vent to tail on underside, using a sharp knife. Place fish on a board, skin side up and with flaps opened out. Press firmly along backbone; turn fish over and lift out backbone.

*Flat Fish* (e.g. dabs, plaice, sole to serve whole)
1. Remove scales, if any.
2. Remove gills and eyes (whole head can be removed if preferred).
3. Make a slit into the body cavity just below the head, on the dark side of the fish; remove gut.
4. Rinse out cavity and remove dark skin by rubbing lightly with salt.
5. Rinse fish in cold water; dry on absorbent kitchen paper.

*To Fillet Flat Fish*

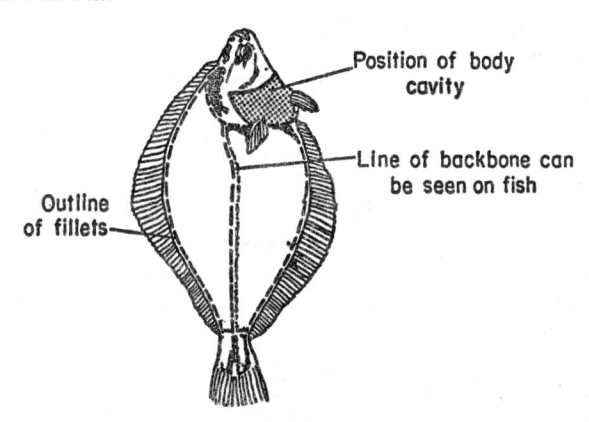

1. Remove scales. Place fish on a board.
2. Using a sharp knife, outline the fillets as shown in diagram.
3. Fillet the pale underside first. Place fish with head away from you; working from the backbone outwards, remove the left fillet cutting

the fish from the bone with long even strokes and keeping the knife flat on the bone. Turn the fish round with head towards you and remove opposite fillet in the same way.
4. Fillet the dark upper side.
5. Rinse fillets in cold water; dry on absorbent kitchen paper.

*To Skin Fillets of Fish:* Place fillet on a board, skin side down and tail towards you. Hold the tail end firmly, using salt on the fingers to avoid slipping. Slide a knife between the flesh and the skin; keeping the knife almost upright, roll the flesh from the skin using a sawing action. It is not necessary to skin all fillets of fish. With flat fish, often only the dark skin is removed. With sole, the fish should be skinned before filleting.

*To Clean Cutlets and Steaks of Fish*
1. Trim fins.
2. With cutlets it may be necessary to remove dark skin, using salt, from inside the 'flaps' of the cavity.
3. Remove bones if necessary, using a pointed knife.
4. Rinse fish in cold water.

**Methods of Cooking Fish:** Fish can be steamed, poached, grilled, baked or fried, or used in 'made up' dishes. Some types of fish are more suitable for certain methods of cooking than others.

**Accompaniments:** In general, fish tends to be rather insipid in flavour and the flesh pale in colour and soft textured. Because of this, accompaniments are important and should provide the necessary colour, flavour and crispness.
  For accompaniments, see individual methods of cooking fish.

## TO POACH FISH

Poaching is suitable for fillets and small pieces of fish (e.g. fillets of haddock, plaice, etc.), for small whole fish (e.g. whiting), and for smoked fish (e.g. finnan haddock, kippers).
  The liquid used for poaching may be water, or milk and water. After poaching, the remaining liquid can be used to prepare a sauce to serve with the fish.

**General Method for Poaching Fish**
1. Prepare fish.
2. Half fill a frying pan with the liquid to be used. Add $\frac{1}{2}$ tsp. salt and 2–3 peppercorns. Bring to the boil.
3. Place fish in pan; cover. Reduce heat and simmer gently until fish is cooked.

**Times for Poaching:** Thick cuts or large pieces—20–30 mins. Thin fillets—6–10 mins. When cooked, the flakes will separate easily and the skin can be lifted from the flesh.

**To serve**

*White fish:* Drain thoroughly; remove skin and bone if necessary. Place on a hot dish and keep hot. Strain liquid and use to make accompanying sauce. Coat fish with sauce, or serve separately. Garnish with slices of lemon and a sprig of parsley. Suitable sauces include anchovy, mushroom, parsley and white sauces.

*Smoked fish:* Drain thoroughly; remove skin and bone if necessary. Place on a hot dish. Garnish with pats of butter.

## TO STEAM FISH

Steaming is a suitable method for cooking whole fish, steaks, cutlets, and fillets (e.g. cod, fresh haddock, hake, halibut, salmon, whiting, etc.). As the water does not come in contact with the fish, less flavour is lost than if the fish were boiled.

**General Method for Steaming Fish**

(a) For whole fish or large pieces:
1. Prepare and weigh fish. Season lightly with salt and pepper.
2. Place fish in steamer and cook over boiling water. Allow 15 mins. per 500 g and 15 mins. over.

(b) For smaller pieces and thin fillets:
1. Prepare fish. Place on a greased heatproof plate.
2. Sprinkle lightly with salt and pepper and lemon juice and dot with margarine or butter.
3. Cover fish with a pan lid or another plate and place over a saucepan of boiling water.
4. Allow to steam until fish is soft, about 10–20 mins. depending on the thickness of the fish.

Test if cooked as for poached fish. When cooked, a white curd-like substance often forms between the flakes of the fish. Serve and garnish as for poached fish. The same accompanying sauces can be used.

## TO GRILL FISH

Grilling is suitable for whole small fish (e.g. herring, mackerel, trout, sole, plaice), and for fillets or cuts of large fish (e.g. sole, halibut, salmon).

**General Method for Grilling Fish**

1. Prepare fish (small whole fish can be grilled with the head on).
2. Heat the grill; grease rack in grill pan with melted butter, margarine or with oil.

3a. For small whole fish such as herring, mackerel, trout—score across flesh on both sides of fish. Brush with melted fat; season lightly. Grill under a moderately hot grill for approx 4–5 mins. on each side.
For small whole flat fish, there is no need to score the flesh. The dark skin can be removed before grilling.

3b. For fillets and cuts of large fish (steaks and cutlets should be about 2 cm thick)—brush both sides with melted fat; sprinkle lightly with seasoned flour.
Grill under a moderately hot grill, turning once only, until golden brown on each side and cooked through.
Cooking time depends on the thickness of fish—for steaks 2 cm in thickness, allow approx. 7–8 mins. each side.

**To serve:** Lift carefully on to a hot dish. Garnish.
**Suitable garnishes:** Grilled tomatoes; watercress or parsley. (Fish served with the head on should have a sprig of parsley over the eye.)
**Suitable sauces:** Mushroom, tartare, served separately. Mustard sauce with grilled herring or mackerel. Alternatively, small pats of maître d'hôtel butter can be placed on the grilled fish.

## TO FRY FISH

Frying is suitable for small whole fish, fillets, cutlets and steaks of fish. Fish can be fried in deep or shallow fat.

**General Method for Frying Fish** (shallow fat)

1. Clean and trim the fish. (Fillets can be skinned if preferred; head should be removed from whole fish.) Wash and dry.
2. Sprinkle fish lightly with salt and pepper.
3. Coat fish.
4. Melt fat in frying pan, sufficient to come half way up the fish, and heat to hazing point.
5. Put coated fish carefully into the frying pan, taking care not to splash the fat; do not overcrowd the pan. (Fillets should be skin side uppermost.)
6. Fry on a moderate heat until golden brown on one side. Turn carefully with a fish slice or palette knife and a fork and fry second side until golden brown.
   *Times for frying:* Thin fillets—allow 2–3 mins. each side; hick pieces, and small whole fish—allow 5–7 mins. each side.
   When cooked, the fish should be soft and the flakes separate easily.
7. Using a perforated fish slice, lift fish from fat and place on absorbent paper.

**To serve:** Serve on a hot dish. Garnish with parsley and slices or quarters of lemon.

Suitable sauces (served separately): Parsley, tartare, tomato.

**Frying Fish** (deep fat)
1. Prepare fish as above.
2. Heat fat to hazing point. (There should be sufficient fat in the deep fat bath to well cover the fish.)
3. Use the basket in the deep fat bath, unless the fish is coated in batter. Cooking times will be shorter than with shallow fat as there is no need to turn the fish.
4. Drain fish well after cooking.
5. Serve and garnish as above.

**Suitable Fats for Frying**

*Shallow frying:* dripping, lard, white cooking fat, cooking oil.
*Deep frying:* white cooking fat, cooking oil.

**To Coat Fish For Frying:** (All 'wet' fish must be coated before frying.)
(a) *Coating with Flour:* This is only suitable for fish to be fried in shallow fat.
1. Clean and dry the fish. Sprinkle lightly with salt and pepper.
2. Sprinkle fish with flour from a dredger, making sure all the fish is covered. Pat flour on firmly; shake off any surplus.

(b) *Coating with Egg and Raspings* (browned breadcrumbs): Suitable for fish to be fried in deep or shallow fat.
1. Clean and dry the fish. Season lightly.
2. Beat egg and pour on to a plate.
   Put raspings on a square of greaseproof paper.
3. Dip fish in beaten egg; brush egg over fish.
4. Lift the fish and drain off any surplus egg.
5. Place fish on raspings and gently shake the paper until fish is completely coated.
6. Lift coated fish on to a board and pat raspings on firmly with a palette knife. Any remaining raspings can be sieved and returned to the storage jar.

(c) *Coating with Batter:* Suitable for fish to be fried in deep or shallow fat.
1. Clean and dry the fish.
2. To make batter:
   50 g *plain flour,*
   ¼ tsp. *baking powder* } (or S.R. flour)
   ¼ tsp. *salt,*
   *approx.* 4 *tablesp. water*

Sieve flour and salt into a basin. Add water gradually to form a smooth batter which will coat the back of the wooden spoon.
3. Dip fish into batter; make sure it is completely coated.
4. Lift fish out using a skewer or a fork. Allow any surplus batter to drain off.
5. Place carefully in the hot fat.

(*d*) *Coating with Oatmeal:* Suitable for herrings and mackerel to be fried in shallow fat.
1. Clean, dry and season the fish. (Fish can be boned or left whole.)
2. Place medium oatmeal on a square of paper, allowing one tablespoonful for each fish.
3. Press fish firmly on to oatmeal, making sure all surfaces are coated. Allow any surplus oatmeal to fall off, but do not shake.

**Kippers, Bloaters:** These may be fried in shallow fat without being coated (or poached in water).

## TO BAKE FISH

Baking is suitable for whole fish, fillets, steaks or cutlets of fish. Often fish baked in the oven is also stuffed. The fish can either be coated and baked in fat, or uncoated and baked in butter or margarine and sometimes milk.

### General Method for Baking Fish

(*a*) *Coated Fish*
1. Heat oven: Regulo 4–5; 180°C (350°F).
2. Prepare fish according to kind. Wash and dry. Coat either in seasoned flour or in egg and raspings.
3. Put cooking fat or dripping into a baking tin and heat to hazing Point. (Fat in tin should be about 5 mm deep.)
4. Place fish in hot fat and baste during cooking.
5. Cook fish until soft.
       Steaks and cutlets, approx. 20–30 mins.;
       small fillets, approx. 10–15 mins;
       whole fish, 10 mins. per 500 g and 10 mins. over.

(*b*) *Uncoated Fish*
1. Heat oven: Regulo 4–5; 180°C (350°F).
2. Prepare fish according to kind. Wash and dry. Stuff if necessary.
3. Season fish lightly with salt and pepper and place in a heatproof dish.
4. Dot with margarine or butter (a small amount of milk can be poured round fish if liked).
5. Cover dish with a lid or greased paper. Bake as above.

# FISH

**To serve:** Lift carefully on to a hot dish. Garnish with parsley and slices of lemon.

**Suitable sauces:** Anchovy, parsley, tartare, tomato.

## To Stuff Fish for Baking

(a) *Steaks and Cutlets:* Using a sharp pointed knife, carefully remove the centre bone. Fill cavity with stuffing. For cutlets it may be necessary to secure flaps with a small skewer or cocktail stick.

(b) *Fillets from Flat Fish:* Skin fillets. Spread stuffing on skinned side. Either roll up from head to tail and bake upright, or fold fillet in three.

(c) *For Larger Fillets:* Cut fish in even sized pieces and spread stuffing on top.

(d) *For Whole Fish*
*Flat Fish:* Clean the fish. (Head can be left on or removed.) Remove fins and tail. The fish can be skinned if preferred. On white side of fish, cut down line of backbone and loosen the fillets on each side to form a centre pocket. Put in stuffing and replace fillets.
*Round Fish:* Scale and gut the fish. Remove eyes and gills. Wash and dry. Fill cavity with stuffing and close with a fine skewer.

## Suitable Stuffings

50 g fresh breadcrumbs
15 g melted margarine
2 tsp. finely chopped parsley
½ tsp. finely chopped thyme

¼ tsp. of salt
Good pinch of pepper
Finely grated zest of ½ lemon
Beaten egg to bind

Mix all ingredients together and add sufficient beaten egg to bind to a stiff consistency. In this recipe, thyme can be replaced by either 25 g finely chopped mushroom, or 25 g finely chopped peeled shrimps.
Allow 50 g breadcrumbs per 500 g fish.

## RECIPES

**Steamed Haddock** (serves 1)

200 g fresh haddock fillet
Salt and pepper
2 tsp. lemon juice

10 g margarine
Garnish: *Parsley*

1. Two-thirds fill a saucepan with water and put to boil.
2. Skin, wash and dry fish; place on a heatproof plate.
3. Sprinkle fish lightly with seasoning and lemon juice, and dot with margarine.
4. Cover with a saucepan lid or another plate. Place over pan of boiling water; allow to steam for approx. 20 mins. or until fish looks opaque and flakes separate easily.

5. Carefully lift fish on to a hot dish. Garnish with parsley.
6. Serve with parsley sauce, handed separately.
(Any liquor from the fish should be added to the sauce.)

**Poached Haddock** (serves 2)

>300 g *fresh haddock fillet*  15 g *margarine*
>250 ml *milk*  1 *tablesp. fresh breadcrumbs*
>¼ *tsp. salt*  1 *tablesp. finely grated cheese*
>4 *peppercorns*
>½ *small onion*  Garnish: *Parsley*
>15 g *plain flour*

1. Skin fish. Place in a frying pan with half the milk. Add salt, peppercorns, and finely sliced onion.
2. Cover pan and poach very gently until fish is just soft (15-20 mins.)
3. Using a fish slice, drain fish and lift carefully into a hot gratin dish. Keep hot.
4. Blend plain flour and cold milk.
5. Strain hot milk in which fish was cooked. Rinse pan. Return strained milk to the pan and bring it to the boil. Add blended flour and bring to the boil, stirring continuously. Cook for ½ min.
6. Remove pan from heat. Gradually add margarine in small pieces and blend in thoroughly, giving a rich creamy sauce.
7. Taste sauce and correct seasoning if necessary.
8. Coat fish with sauce.
9. Sprinkle with cheese and breadcrumbs. Grill until golden brown.
10. Garnish with parsley.

**Grilled Halibut** (serves 2)

>1 *steak of halibut,* 2 *cm thick (approx.* 300-400 g)
>*Salt and pepper*
>15 g *butter or margarine*  Garnish: 15 g *maître d'hôtel butter*
>1 *tsp. plain flour*  (see p. 103).

1. Trim fish. Wash and dry.
2. Brush on both sides with melted butter and sprinkle lightly with seasoned flour.
3. Heat grill. Grill fish under a moderately hot grill until golden brown; turn carefully and grill second side.
Allow 5-7 mins. each side.
4. Serve on a hot dish. Garnish with chilled maître d'hôtel butter.

**Grilled Mackerel** (serves 2)

>2 *medium sized mackerel*  Garnish: *Parsley*
>10 g *margarine*
>*Salt and pepper*

1. Scale, trim and gut the fish. Remove gills and eyes. Wash and dry.
2. Brush with melted margarine on both sides. Season lightly.
3. If fish are very thick, score across flesh on both sides.
4. Heat grill. Grill fish under a moderately hot grill for 4–5 mins on each side. Turn once only during cooking.
5. Serve on a hot dish. Garnish with parsley.
6. Serve with mustard sauce, handed separately.
The recipe is also suitable for Herring.

**Fried Fillets of Plaice** (serves 2)

1 *medium sized plaice*  *Fat for frying*
*Salt and pepper*  Garnish: *Parsley*
To coat: 1 *egg*  4 *slices lemon*
4 *tablesp. raspings*

1. Fillet plaice. Wash and dry fillets and season lightly.
2. Coat in egg and raspings. (Any remaining raspings should be sieved and returned to storage jar.)
3. Heat fat to hazing point. Carefully put in fillets, skin side uppermost, and fry gently until golden brown (about 2 mins.) Turn fish and fry second side until brown.
4. Lift fish from pan on fish slice. Place on absorbent paper on a baking tin. (Keep hot while any remaining fillets are fried.)
5. Serve on a hot dish. Garnish with parsley and place a slice of lemon on each fillet.
6. Serve with tartare sauce, handed separately.

**Baked Stuffed Cod Steaks** (serves 3)

3 *cod steaks*  Garnish: *Parsley*
*Ingredients for Stuffing, using*  2 *slices lemon*
50 *g breadcrumbs*  3 *tomatoes*
15 *g margarine*
*Salt and pepper*
3–4 *tablesp. milk*

1. Prepare cod steaks; remove bone; wash and dry. Sprinkle lightly with seasoning.
2. Make stuffing. Stuff centre of steaks.
3. Place in a heatproof dish; dot with margarine and pour milk round.
4. Cover dish with a lid or greased paper.
5. Bake a third of the way down the oven, Regulo 4–5 or 180°C (350°F), for 20–30 mins. or until fish is just soft and flakes separate easily.
6. Lift steaks on to a hot dish. Garnish with parsley, slices of lemon and baked tomatoes (see p. 89).
7. Serve with parsley sauce, handed separately. (Any liquor after cooking fish should be added to sauce.)

## Soused Herrings (serves 2)

| | |
|---|---|
| 2 medium sized or 4 small herrings | 1 blade mace |
| Salt | 2 thin slices onion |
| 125 ml water | For serving: ½ small lettuce |
| 125 ml vinegar | Watercress |
| 4 peppercorns | 1–2 tomatoes |
| 1 bay leaf | |

1. Scale and trim fish; remove head and gut. Split open and remove backbone (see p. 42).
2. Wash and dry fish and sprinkle with salt.
3. Roll up from head to tail. Pack side by side into a heatproof dish, tails uppermost.
4. Pour over sufficient vinegar and water to cover. Add seasonings, spices and onion.
5. Cover dish and bake half way down the oven, Regulo 4 or 180°C (350°F), for 30–40 mins. or until soft.
6. Remove from liquor, drain and allow to cool.
7. Serve on a bed of green salad and garnish with tomato.

The recipe is also suitable for Mackerel.

## Russian Fish Pie (serves 2–3)

150 g Rough Puff or Flaky Pastry (see pp. 141–3)
Filling: 200 g cod fillet
½ tsp. salt
Pepper                        Garnish: Beaten egg
2 tsp. lemon juice                      Parsley
1 tsp. chopped parsley
100 ml white sauce (coating consistency; see p. 97)

1. Prepare pastry. Roll out to a 20 cm square.
2. Make filling; flake fish. Add seasoning, lemon juice, parsley, and sufficient white sauce to bind the mixture together.
3. Place fish mixture in centre of pastry:

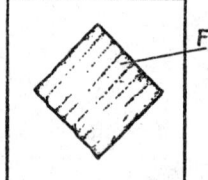

*Filling placed in centre of pastry*

4. Damp edges of pastry and fold to form an envelope shape. Decorate with pastry leaves. Brush with beaten egg.
5. Bake 40–50 mins. a third of the way down oven, Regulo 7 or 220°C (425°F) until pastry is brown (15–30 mins.); then reduce to Regulo 3 or 150°C (300°F) for remainder of time.

FISH

6. Lift on to a hot dish. Garnish with parsley.
7. Serve with anchovy, parsley or tomato sauce, handed separately.

VARIATIONS: Thinly sliced tomato or hard boiled egg can be placed on top of the fish mixture inside the 'envelope'.

## Herring Roes on Toast (serves 2)

200 g soft herring roes
25 g plain flour
½ tsp. salt
Pepper

Fat for frying
2 slices bread, 5 mm thick
15 g butter
Garnish: *Parsley*

1. Wash and dry roes. Coat in seasoned flour.
2. Put into shallow fat which has just reached hazing point. Fry gently for 3–4 mins. until golden brown, turning once during cooking.
3. Drain well.
4. Serve on hot buttered toast. Garnish with parsley.

## Fish Cakes (makes 4–6)

250 g cooked white fish
250 g potatoes, creamed (see p. 86)
1 tsp. finely chopped parsley
2 tsp. lemon juice
1 level tsp. salt, 2–3 shakes pepper

2 tablesp. thick white sauce, or beaten egg to bind
To coat: *beaten egg and raspings*
*Deep fat for frying*
Garnish: *Slices of lemon*
*Parsley*

1. Prepare and boil potatoes (see p. 86).
2. Prepare fish; steam between two plates, over the potatoes.
3. Remove any skin or bone from the fish and flake it up.
4. Drain potatoes when soft and cream them (see p. 86). (If potatoes were 'left over,' mash, and reheat with margarine, milk and seasoning as for creamed potatoes.)
5. Add potatoes to fish, also chopped parsley, lemon juice, seasoning and sufficient white sauce or beaten egg to bind the mixture together.
6. Turn mixture on to a floured board; shape into a thick roll. Divide equally into 4–6 'cakes'.
7. Shape each cake into a round about 2 cm thick, using the hand and a palette knife.
8. Brush with beaten egg, then coat in raspings. Reshape on the board with a palette knife, patting the raspings on well.
9. Fry in deep fat which has just reached hazing point, for 3–5 mins, or until golden brown. (They can be cooked in shallow fat if liked.) Serve on a hot dish, garnished with parsley and slices of lemon. Hand parsley sauce separately.

**Kedgeree** (serves 2)

    250 g *cooked smoked haddock*     *Salt and pepper*
    80 g *Patna rice*     Garnish: 1 *hard boiled egg*, or
    40 g *margarine*     1 *tsp. chopped parsley*

1. Boil rice (see p. 89). Poach haddock (see p. 50).
2. Remove any skin and bone from the fish and flake it.
3. Melt margarine in a saucepan; add rice, flaked fish, salt and pepper. Heat very thoroughly, for 15–20 mins.
4. Pile in a cone shape on a heated dish.

Garnish: *Either:* chop egg white; sieve the yolk and sprinkle them separately on top of the kedgeree.
    *Or:* sprinkle over finely chopped parsley.

## SHELL FISH

All shell fish must be used when very fresh. They should be bought and eaten on the same day and not kept overnight. Unless obtained directly from the fisherman, shellfish are usually sold ready boiled. Oysters are sold raw and the shells should be tightly closed.

**Crab:** a good crab should feel relatively heavy in proportion to its size. The male crab is best having larger claws. Ask the fishmonger to break open the crab; the meat should be firm and pinkish in appearance, have no unpleasant smell and the meat not at all wet.

**Shrimp Patties** (makes 8–10)

    150 g *Rough Puff or Flaky Pastry*     Garnish: *Parsley*
    Filling: 150 ml *white sauce (panada)*     *Whole shrimps*
       (see p. 96)
    *Salt and pepper*
    1 *tsp. lemon juice*
    50 g *peeled shrimps*

1. Make pastry (see p. 141).
2. Prepare patty cases (cut out as for 'Jam Puffs'—see p. 162). Brush with beaten egg. Bake patty cases and lids a third of the way down oven, Regulo 7 or 220°C (425°F), for 15–20 mins. or until golden brown and firm to touch.
3. Remove from oven; using the handle of a teaspoon, carefully take out any soft pastry from the centre of the cases. Return to oven for 1–2 mins. to dry off pastry.
4. Cool patty cases and lids on a wire tray.
5. Peel and chop shrimps.
6. Prepare panada. Season well with salt, pepper and lemon juice. Stir in chopped shrimps.

7. Fill each patty with sauce and put a 'lid' on each. Garnish each with a very small piece of parsley just underneath the lid.
8. Arrange neatly on a dish with a d'oyley or oval dish paper. Decorate dish with whole shrimps and parsley.
The recipe is also suitable for prawns.

**Prawn Curry** (serves 2)

| | |
|---|---|
| 100 g *peeled prawns* | Garnish: *Parsley* |
| 300 ml *curry sauce* (see p. 103) | *Slices of lemon* |
| 80 g *Patna rice* | 4 *prawn heads* |

1. Prepare curry sauce (see p. 103). Simmer 20–30 mins.
2. Peel prawns. Add to sauce and allow to simmer in sauce for 10 mins.
3. Meanwhile, boil the Patna rice (see p. 89). Drain, rinse and dry.
4. Pour prawn curry into serving dish.
5. Arrange a border of rice round dish.
6. Garnish curry neatly with parsley and slices of lemon.
Prawn heads can be used to garnish border of rice if liked.

# 12. Meat

### Food Value

*1st Class Protein:* a good source.
*Fat:* the amount varies with the cut of meat.
*Carbohydrate:* meat contains no carbohydrate.
*Vitamins:* Vitamin A is found especially in liver, heart, and kidney. Vitamin $B_1$ is found in meat, especially pork products. Liver, kidney, heart are rich in Vitamin $B_2$.
*Mineral elements:* lean red meat, also liver, kidney and corned beef are good sources of iron. Meat is a good source of phosphorus.
*Water:* meat is composed of approx. 60–70% water. In fat meat, fat replaces water.

**Structure of Meat:** Lean meat, as we know it, is really muscle tissue. Muscles are made up from bundles of muscle fibres (containing protein and meat juices) and the fibres are held together by connective tissue. This connective tissue is in the form of collagen, which can be converted to gelatine during cooking, so that cooking renders the meat tender.

Fat 'cells' are interspersed in the connective tissue, often giving the lean meat a 'marbled' appearance.

**Toughness of Meat:** In general, those parts of the animal where there is most movement, so that muscles are well developed (such as the lower leg and neck) give the toughest cuts of meat. The muscle fibres are long and thick, the connective tissue is dense, often forming gristle in the meat, and there may be a lot of fat.

Tough meat needs long, slow, moist cooking to make it tender; stewing or cooking in a casserole are the most suitable methods. Tender cuts of meat come from the part of the animal where there is least muscular movement (such as the centre of the back and the hind quarters). The muscle fibres are short and fine and there is relatively little connective tissue. Tenderness (and toughness) is also affected by the age of the animal and the way it was reared. Tender meat can be cooked by quick, dry methods of cooking such as roasting, grilling or frying.

There are a few cuts of meat (e.g. breast of mutton, brisket, silverside, etc.) which cannot be regarded as 'tough' cuts, but dry methods of cooking do not always leave them very tender. Such cuts can be successfully cooked by braising or boiling.

**Cuts of Meat and Methods of Cooking:** See pp. 57–65.

## CUTS OF BEEF

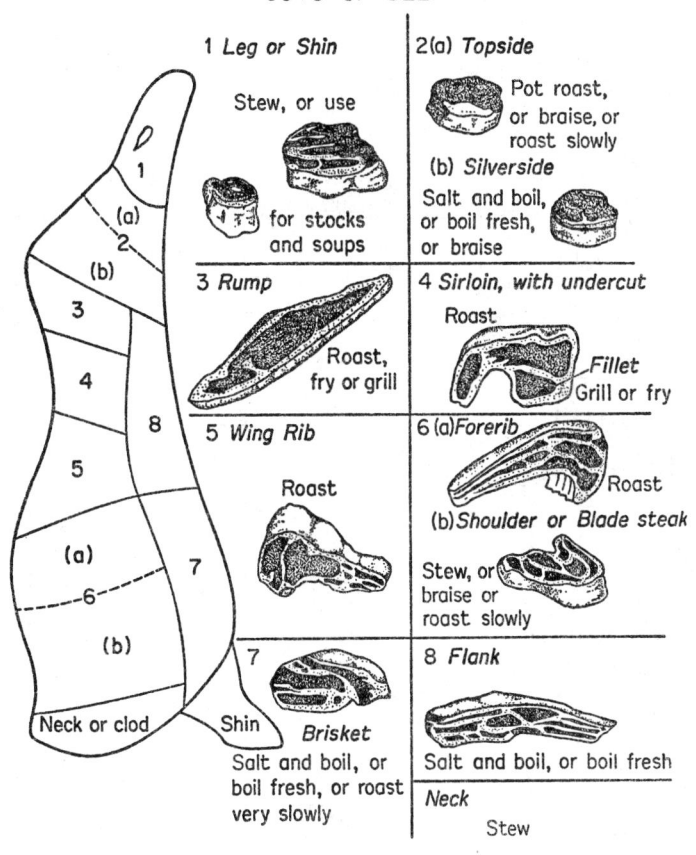

| | |
|---|---|
| 1 **Leg or Shin**<br>Stew, or use for stocks and soups | 2(a) **Topside**<br>Pot roast, or braise, or roast slowly<br>(b) **Silverside**<br>Salt and boil, or boil fresh, or braise |
| 3 **Rump**<br>Roast, fry or grill | 4 **Sirloin, with undercut**<br>Roast<br>*Fillet* Grill or fry |
| 5 **Wing Rib**<br>Roast | 6 (a) *Forerib*<br>Roast<br>(b) **Shoulder or Blade steak**<br>Stew, or braise or roast slowly |
| 7 **Brisket**<br>Salt and boil, or boil fresh, or roast very slowly | 8 **Flank**<br>Salt and boil, or boil fresh<br>**Neck**<br>Stew |

## CUTS OF MUTTON AND LAMB

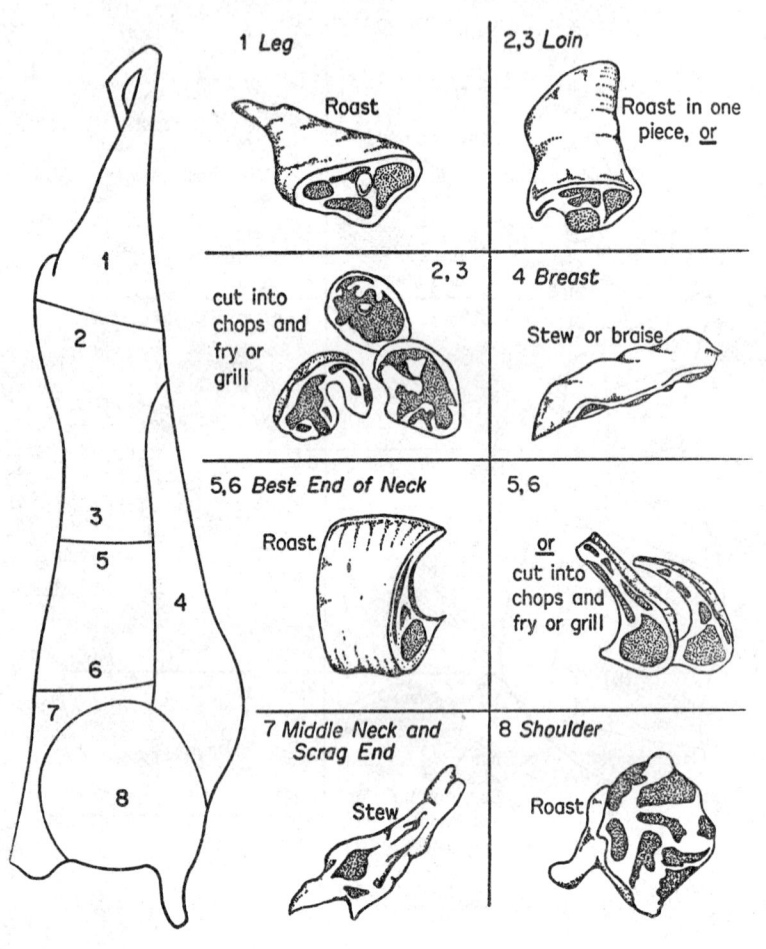

| | |
|---|---|
| **1 Leg** — Roast | **2,3 Loin** — Roast in one piece, or |
| **2, 3** cut into chops and fry or grill | **4 Breast** — Stew or braise |
| **5,6 Best End of Neck** — Roast | **5,6** or cut into chops and fry or grill |
| **7 Middle Neck and Scrag End** — Stew | **8 Shoulder** — Roast |

## CUTS OF PORK

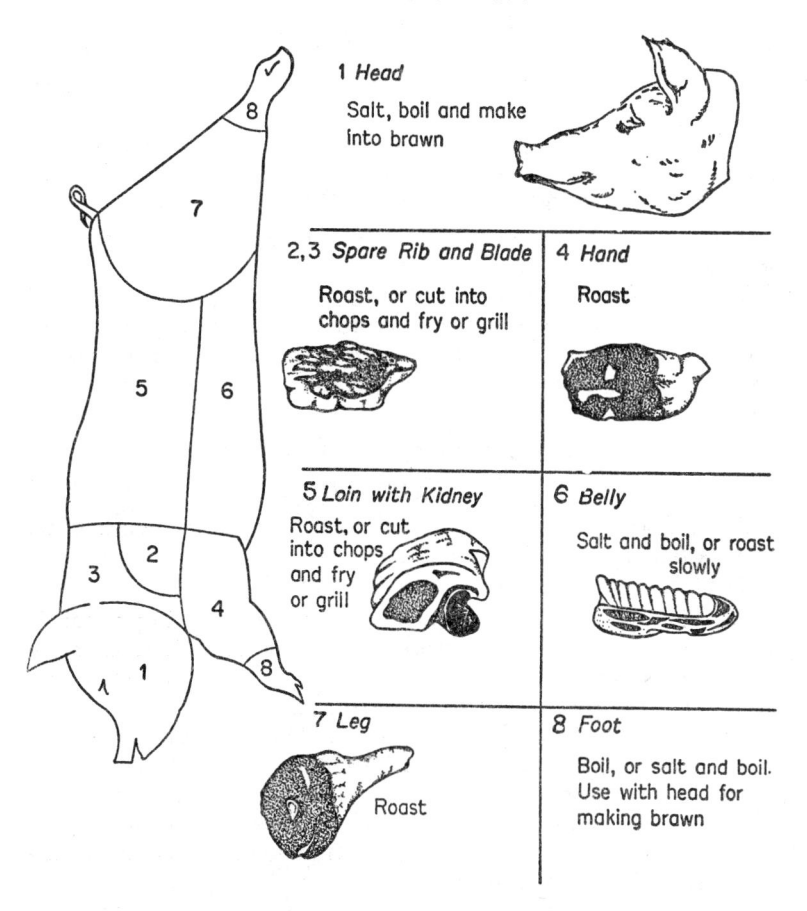

**1 Head**

Salt, boil and make into brawn

---

**2,3 Spare Rib and Blade**

Roast, or cut into chops and fry or grill

**4 Hand**

Roast

---

**5 Loin with Kidney**

Roast, or cut into chops and fry or grill

**6 Belly**

Salt and boil, or roast slowly

---

**7 Leg**

Roast

**8 Foot**

Boil, or salt and boil. Use with head for making brawn

## Buying Meat

Buy meat from a reliable butcher. Good meat is dear, but it is not worth buying poor quality meat just because it is less expensive. Cheap cuts of good quality meat are preferable to prime cuts of poor quality meat.

Whenever possible, choose 'home fed' and 'home killed' meat. Although imported chilled meat is usually of very high quality, it often has less flavour than home produced meat. Get to know the look of good quality fresh meat:

(a) Beef should have deep red flesh and firm creamy coloured fat.
(b) Mutton and lamb should have pinky-fawn flesh and hard, white fat.
(c) Pork lean should be pale pink, and the fat soft and white.

There should be no smell to the meat; stale meat smells sour and must not be used.

Try to choose your own joint of meat and, whenever possible, have it specially cut. Select your joint according to the way you want to cook it. If you are using a cheap cut of meat, make sure it is going to be economical, and that you are not, in fact, paying for a lot of bone, skin and waste.

## THE COOKING OF MEAT

### 1. *ROASTING*

Roasting (or rather baking) is only suitable for prime tender joints of meat (see diagrams for cuts of meat).

There are several different methods of roasting:

(i) Place the prepared joint in a very hot oven, Regulo 7 or 220°C (425°F) for 15–20 mins. to seal the outside and help retain meat juices. Reduce heat to Regulo 4–5 or 180°C (350°F) and continue cooking for the required time.

(ii) Place the prepared joint in a moderate oven, Regulo 4–5 or 180°C (350°F), and cook at this temperature throughout.

(iii) As (ii), but place the meat in a slow oven, Regulo 3 or 150°C (300°F), and cook at this temperature throughout. (This method of roasting helps to make 'firm' joints tender, and is also suitable for small roasts.)

In all the above methods, the joint is placed in an open baking tin, and cooked half way down the oven.

Some people prefer to roast meat in a covered tin, so that the outside does not become dry. For this, use method (ii) above.

### Times for Roasting

*Beef and lamb:* allow 20 mins. per 500 g and 20 mins. over.
*Mutton:* allow 25 mins. per 500 g and 25 mins. over.
*Pork:* allow 30 mins. per 500 g and 30 mins. over.

MEAT 61

When cooking in a covered baking tin, allow an extra ½ hour. However small the joint, it should not be roasted for less than one hour, so that heat can penetrate to the centre of the joint.

### To Prepare Meat for Cooking

1. When buying, ask the butcher to bone the joint if necessary.
2. Remove any dry or tough skin from the outside of the joint. Trim off excess fat or gristle; remove white spinal cord from neck and loin cuts.
3. Rinse meat quickly under the cold tap, and dry on clean absorbent kitchen paper.
4. Tie or skewer into shape if necessary.
5. Weigh the joint and calculate cooking time.

### To Roast Meat

1. Place the prepared and weighed meat either directly in the baking tin, or stand it on a rack in the tin.
2. If the joint is very lean, spread 25–30 g dripping over it.
3. Place in pre-heated oven and bake for the required time. For very lean meat, baste every 20–30 mins. during cooking. If potatoes are to be baked round the joint, they should be put in for the final 1–1¼ hour of the cooking time. Potatoes need frequent basting to brown them.
4. When cooked, dish the roast meat and potatoes and keep them hot while gravy is made.

### To Make Gravy

Carefully pour off all the dripping into a basin (or use a metal spoon and skim off) leaving the meat juices in the baking tin.

*Method 1:* Place baking tin containing meat sediment over a low heat. Stir in 15 g plain flour and cook gently until golden brown. Add 250 ml stock or water; bring to the boil, stirring all the time and cook for 1 minute. Flavour with salt and pepper. Colour if necessary with a few drops of gravy browning.

*Method 2:* Blend 15 g plain flour gradually with 250 ml stock or water. Add the blended flour to the meat juices in the tin. Stirring all the time, bring to the boil and cook for 1 minute. Season and colour with gravy salt. Alternatively, commercially prepared flavoured gravy thickenings may be used.

### Accompaniments for Roast Meats

*Beef:* Yorkshire pudding (see p. 124); horseradish sauce; roast potatoes; gravy.

*Mutton:* Redcurrant jelly; onion sauce (see p. 98); roast potatoes; gravy.

*Lamb:* Mint sauce (see p. 103): roast or new potatoes; gravy.

*Pork:* Apple sauce (see p. 102); sage and onion stuffing (see p. 78); roast potatoes; gravy.

## 2. *GRILLING*

Grilling is only suitable for cooking thin and very tender cuts of meat.

### Times for Grilling

*Chops (lamb, mutton, pork):* 15-20 minutes
*Steak:* fillet, 7-10 minutes
    rump, 10-15 minutes
(N.B. Steak should be served 'rare', i.e. slightly underdone and red in the centre.)
*Liver:* 10-15 minutes
*Kidneys (lamb, sheep, pigs):* 5-15 minutes
*Bacon rolls (or rashers):* 3-5 minutes
*Slices of gammon:* 5-10 minutes
*Sausages:* 10-15 minutes

All the above times depend on the thickness of the meat.

### To Prepare Meat for Grilling

*Chops:* Trim off excess fat. Remove any small splintered pieces of bone from chump chops. Skewer into a neat shape if necessary. Season lightly with salt and pepper on both sides.

*Steak:* Trim fat if necessary. Beat steak on both sides using a rolling pin or a steak bat. (This helps to break up the fibres and tenderize the steak.) Brush with melted fat and season with salt and pepper on both sides.

*Liver:* Remove skin if possible. Cut out any large pipes, using sharp scissors. Wash thoroughly in cold water; dry on absorbent paper. Brush with melted fat; season with salt and pepper on both sides.

*Kidneys:* Remove suet; skin the kidney and cut off any tubes. Using a sharp knife, split the kidney almost in half, cutting from the outer towards the inner edge. Remove core and tubes with pointed scissors. Soak the kidney 10-15 mins. in cold water. Dry. Brush with melted fat and season with salt and pepper.

*Sausages:* Prick well before grilling.

*Bacon and Gammon:* Trim off rind. To grill rashers, snip fat at 2 cm intervals. To make bacon rolls; place bacon on a board. Remove rind. Firmly stroke with a knife to 'thin out' the meat. Cut in 5-7 cm lengths, roll up and stick along a skewer.

### To Grill Meat

1. Prepare meat and place on grill rack.
2. Preheat the grill until red hot.

3. Place meat under grill; cook for 1–2 mins. on each side until the meat changes colour and the surfaces are sealed.
4. Reduce the heat of the grill, and cook more gently until the meat is cooked through. Use two spoons for turning the meat during cooking, taking care not to puncture the surface of the meat. Turn as necessary to prevent burning.

### Accompaniments for Grilled Meats

Grilled tomatoes and mushrooms (see pp. 88–9)
Maître d'hôtel butter (see p. 103)
Watercress
Game chips (potato crisps)
Chipped potatoes (see p. 87)
With grilled gammon, serve grilled slices of pineapple. With grilled pork chops, serve grilled apple rings.

### 3. FRYING

All meats suitable for grilling can also be fried. Preparation of the meat and times for cooking are the same as for grilling.

**Chops, steak, liver, kidneys:** Dip in seasoned flour to coat the meat. Chops can be coated in egg and raspings. Fry in shallow fat (see p. 26).

**Bacon, sausages:** No extra fat should be needed for frying bacon or sausages. Place meat in a cold pan and heat very gently to draw out the fat (see dry frying, p. 26).

**Accompaniments for Fried Meats:** Fried potatoes; fried tomatoes and mushrooms; fried onion rings; fried eggs.

Accompaniments (except for eggs) should be fried in the clean fat before the meat, and kept hot while the meat is cooked.

Egg fried to accompany meats other than bacon may have to be fried in a separate pan in clean fat. Eggs cannot be kept hot, or they will go hard (see fried bacon and egg, p. 75).

### 4. STEWING

Stewing is a very slow, moist method of cooking and used for cooking the tough cheaper cuts of meat to make them tender. Stews can be made either in a saucepan or stew pan on top of the stove, or in a casserole in the oven. In both cases, the pan must have a well fitting lid. The relatively small amount of liquid used in stewing forms the gravy, and since all the meat and vegetable extracts cook into the liquid, stews develop a very good flavour. There are two main methods of making stews:

(a) **Fried stews:** In these the prepared meat is fried quickly in the dripping until brown, then removed. Onions are fried and browned, the flour is added and cooked over a gentle heat to give a light brown roux. Stock or water are added, and the sauce brought gently to boiling point, stirring all the time.

The meat and prepared vegetables and seasoning are added to the stew and the whole cooked very gently indeed on top of the stove, or in the oven, Regulo 3, or 150°C (300°F) until the meat is tender. The time varies slightly according to the cut of the meat, and whether it is cooked on top or in the oven.

(See individual recipes: Brown Stew, p. 66; Beef Olives, p. 67.)

(*b*) **Simple or 'Cold Water' Stews:** The prepared meat is tossed in seasoned flour. Meat and vegetables are arranged in the casserole or stewpan, and cold stock or water is added to come ¾ of the way up the ingredients. The stew is brought gently to boiling point, then simmered very slowly until the meat is tender.

Better flavours are developed when these stews are prepared in a casserole and cooked in the oven.

(See individual recipes: Hot Pot, p. 68 and Irish Stew, p. 68.)

### 5. BRAISING

See notes on Braising, p. 24. Times allowed for braising meat are similar to those for oven stews. See Braised Stuffed Breast of Lamb, p. 69.

### 6. BOILING

Boiling is a suitable method of cooking joints of medium tenderness. In particular, it is the method used for salted meat (e.g. salt beef, salt pork, bacon joints, etc.).

**Times for Boiling Meat**

*Fresh Beef, Mutton:* 25 mins. per 500 g and 25 mins. over.
*Salt Beef, Pork, Ham, Bacon:* 30 mins. per 500 g and 30 mins. over.
For smaller joints, never boil for less than 1½ hours.

**To Boil Fresh Meat**

1. Trim off any hard skin, gristle or excess fat. Skewer into shape if necessary. Rinse joint quickly in cold water.
2. Weigh joint and calculate the cooking time.
3. Put meat into a saucepan large enough to hold meat and any vegetables which may be added later. Almost cover with cold water; add 1–2 tsp. salt, 1 bay leaf and 6 black peppercorns.
4. Bring the liquid very slowly to boiling point, reduce heat and simmer very gently for the required cooking time.
5. 1½ hours before the end of cooking, add whole onions and carrots to serve with the meat.
   Any dumplings should be added 20–30 mins. before the end of cooking time.

## To Boil Salt Meat
1. Prepare the meat and calculate the cooking time as above.
2. Put meat in the pan, cover with cold water; bring to the boil slowly, then pour off the water.
3. Recover with cold water and continue as for fresh meat. Do not add salt with the seasonings.

For bacon and ham joints, which may be very salty, they may be soaked in cold water overnight before boiling. Joints of bacon and ham can be served hot with vegetables and dumplings; alternatively, they can have rind removed and be allowed to go cold. When cold, coat any cut fat surface in raspings.

### Accompaniments for Boiled Meats
Whole root vegetables (carrots, onions, small turnips) boiled with the meat.

Dumplings (with beef).

*Sauces:* with beef—liquid in which meat was cooked; with mutton—caper or onion sauce; with bacon and ham—parsley sauce.

**To Serve Boiled Meat Hot:** Serve meat on a heated dish; pour some of the cooking liquid round beef. Put vegetables and dumplings round the joint. Hand sauce separately.

Any remaining cooking liquid can be used for stock or in soup, though care is needed when using liquid from salted meat.

## 7. *STEAMING*
Joints of ham, bacon, or whole 'boiling' fowl can be steamed instead of boiled. Whole vegetables can be placed around the joint in the steamer to give flavour. For steaming, allow half as long again as the time allowed for boiling.

## RECIPES
### Mixed Grill (serves 4)
Either 4 *pieces fillet or rump steak* (100–150 *g each*)
Or 4 *best end of neck of lamb chops*
2 *lamb's kidneys*
4 *slices lamb's liver*
2 *rashers of bacon, to make bacon rolls*
100 *g mushrooms*
2 *large tomatoes*
1 *bunch of watercress*
Garnish: *Maître d'hôtel butter* (using 25 g butter, see p. 103)
*Game chips* (potato crisps)

1. Prepare maître d'hôtel butter (see p. 103). Leave in a cool place.
2. Prepare, wash and drain watercress (see p. 91). Leave in a cool place.
3. Prepare meat for grilling according to kind (see p. 62).
4. Wash tomatoes; cut in half across the stalk. Peel mushrooms. Brush both with melted fat and season lightly.

5. Heat the grill. Put crisps on a baking tin in a slow oven to heat.
6. Place tomatoes, cut side up, in the bottom of the grill pan, and mushrooms dark side uppermost.
7. Place meat (except kidney and bacon rolls) on the grill rack, above the vegetables. Grill.
(For Methods of Grilling and Times, see p. 62).

Kidney and bacon rolls should only be placed under the grill 5-7 mins. before the end of cooking. During cooking, fat will drip from the meat and baste the tomatoes and mushrooms.

As pieces of meat cook, they may be removed from under the grill and kept hot in a slow oven, Regulo 1 or 120°C (200°F) or placed beneath the grill rack.

To serve the whole grill: Use a large oval meat dish, ready heated. Arrange the main pieces of meat on neatly; place a small piece of maître d'hôtel butter on each. Garnish with tomatoes, mushrooms, and bacon rolls. Watercress should be placed in small neat bunches and game chips grouped at the ends of the dish. The whole dish should be very neat and tidy.

Serve with chipped potatoes and a green vegetable.

**Fried Steak and Onions** (serves 2-3)

    400 g rump or fillet steak (15 mm thick)    Fat for frying
    200 g onions    Garnish: Parsley
    1 tsp. plain flour; seasoning

1. Skin onions; slice thinly into rings.
   Melt fat in the frying pan to be approx. 5 mm deep. Heat to low hazing point.
2. Put onion rings carefully into hot fat; fry gently until golden, turning as necessary. Drain well on a slice; keep hot in a cool oven.
3. While onions are cooking, prepare steak. Trim off unnecessary fat; beat steak well on both sides. Coat in seasoned flour.
4. Fry steak immediately after the onions, using the same fat. Place steak in hot fat; cook gently for 5-7 mins.; turn carefully with a spoon and slice, and fry the second side.
5. To serve, lift steak from fat on a perforated slice and allow the fat to drain off. Place steak on a heated oval dish; place fried onions neatly at the ends of the dish. Garnish meat with a sprig of parsley.

**Brown Stew and Dumplings** (serves 4)

    500 g blade steak    25 g dripping
    1 medium sized onion    25 g plain flour
    1 large carrot    400-500 ml stock or water
    1 small turnip    1 level tsp. salt; pepper
    Dumplings: For ingredients, see p. 67

MEAT 67

1. Trim the meat; cut into 2 cm pieces.
2. Prepare vegetables. Slice carrot and turnip thinly, or dice. Slice onion into rings.
3. Melt dripping in a saucepan or stewpan.
4. Add prepared meat and fry quickly until brown, turning with a metal spoon. Remove meat and put on a plate.
5. Add onion and fry gently until limp.
6. Add flour; mix in to form a roux. Cook very gently, stirring all the time until golden.
7. Add stock and bring slowly to the boil, stirring all the time.
8. Add meat, carrot, turnip and seasoning. Reduce heat and simmer very gently for about 2 hours, or until the meat is tender.

When cooking is complete, add a few drops gravy browning if necessary. Taste gravy; correct seasoning.

**Dumplings**

100 g S.R. flour
¼ tsp. salt

50 g suet
Water (approx. 2 tablesps.)

1. Prepare suet pastry (see p. 141).
2. Turn on to a floured board and form into a roll.
3. Divide pastry into either 4 or 8 equal sized pieces. Roll each into a ball.
4. Put dumplings on top of the brown stew and cook for the final 20–30 mins. of cooking time.

Serve stew in a heated dish; place dumplings on top.

**Beef Olives** (serves 4)

500 g topside of beef
1 medium sized onion
25 g dripping
25 g plain flour
400 ml stock or water
1 level tsp. salt; 2–3 shakes pepper

Veal forcemeat (see p. 78)
Garnish: 1 medium carrot
½ small turnip
Parsley

1. Make veal forcemeat (see p. 78). Prepare and slice onion.
2. Trim meat if necessary. Cut the meat into thin slices, cutting across the grain. The slices should be about 5 mm thick, 7 cm wide and 10 cm long.
3. Spread forcemeat down the centre of each slice of meat; roll up and tie with cotton.
4. Melt dripping in a saucepan; fry meat until brown. Remove from pan.
5. Fry onion lightly. Add flour, and brown very gently, stirring all the time.
6. Add stock. Bring the sauce gradually to the boil, stirring all the time.

7. Add beef olives and seasoning. Simmer very gently for 1½–2 hours, until the meat is tender.

*Garnish*: Prepare carrot and turnip. Cut in 5 mm dice. Boil vegetables together (see p. 84), allowing 5 mins. longer for the carrot to cook. Wash and dry parsley, and chop very finely. (Have the garnish ready for when the beef olives are cooked.)

*To Serve:*
1. Remove beef olives from gravy; take off cotton. Arrange in a heated dish. Taste gravy and correct seasoning if necessary. Add a few drops gravy browning if needed.
2. Strain gravy over beef olives.
3. Arrange mixed diced vegetables at ends of the dish and sprinkle lightly with parsley.

**Irish Stew** (serves 4)

| | |
|---|---|
| 500 g *scrag-end or middle neck of mutton* | 400–500 *ml water* |
| 750 g *potatoes* | 1 *level tsp. salt;* 2–3 *shakes pepper* |
| 2 *onions* | Garnish: *Chopped parsley* |

1. Wash the meat; joint it into neat pieces.
2. Peel the onions and half the potatoes. Slice both thinly.
3. Put meat and cold water into a saucepan large enough so that it is only ½ full. Bring to boiling point. Reduce heat and simmer gently.
4. Add sliced vegetables and seasoning. Simmer gently for 2–2½ hours.
5. Prepare remaining potatoes (cut in half if large). Place on top of the stew and cook gently for the final ¾ hour.
6. To serve, place meat in centre of a heated dish. Taste gravy and correct seasoning if necessary. Pour over the meat. Arrange whole potatoes at ends of dish and sprinkle with finely chopped parsley.

**Hot Pot** (serves 4)

| | |
|---|---|
| 500 g *neck or skirt of beef* | 2–3 *shakes pepper* |
| 2 *onions* | 300 *ml stock or water* (approx.) |
| 2 *medium sized carrots* | 500 g *potatoes* |
| 1 *rounded tsp. salt* | |

1. Wash and trim meat. Cut into 2 cm cubes.
2. Prepare vegetables. Slice carrots and onions thinly into rings; cut potatoes in 5 mm slices.
3. Arrange alternate layers of carrot, onion, and meat in a casserole large enough to hold all the ingredients.
4. Season; add stock just to cover these ingredients.

MEAT

5. Arrange all the sliced potatoes neatly on top to form a thick layer. Cover the casserole with the lid.
6. Cook half way down the oven, Regulo 3 or 150°C (300°F), for 2½–3 hours, until meat is tender. For the final ½ hour, remove the lid to brown the potatoes.
7. Serve in the casserole in which it was cooked. Serve with a green vegetable.

### Braised Stuffed Breast of Lamb (serves 4)

| | |
|---|---|
| 1 *breast of lamb* (¾–1 kg) | 350–400 *ml stock* (*approx.*) |
| *Veal forcemeat* (see p. 78) | 15 *g dripping* |
| Mirepoix: 2 *onions* | 1 *level tsp. salt* |
| 2 *carrots* | For the gravy: |
| 1 *small turnip* | 15 *g plain flour* |
| 1 *bacon rasher* | 2 *tablesp. cold water* |
| *Bouquet garni* | |

1. Remove any tough outer skin from meat. Trim off any excess fat, then bone the breast of lamb.
2. Prepare veal forcemeat. Spread down the centre of the breast of lamb. Roll up and tie with string or skewer securely.
3. Weigh the joint and calculate cooking time (as for roasting).
4. Peel vegetables. Leave whole or cut in half if very large. Cut bacon in slices.
5. Melt dripping in a double roasting tin. Fry bacon lightly and remove. Fry joint, browning on all sides, then remove. Fry the vegetables gently until golden brown on all sides (about 5–7 mins.).
6. Add enough stock just to cover the vegetables; add seasoning and bouquet garni. Bring to the boil.
7. Place meat on top of vegetables. Cover the pan. Reduce heat and simmer gently for ¾ of the total cooking time, or place in a moderate oven.
8. Remove lid from pan (if cooked on top of stove, place the pan half way down the oven, preheated to Regulo 6 or 200°C (400°F); bake for the remainder of cooking time without lid.

*To Serve:*

1. Lift meat on to a heated dish; remove skewers or string. Arrange vegetables round meat.
2. Skim the liquid to remove fat. Blend flour with cold water to form a smooth paste. Bring liquid to the boil; add blended flour. Boil, stirring all the time, and cook for 1 min.
3. Taste and correct seasoning. Add a few drops of gravy browning if necessary. Strain gravy into a sauce boat and hand separately.

## Steak Pie (serves 4)

500 g blade steak  
1 onion  
15 g plain flour  
1 level tsp. salt  
⅛ tsp. pepper  
250 ml stock  
100 g Rough Puff or Shortcrust pastry

1. Wash the steak and dry on absorbent paper. Cut the meat into 2 cm pieces.
2. Mix flour and seasonings together on a plate. Toss meat in seasoned flour.
3. Skin onion and slice very thinly.
4. Put meat and sliced onion in a small casserole. Add stock just to cover the meat.
5. Cook very gently, half way down the oven, Regulo 3 or 150°C (300°F), for 2–2½ hours, until meat is tender.
6. Taste gravy and correct seasoning. Add a few drops of gravy browning if necessary to give a rich brown colour.

*To Shape the Pie*

1. Put cooked meat in a 500 ml pie dish. (Use a pie funnel if necessary to keep the centre of the pastry up.) Add enough gravy to come two-thirds of the way up the meat.
2. Roll out the prepared pastry to the shape of the dish, but 15 mm wider all round.
3. Cut a 15 mm strip of pastry from round the edge and use to line the rim of the pie dish. Damp the pastry edge.
4. Lift the pastry top on to the pie. Press damp edges together at the rim. Trim the edges with a knife.
5. Flake the edges of the pastry, and decorate with large flutes.
6. Roll any remaining pastry thinly into a strip; trim to 3 cm wide. Cut across diagonally to form leaves. Mark 'veins' with the back of a knife.
7. Damp leaves and arrange on pie. Make a hole for steam to escape in the centre of the pie.
   Brush with beaten egg or milk to glaze.
8. Bake half way down the oven, Regulo 7 or 220°C (425°F) for 15–20 mins. to cook the pastry. Reduce heat to Regulo 4 or 160°C (325°F) and cook for a further 20–30 mins. to thoroughly heat the meat.

## Steak and Kidney Pudding (serves 4)

200 g suet crust pastry  
500 g neck or skirt of beef  
1 sheep's kidney, or 50 g ox kidney  
15 g plain flour  
1 level tsp. salt  
⅛ tsp. pepper  
2 tablesp. water

1. Prepare steamer; put on a large saucepan ⅔ full of water to boil. Grease a 750 ml basin.
2. Prepare kidney (see p. 62). Soak in cold water. Trim stewing beef if necessary. Cut beef and kidney in 2 cm pieces.
3. Mix flour and seasoning on a plate; toss meat in seasoned flour.
4. Prepare suet crust pastry. Line the basin with two-thirds of the pastry. Roll remaining pastry to fit the top of the basin.
5. Put filling in the basin. Add 2 tablespoons water. Damp edge of pastry and press lid on top. Cover with double greased greaseproof paper and tie down firmly.
6. Place basin in steamer. Steam gently for 4 hours.
7. Turn out on to a heated dish; garnish with parsley.

## THE USE OF OFFAL

'Offal' is the name given to those internal parts of the animal which can be used for food. It includes liver, kidney, heart, sweetbreads, tripe, brains, etc. All offal must be used when very fresh. It needs to be cleaned carefully and very thoroughly.

**Liver:** Lamb's and calves' liver are tender and have the best flavour. They are the most suitable for grilling and frying.

Pig's liver can be used, but is very coarse in texture.

Ox liver is often strong flavoured and should be soaked for ½ hour in cold water before cooking. It is sometimes very coarse and needs slow and careful cooking to make it tender. It is best cooked in a stew or casserole.

For preparation of liver, see p. 62.

**Kidney:** Lamb's and sheep's kidneys are the best for frying and grilling. Pig's kidney is often very strong in flavour and should be soaked before cooking.

Ox kidney needs careful preparation to remove the central 'core', and also needs to be soaked for half an hour before cooking. Ox kidney is only suitable for stewing or cooking in a casserole, as it requires long slow cooking to make it tender.

For preparation of kidneys, see p. 62.

**Heart:** Lamb's and sheep's hearts are the most tender, and are usually stuffed and served whole. Ox heart is tough; it should be sliced and stewed gently, or cooked in a casserole.

*To prepare heart:* using scissors, remove the tubes from the top of the heart, and the thin walls dividing the cavities. Trim off any fat. Soak the heart for 10 mins. in salted water. Wash well under cold running water to remove all blood. Leave small hearts whole; slice ox heart thinly.

**Sweetbreads:** Lamb and calf sweetbreads are the most tender and have the best flavour. To blanch sweetbreads: place sweetbreads in a small saucepan, cover with cold water and bring to the boil. Drain off the boiling water, then cover again with cold water. When the sweetbreads have gone cold, carefully remove any fat from the outside.

Sweetbreads can be stewed or fried. For frying, poach the sweetbreads in salted water for 10 mins. Drain well. Slice if necessary; coat in egg and raspings. Fry in shallow fat.

**Tripe:** As sold in this country, tripe is usually cleaned and partly cooked. It can be used without further preparation but is more usually stewed.

**Brains:** Lamb's or sheep's brains are the most suitable for cooking. They need careful preparation. Soak well in salted water to remove all blood; then rinse in clear water. Remove skin where possible.

Brains can be coated in seasoned flour and fried in shallow fat; alternatively, poach brains lightly in salted water, drain well, and serve on thin buttered toast.

### RECIPES USING OFFAL

**Stuffed Liver** (serves 3)

200–250 g ox liver
2 rashers bacon
Veal forcemeat (see p. 78) ½ quantity
250 ml stock or water

Salt and pepper
1 tsp. plain flour
Garnish: Parsley

1. Prepare liver (see p. 62). Cut into 3 slices, 15 mm thick.
2. Make veal forcemeat (see p. 78).
3. Place slices of liver in a shallow tin or fire proof dish; spread each piece with stuffing.
4. Trim rind from bacon. Cut each rasher in half and place a piece of bacon on each slice of liver.
5. Pour enough stock or water into the dish to just cover the liver. Season lightly. Cover with greaseproof paper.
6. Bake half way down the oven, Regulo 4 or 160°C (325°F), for 40–50 mins. until liver is tender.
7. Lift liver on to a heated dish. Keep hot.
8. Blend plain flour with 2 tablespoons cold water. Boil stock, add blended flour, and bring to the boil, stirring all the time. Add a few drops gravy browning if necessary. Taste and correct seasoning.
9. Strain the gravy round the liver. Garnish with parsley.

**Liver Casserole** (serves 3)

200–250 g lamb's liver
1 medium sized onion
2–3 tomatoes
50 g mushrooms

½ level tsp. salt; 2–3 shakes pepper
15 g plain flour
125–250 ml stock or water

MEAT

1. Prepare liver (see p. 62). Cut into 6 thin slices.
2. Prepare vegetables; slice onion and tomatoes into thin rings. Peel mushrooms, slice stalks and cut mushrooms in half if large.
3. Mix flour and seasonings. Toss liver in seasoned flour.
4. Arrange a layer of onions in the bottom of a 750 ml casserole, then alternate layers of liver, tomatoes and mushrooms, and finally onion.
5. Pour over stock to just cover ingredients. Cook half way down the oven, Regulo 3 or 150°C (300°F), for $1\frac{1}{4}$ hours, or until liver is tender.
6. Taste the gravy; reseason and add a few drops gravy browning if necessary.

**Fried Liver and Bacon** (serves 3)

200 g lamb's liver
3 rashers streaky bacon
15 g plain flour

For gravy: 15 g plain flour
250 ml stock or water
$\frac{1}{4}$ tsp. gravy salt

1. Prepare liver and cut into 15 mm slices. Dip in plain flour.
2. Prepare and fry bacon. (see p. 75). Lift from pan; drain well. Place on a heated plate and keep hot.
3. Fry the liver in the bacon fat adding extra fat if necessary. Cook gently for 10–15 mins, turning once, until liver is brown on the outside and cooked through. Drain and arrange on a heated dish; place bacon on top. Keep hot.

*To Make the Gravy:*
4. Drain all fat from the frying pan, leaving only $\frac{1}{2}$ tablespoon fat, and any meat juice.
5. Heat fat; sprinkle in flour and brown gently over a low heat, stirring all the time. Add stock gradually and bring to the boil, stirring continuously. Cook for 1–2 mins, then stir in the gravy salt. Taste and reseason if necessary.
6. Strain gravy round liver, or serve separately in a sauce boat.

**Pot Roast Hearts** (serves 2–4)

2 sheep's hearts
Veal forcemeat (see p. 78)
50 g dripping
Garnish: Parsley

For Gravy: 15 g plain flour
250 ml stock or water
$\frac{1}{4}$ tsp. gravy salt

1. Prepare and trim hearts (see p. 71). Soak in salt water.
2. Make veal forcemeat (see p. 78).
3. Wash hearts well under cold running water. Drain well and dry on absorbent paper.
4. Stuff hearts; secure 'flap' on each heart with a skewer.

5. Choose a saucepan just large enough to hold the hearts. Melt fat and heat until smoking hot.
6. Brown the hearts quickly in the fat, turning with a spoon and fork. (Take care not to prick them.)
7. Cover the saucepan. Reduce the heat and cook very gently indeed for 1 hour, turning occasionally, until the hearts are tender.
8. Remove hearts, drain well and place on a heated dish. Remove skewers. Keep the meat hot.
9. Make gravy (as for Fried Liver and Bacon above, Nos. 4–6).

Strain some gravy round the hearts. Garnish each with a small spray of parsley. Serve remaining gravy separately in a sauceboat.

## ADDITIONAL RECIPES USING MEAT

**Mince** (serves 2–3)

250 g *raw minced beef* (e.g. *skirt*)
1 *small onion*
15 g *dripping*
15 g *plain flour*
1 *level tsp. salt;* 2–3 *shakes pepper*

150–200 *ml stock*
1 *tsp. Worcester sauce or tomato ketchup*
Garnish: *Parsley*
*Triangles of toasted bread*

1. Peel onion; chop very finely.
2. Melt dripping in a small saucepan. Fry onion gently until golden brown.
3. Add mince and fry lightly, turning with a metal spoon until the meat is no longer red.
4. Add flour, and mix with the meat. Pour in stock and bring gradually to the boil, stirring all the time.
5. Add seasoning; cover pan, and cook very gently for ¾–1 hour, until the meat is tender.
6. Stir in Worcester sauce or ketchup; taste and correct seasoning. Add a few drops of gravy browning if necessary.
7. Serve mince in a heated dish. Garnish with parsley and place small triangular croûtes of toasted bread around the edges of the dish.

**Cornish Pasties** (makes 4)

200 g *Shortcrust pastry*
Filling:

150–200 g *raw minced beef*
1 *small sized onion or leek*

1 *medium sized potato*
1 *level tsp. salt;* 2–3 *shakes pepper*

1. Prepare shortcrust pastry (see p. 139).
2. Peel onion and potato. Chop onion very finely. Cut potato in 5 mm dice.
3. Mix minced beef, chopped onion, diced potato and seasonings together.

## MEAT

4. Divide pastry in four equal pieces; shape and roll each piece carefully to a 15 cm round.
5. To shape each pasty, place filling on half the circle of pastry. Damp edges. Fold pastry over and seal the edges. Brush with milk. Make a small hole in the top of each pasty for steam to escape.
6. Place pasties on a flat baking sheet; bake half way down the oven, Regulo 7 or 220°C (425°F) for 15–20 mins. until the pastry is brown; reduce to Regulo 3 or 150°C (300°F), and cook for a further ¾–1 hour, until the meat is tender.

### Spaghetti alla Bolognese (serves 2)

100 g spaghetti (or macaroni)
Meat sauce:
  100 g raw minced beef
  50 g mushrooms
  1 small onion
  4 tomatoes
1–2 tsp. tomato paste
¼ tsp. salt; 2–3 shakes pepper
1 tablesp. olive oil, or 15 g butter
Garnish: 15 g butter
  25 g finely grated cheese

1. Peel mushrooms and onion; chop very finely.
2. Skin tomatoes in boiling water; slice up roughly.
3. Heat olive oil or butter in a small saucepan; add chopped onion and fry lightly.
4. Add minced beef and fry gently, turning all the time until no longer red.
5. Add mushrooms, tomatoes, tomato paste and seasoning. Cover pan, and simmer very gently for approx. ¾ hour, until the meat is tender. Stir periodically to prevent burning.
6. Cook spaghetti when the meat sauce has been simmering for 20 mins. Choose a fairly large saucepan; half fill with water; add 1 tsp. salt and bring to the boil.
7. Gently lower the spaghetti into the boiling water, curling it round the pan to avoid breaking it. Cook fairly briskly with no lid on the pan, for 15–20 mins. until the spaghetti is soft. Drain well.
8. Pile the spaghetti on a heated dish. Pour the meat sauce on top. Sprinkle the top with grated cheese and place a piece of butter in the centre.

### Fried Bacon and Egg (serves 1)

2 rashers bacon
1 egg
½ slice bread, 1 cm thick

1. Trim off bacon rind using scissors. Snip the bacon fat at 1 in. intervals, so the bacon lies flat in the pan.
2. Place bacon in a cold frying pan; heat gradually to draw fat out of the bacon. Fry gently, turning as necessary until bacon fat is pale golden. Drain on a slice; lift on to a heated plate and keep hot.

3. Break egg into a cup. Lower into the hot fat and cook very gently for 1-2 mins, basting the egg yolk with hot fat while frying. (If insufficient fat comes from the bacon, it may be necessary to add a small nut of cooking fat, and melt it before frying the egg.)
4. Carefully lift the egg on to the hot plate with a slice.
5. For fried bread: increase heat under frying pan; put in bread and fry quickly until golden brown on one side. Fry second side if liked. Lift egg carefully on to the fried bread. Serve immediately.

**Sausage Rolls** (makes approx. 12—16 rolls)

    200 g *Rough Puff or Flaky pastry* (see pp. 141-3)
    250 g *sausage meat*

1. Prepare pastry.
2. Roll pastry out to a rectangle, 20 cm wide and 30 cm long. Trim edges. Cut down the centre into 2 strips, 10 cm wide. Turn pastry over.
3. Divide sausage meat in two equal parts. Roll each to a coil, 30 cm long.
4. Place sausage meat down each piece of pastry, and damp edges. Either fold pastry over; press edges together, then flake and flute the edges.
   Alternatively, roll the pastry round the sausage meat, and turn with join underneath.
5. Brush along with beaten egg or milk. Score the top at intervals.
6. Cut rolls into even sized pieces. Place on a flat baking sheet. Bake a third of the way down the oven, Regulo 7 or 220°C (425°F), until well risen and golden brown. (Approx. 20-25 mins.) Cool on a wire tray.
7. To serve, pile neatly on an oval dish, on a d'oyley or dish mat. Garnish with sprays of parsley. They can be served hot or cold.

**Sausage and Mash** (serves 3)

    250 g *pork sausages*    *Seasoning*
    500 g *potatoes*    3 *tomatoes*
    15 g *margarine*    Garnish: *Parsley*
    2 *tablesp. milk*

1. Peel potatoes; place in cold salted water. Bring to the boil and simmer gently for 15-20 mins., until soft.
2. Prick sausages well. Place in a frying pan. Heat gently to draw fat from the sausages. Fry for 10-15 mins, turning the sausages to get them evenly browned.
3. Drain the sausages; put on a plate and keep hot.
4. Cut tomatoes across in half. Place cut side up in the hot fat; fry for 2-3 mins., turn and fry the second side.

5. Drain and cream potatoes (see p. 86).
6. Pile the creamed potatoes in the centre of a hot dish. Fork into a neat shape, or smooth with a palette knife. Arrange sausages and tomatoes round the potatoes. Garnish with parsley.

**Toad in the Hole** (serves 3)

*200–250 g sausages, or sausage meat*
*250 ml batter* (see p. 123)

1. Make batter (see p. 123).
2. Rinse the sausages under the cold tap. Slit the skins from end to end and remove. Place sausages in a heat proof dish. Bake a third of the way down the oven, Regulo 7 or 220°C (425°F), for 5-10 mins., until the fat has been drawn out of the sausages. (In the meantime, beat the batter thoroughly.)
3. Pour the prepared batter over the heated sausages; return to the oven and bake for 30-45 mins., until well risen and golden brown, and firm to touch.

Serve straight away.

## POULTRY

**Points to look for when buying poultry:** If the poultry is 'ready dressed', the skin should be fresh and clear in colour, and the flesh firm and plump. There should be no unpleasant smell. If the bird is young, its feet will be smooth. With chicken, the end of the breast bone should be soft and pliable. If the poultry still has the feathers on, buy it from a reliable source, so that you know when it was killed. Usually the poulterer will dress the bird for you if asked. Deep frozen poultry is usually of good quality and well prepared. It should be allowed to thaw gradually before cooking.

### Accompaniments for Roast Poultry

*Chicken and Turkey:* Veal forcemeat (see p. 78), chippolata sausages, bacon rolls, gravy, bread sauce (see p. 102), watercress to garnish. Green salad may be served with the roast poultry.

*Duck:* Sage and onion stuffing, (see p. 78), gravy, apple sauce (see p. 102), Green salad, garnished with slices of fresh orange.

*Goose:* Sage and onion stuffing, gravy, apple sauce.

### Roast Chicken

*1 roasting chicken, 1½–2 kg*
*Veal forcemeat* (see p. 78)
*200 g chippolata sausages*
*3 rashers bacon*
*25 g dripping*

Garnish: *Watercress*
Accompaniments:
　*Green salad* (see p. 93)
　*Bread sauce* (see p. 102)

1. Prepare chicken; wash and drain well.
2. Make veal forcemeat. Place some of the stuffing underneath the neck skin in the hollow of the wishbone. Pull the skin across; tuck underneath and secure with the wing tips. Stuff the body cavity with the remaining stuffing. Truss the bird and tie with string.
3. Weigh the bird and calculate cooking time. Allow 20 mins. per 500 g and 20 mins. over.
4. Place the bird in a roasting tin; spread the breast and legs with dripping (or any layer of fat which was in the body cavity).
5. Place half way down a preheated oven, Regulo 4 or 180°C (350°F). Baste frequently during cooking.
6. Prepare bread sauce; wash salad vegetables. Prepare French dressing for green salad.
7. Prepare bacon rolls; prick sausages. $\frac{1}{2}$ hour before the end of cooking time, place sausages in a separate tin and bake in the oven; add bacon rolls and cook for the final 15 mins.
8. Immediately before the chicken is removed from the oven, finish and toss the green salad in French dressing.
9. Dish the chicken (remove string); garnish with sausages and bacon rolls; keep hot.
10. Make gravy (see p. 61). Pour into a sauce boat.
11. Garnish chicken with a neat bunch of watercress at the tail end. Serve roast chicken and gravy. Hand bread sauce and green salad separately.

(N.B. Potatoes can be roasted round the bird, as for Roast Meats.)

## Veal Forcemeat

| | |
|---|---|
| 50 g fresh white breadcrumbs | $\frac{1}{4}$ tsp. finely grated zest of lemon rind |
| 15 g shredded suet (or margarine) | $\frac{1}{4}$ tsp. salt |
| 2 tsp. finely chopped parsley | $\frac{1}{8}$ tsp. pepper |
| 1 tsp. chopped thyme | 1 small egg |

1. Prepare breadcrumbs and put in a basin.
2. Add suet, grated zest of lemon rind, and seasonings.
3. Wash herbs and dry thoroughly; discard stalks. Chop leaves finely, and add to dry ingredients.
4. Beat egg and add sufficient to bind the ingredients together. Use as needed to stuff poultry, fish, meat, etc.

## Sage and Onion Stuffing

| | |
|---|---|
| 50 g fresh white breadcrumbs | 2 tsp. finely chopped sage leaves |
| 3 medium sized onions | $\frac{1}{4}$ tsp. salt |
| 15 g margarine | $\frac{1}{8}$ tsp. pepper |

1. Peel and slice onions. Cook in boiling salted water until tender (20–30 mins.). Drain well and chop.
2. Add breadcrumbs, margarine, sage and seasoning and mix well. Use as needed, to stuff pork, duck and goose.

# 13. Vegetables

**Types of Vegetables:** For culinary purposes, vegetables can be grouped as follows:
(a) *Green vegetables:* e.g. cabbage, Brussels sprouts, spinach, cauliflower, lettuce, watercress, etc.
(b) *Legumes and pulses:* e.g. peas and beans. The dried seeds of peas, beans and lentils are known as 'pulses'.
(c) *Root vegetables:* e.g. beetroot, carrots, parsnips, swedes, turnips, potatoes, etc. Also the bulbous roots such as onions, leeks.
(d) *Blanched stems:* e.g. celery, chicory.

## Food Value

*2nd Class Protein:* Pulses are a good source. Root vegetables have a very small quantity.

*Fat:* Most vegetables contain no fat.

*Carbohydrate:* Starch is found in potatoes and pulses. Sugar is found in peas, beans, beetroot, onions, tomatoes, etc.

*Vitamin A:* Found in the form of carotene in all yellow, orange and green vegetables, e.g. carrots, cabbage, tomatoes, etc.

*Vitamin B:* All vegetables contain a little; there is a fair quantity in pulses.

*Vitamin C:* Fresh green vegetables, potatoes and tomatoes are rich sources.

*Vitamin D:* None.

*Vitamin E:* A small amount found in green vegetables.

*Mineral Elements:* Calcium found in leafy green vegetables. Iron found in spinach, watercress, parsley, pulses, though it is not always in a form which can be absorbed by the body. Sulphur found in green vegetables, onions.

*Water:* Fresh vegetables contain a large amount, often as much as 70–90%.

*Roughage:* A valuable source—skins, seeds, pips, stalks and ribs of leaves, etc.

Much of the food value of vegetables can be destroyed if they are carelessly stored after purchase, or if they are badly cooked.

## Buying and Storing Vegetables

Whenever possible, it is best if vegetables can be cut or dug from the garden and used straight away. If this is not possible, choose vegetables carefully when buying.

VEGETABLES 81

Green vegetables should be a good fresh green in colour; the leaves should be crisp, and the heart of cabbage or lettuce firm. Peas and beans should also be crisp and firm and not appear wrinkled. Yellowing and soft leaves are signs of staleness. Avoid vegetables which have had their outer leaves stripped off (such as cauliflower and lettuce). There is no need to strip fresh vegetables; also the dark outer leaves have the highest food value. Green vegetables should be used as quickly as possible. They do not keep well, and Vitamin C is lost during storage. If it is necessary to keep them, either put them in the vegetable drawer of the refrigerator, or in a polythene bag in a cool place, or in a saucepan or tin with a well fitting lid.

Root vegetables should be firm to touch, a good colour and the skins free from blemishes. Try to choose ones of medium size. Very large vegetables can be coarse and woody. Avoid root vegetables which feel soft or look withered; also avoid those with a large amount of earth on as this weighs heavily. At home, store root vegetables in a cool dark place where air can circulate round them, preferably in a vegetable rack.

**Vegetables in Season**

| | |
|---|---|
| Broad Beans | June–July |
| Beetroot | All the year |
| Brussels Sprouts | October–March |
| Cabbage | All the year |
| Carrots (new) | April–September |
| Carrots (old) | September–April |
| Cauliflower | All the year (often imported in winter) |
| Celery | November–February |
| Leeks | September–March |
| Lettuce | April–October (imported ones are best in winter) |
| Marrow | August–September |
| Onions | All the year |
| Parsnips, Turnips | September–March |
| Peas | June–September |
| Potatoes (new) | April–August |
| Potatoes (old) | September–April |
| Spring Greens | February–May |
| Tomatoes | June–October (imported all the year) |

When buying vegetables, try to use those which are 'in season' as then they are at their cheapest and best.

**Frozen Vegetables:** Many vegetables, especially the green ones can now be bought frozen. Although these seem expensive, there is no waste at all, and no preparation involved. It also enables you to use these vegetables at a time of year when they are not normally available. Though the flavour is good, it is not as good as that of fresh vegetables.

## PREPARING AND COOKING VEGETABLES

### GREEN VEGETABLES

**Preparing Green Vegetables:** It is best to prepare green vegetables quickly just before they are cooked. Only discard any tough or discoloured outer leaves; the dark outer leaves are rich in vitamins.

Vitamin C is easily lost from green vegetables. It is soluble in water and can be lost if vegetables are soaked during washing; they should be washed thoroughly but quickly in two or three lots of cold water. Vitamin C is also destroyed if exposed to the air, so more is lost if vegetables are cut or shredded a long time before cooking. (For preparation, see notes on individual vegetables.)

**Cooking Green Vegetables:** Green vegetables need careful cooking to retain all possible Vitamin C. They should be cooked quickly in as little water as possible until they are just tender.

**General Method for Boiling Green Vegetables**
1. Choose a saucepan just large enough to hold the vegetables. Quarter fill with water, add 1 level tsp. salt and bring to the boil.
2. Put in prepared green vegetables gradually, so that the water does not go off the boil.
3. Cover pan and boil steadily until the vegetables are tender. (Test the stalk with a skewer or vegetable knife.)
4. Drain well through a colander.
5. Garnish if necessary and serve at once.

The water left after cooking green vegetables should be used to make gravy whenever possible.

**Bicarbonate of Soda:** Bicarbonate of soda should not be added to water for cooking green vegetables as it destroys food value. Provided vegetables are put into fast boiling water and cooked quickly, they will remain green.

**Amount to Serve:** Allow approx. 500 g green vegetables for 3 people.

**Brussels Sprouts:** Discard tough or discoloured outer leaves. Cut large sprouts in half; cut a cross in the stalk of whole sprouts to speed cooking. Wash quickly in cold water. Boil for 10–15 mins. until just tender. Drain well; serve in a covered dish with a knob of butter.

**Cabbage:** Discard tough or discoloured outer leaves. Cut cabbage in four and wash thoroughly in cold water. Using a sharp knife, shred up finely immediately before cooking. Boil 10-15 mins. until just tender. Drain well; serve in a covered dish.

**Cauliflower:** Discard the very large and tough outer leaves. Cut cauliflower in sprigs, or leave whole. Cut a cross in the bottom of the thick stalk. Wash well in cold water; if there are insects in the flower, soak for 10-20 mins. in cold salted water. Boil for 15-20 mins. until the stalk is just tender and the flower unbroken. (Place the whole cauliflower flower uppermost in pan.) Drain well. Put in an open vegetable dish; coat with white sauce. (Allow 300-400 ml white sauce for 1 large cauliflower.)

Cauliflower can also be coated in cheese sauce and served 'au gratin' (see p. 109).

**Spinach:** Discard very tough leaves. With a sharp knife, remove thick stalks. Wash very thoroughly.

Pack tightly into a saucepan, sprinkle lightly with salt, and cook gently for 10-15 mins. (No water need be added as there will be enough left on the leaves after washing.) When cooked, drain well; return to the pan. Add a small knob of butter and chop finely with a knife. Serve in a covered dish.

**Spring Greens:** Discard tough or discoloured outer leaves, or any coarse ribs from the leaves. Wash thoroughly, opening out the leaves. Using a sharp knife, shred finely immediately before cooking. Cook and serve as for cabbage.

**Beans**
1. *Broad Beans:* Shell the beans. Boil for 10-20 mins. until the skins are tender. Drain well. Put in an open dish. Coat with parsley sauce, or toss in butter.
2. *French Beans:* Wash well. Leave whole (or cut in half if very long). Boil for 10-15 mins. until just tender. Drain well. Serve in a covered dish.
3. *Runner Beans:* 'String' the beans by cutting off the edges thinly. Wash in cold water. Shred finely immediately before cooking. Boil for 10-15 mins. until just tender. Drain well. Serve in a covered dish.

**Peas:** Shell the peas. To the boiling salted water for cooking the peas, add 1 level tsp. sugar and a sprig of mint. Boil peas for 10-15 mins. until just tender. Drain well. Serve in a covered dish.

## ROOT VEGETABLES

Care should be taken to prepare root vegetables as cleanly as possible. They should be scrubbed or washed before peeling to remove all mud. On no account should they be peeled in a bowl of muddy water.

There should be no undue waste when preparing root vegetables. Young vegetables with thin skins (such as new potatoes and carrots) should only be scraped, old potatoes peeled thinly, and only vegetables with very tough skins (such as swedes) should be thickly peeled. After vegetables have been peeled, they should be put into clean cold water to prevent discolouring. Try to prepare them just before cooking. Some of the soluble nutrients are soaked out (especially Vitamin C from potatoes) if the vegetables are kept in water too long.

**Cooking Root Vegetables:** Root vegetables can be boiled, or cooked by the conservative method; most can be baked, and some fried. All root vegetables can be steamed.

### General Method for Boiling Root Vegetables
1. Prepare vegetables and cut into even sized pieces.
2. Put vegetables in a saucepan large enough so that they ⅔ fill the pan. Pour in boiling water to come ¾ of the way up the vegetables. Add 1 tsp. salt for each 500 g vegetables.
3. Cover pan and simmer very gently until vegetables are just tender. (Test with a skewer or vegetable knife.)
4. Drain well. (Use any cooking water in gravy whenever possible.)
5. Garnish if necessary, and serve at once.

### Conservative Method of Cooking Root Vegetables
1. Prepare vegetables and cut into even sized pieces.
2. To 500 g vegetables allow: 15 g margarine, 100 ml water, 1 level tsp. salt.
3. Choose a saucepan just large enough to hold the vegetables, and with a well fitting lid.
4. Melt fat in saucepan and 'sweat' the vegetables over a gentle heat until fat has been absorbed (approx. 3–5 mins.).
5. Add boiling water and salt. Replace lid on pan.
6. Simmer the vegetables very gently until tender.
7. Serve the vegetables in their own liquid. Garnish with chopped parsley. (Parsley can be cut with scissors for speed.)

Instead of cooking in a saucepan on top of the stove, root vegetables can be cooked by the Conservative Method in a covered casserole in the oven. The oven should be at Regulo 4 or 160°–180°C (325–350°F) and the vegetables will take approx. ¾–1 hour to cook.

### General Method for Baking Root Vegetables in Fat
1. Heat the oven to Regulo 6 or 200°C (400°F).
2. Prepare vegetables and cut into even sized pieces. Leave onions whole.
3. Melt 50 g dripping in a baking tin.

# VEGETABLES 85

4. Put the prepared vegetables into the hot fat. Baste well.
5. Bake half way down the oven for 1–1½ hours, until soft and golden brown. Baste from time to time during cooking.

If time is limited, vegetables can be 'par-boiled' for 5–7 mins., then drained before baking. Potatoes, especially, are often roasted in the fat round 'roast meat'.

**Beetroot:** Cut off the leaves, leaving 5 cm leaf stalk on the beetroot. Wash beetroot carefully to remove soil. Take care not to break skin. Boil 1–1½ hours, according to the size of the beetroot. (When cooked, the skins should peel off easily.)
(a) Put in an open vegetable dish. Coat with white sauce and serve hot. (Leave small beetroot whole; cut larger ones in 5 mm slices.) Or;
(b) Allow to cool. Slice thinly and cover with vinegar. Serve with salad or cold meat.

**Carrots:** Scrub to remove mud. Scrape new carrots or thinly peel old ones. If new carrots are very small, leave whole. For old carrots, slice thinly into rings or cut in 1 cm dice.
*either:* Boil 20–40 mins. until just tender. Drain well. Add a knob of butter and toss carrots in butter. Serve sprinkled with chopped parsley.
*or:* Cook by the Conservative Method (20–40 mins.). Serve in their own juice, sprinkled with chopped parsley.
*or:* Bake in fat. (See General Method, p. 84.)

**Parsnips:** Prepare as for carrots. Cut in 5 mm thick slices.
*either:* Boil 30–40 mins. until just tender. Drain well. Add a knob of butter, salt and pepper and mash well. Serve sprinkled with chopped parsley.
*or:* Cook by the Conservative Method (30–40 mins.) Serve as for carrots.

**Swedes and Turnips:** Scrub well. Peel thickly.
*either:* Cut in 1 cm thick slices. Boil and mash as for parsnips.
*or:* Cut in 1 cm dice. Cook by the Conservative Method.
Swede and carrot can be cooked and served together.

## BULBOUS ROOT VEGETABLES

**Onions**
*To Prepare:* Cut off the root (and green top if any) and remove the outer skin. Rinse in cold water.
*To Cook:*
*either:* Boil whole for 20–40 mins. (depending on size). Drain well. Put in an open vegetable dish. Coat with white sauce.
*or:* Cook by the Conservative Method (20–40 mins.)

*or:* Slice in 5 mm thick rings. Fry in shallow fat at hazing point until gold brown. Serve with fried liver, steak, etc.

*or:* Bake in fat. (See General Method, p. 84.)

**Leeks**

*To Prepare:* Slice off the root thinly. Cut any coarse green leaves off at the top. Remove one outer layer. Cut the leek in half lengthways and wash very thoroughly between the leaves with cold water.

*To Cook:* Boil for 20–40 mins. until just tender. Drain well. Put in an open vegetable dish. Coat with white sauce.

Onions and leeks can also be coated with cheese sauce and served 'au gratin' as a main dish.

**Potatoes**

*To Prepare:*
1. Scrub to remove mud.
2. Scrape new potatoes; peel old ones thinly. Remove 'eyes' with a vegetable knife.
3. Put into clean cold water as they are peeled. Cook straight away. (Potatoes should not be prepared in advance and kept in water as Vitamin C will be lost.)

Allow 500 g potatoes for 3–4 people.

**Boiled Potatoes:** Prepare potatoes. Leave new potatoes whole; cut old ones in half if very large. (Try to use potatoes which are fairly even in size so that they cook at the same rate.)

*For New Potatoes:* Put in a saucepan large enough so that they two-thirds fill the pan. Pour in boiling water to come ¾ of the way up the vegetables. Add 1 tsp. salt. Cover the pan and simmer gently until potatoes are soft. (20–30 mins.) Drain well using the saucepan lid. Toss in butter. Serve sprinkled with finely chopped parsley.

*For Old Potatoes:* Put potatoes in a saucepan. Put in cold water to come ¾ of the way up the potatoes; add 1 tsp. salt. Cover pan, bring to the boil, then reduce heat and simmer gently until potatoes are soft (20–40 mins.). Drain well, using the saucepan lid. Heat the pan gently for about 1 minute to dry off the vegetables.

Potatoes can be left whole or mashed with a potato masher. Serve in a covered dish.

**Creamed Potatoes:** Use old potatoes. Boil (as above), drain and dry off. Mash with a potato masher or fork. To 1 lb potatoes add:

15 g margarine,
1 tablesp. top of milk,
¼ tsp. salt, 2–3 shakes pepper.

Using a wooden spoon, beat potatoes, fat, milk and seasoning together well over a gentle heat until creamy. Put into a dish; fork or smooth into a neat shape. Garnish with a sprig of parsley (or chopped parsley).

VEGETABLES 87

**Duchesse Potatoes:** Use old potatoes. Boil (as above), drain and dry off. Mash very thoroughly or press through a sieve.
To 500 g potatoes add:
 15 g margarine,
 1 small egg, beaten,
 ¼ tsp. salt,
 2-3 shakes pepper, 1-2 tablesp. milk, if necessary.
Using a wooden spoon, beat potatoes, fat and seasoning together over a gentle heat. Add most of the beaten egg (and a little milk if necessary) to give a soft consistency.
Fit a forcing bag with a star potato pipe. Pipe in neat shapes on to a greased baking sheet. Bake in a hot oven, Regulo 6 or 200°C (400°F), for 15-20 mins. until golden brown.
Serve hot in an open vegetable dish.

**Baked Potatoes (in Jackets):** Choose medium to large sized potatoes without blemishes. Scrub well.
Prick skins in several places with a fork to prevent them bursting during cooking. Rub the skins with a 'lard' paper or brush with melted lard.
Place on the bars of the oven shelf half way down the oven. Turn on the oven, Regulo 4 or 180°C (350°F) and bake for 1-1½ hours, until soft when tested with a skewer. Pile in a vegetable dish. Serve with pats of butter.

**Roast Potatoes:** Prepare potatoes. Follow the General Method for baking root vegetables in Fat.
Serve in an open vegetable dish, or arranged round a roasted joint of meat.

**Chipped Potatoes:** Prepare potatoes. Slice into 7 mm 'chips', the length of the potato.
Rinse well in cold water; dry on a clean tea towel. Place chips in a frying basket. Lower gently into deep fat at hazing point. Cook until chips are soft all through, crisp and golden brown on the outside (10-20 mins.).
Remove basket of chips from the fat. Drain well, then drain on absorbent paper. Serve very hot in an open dish.

**Potatoes Fried in Shallow Fat:** Prepare potatoes; slice thinly into rings. Rinse and dry.
Melt 1 cm of dripping or cooking fat in a frying pan and heat to hazing point. Carefully put potatoes into hot fat and fry gently, turning them as necessary, until crisp and golden brown (10-15 mins.). Remove from fat with a perforated slice or draining spoon. Drain well on absorbent paper.

Serve very hot in an open vegetable dish.

For shallow frying, potatoes can be 'parboiled' first for 5–7 mins., then sliced. This reduces the time for frying.

## OTHER VEGETABLES

**Celery:** Discard very coarse outer pieces. Trim the root; discard leaves. Break celery into separate sticks, and scrub well in cold water. (Retain the heart to eat raw.)

Cut the celery in even lengths. Boil (as for carrots.) for 15–20 mins. Drain very well. Put in an open vegetable dish. Coat with white sauce.

*Alternatively:* Prepare celery. Cut into 2 cm lengths. Cook as for carrots by the Conservative Method. Serve celery in own juice. Sprinkle with chopped parsley.

**Marrow:** Cut marrow into 3 cm rings and remove seeds. Peel marrow thickly. Cut marrow into 2 cm pieces; rinse in cold water. Place in a perforated steamer and sprinkle lightly with salt. Steam over boiling water until soft (30–40 mins.). Drain well. Place in an open vegetable dish. Coat with white sauce.

**Mushrooms** (Allow 100 g mushrooms for 2 people.):

*To Prepare:* Peel skin from mushrooms; remove stalk or slice off end. Mushrooms can be fried, grilled or served in sauce.

*To Fry:* Prepare mushrooms; remove stalk. Melt 30 g butter or margarine in a frying pan, without allowing it to brown (or fry in fat after cooking bacon). Place mushrooms in fat, cap side down, and fry gently for 3–4 mins. Turn carefully and fry for a further 2–3 mins.

Remove carefully. Drain off fat. Serve on toast, or to accompany fried bacon, steak, or chops.

*To Grill:* Prepare mushrooms; trim or remove stalks. Place in grill pan, gill side up. Brush with melted butter or margarine. Sprinkle lightly with salt and pepper.

Heat grill. Grill mushrooms under a gentle heat for 5–10 mins. until soft. Serve with grilled meats.

**Mushrooms in Sauce** (serves 2–3)

| | |
|---|---|
| 100–150 g *mushrooms* | 250 *ml milk* |
| 25 g *margarine* | ¼ *tsp. salt, 2–3 shakes pepper* |
| 25 g *plain flour* | |

1. Prepare mushrooms. Trim stalk. Slice mushrooms thinly.
2. Melt fat in saucepan. Sweat mushrooms very gently with a lid on the pan for approx. 5 mins. without browning.
3. Add flour, and cook gently, stirring all the time, for 1–2 mins.
4. Remove from heat. Gradually blend in milk.

5. Return to the heat. Stirring all the time, gradually bring to the boil. Reduce heat and simmer for 2–3 mins.
6. Serve as a vegetable with fish, meat or bacon; alternatively, serve on hot buttered toast, as a High Tea or supper dish.

**Tomatoes** (Allow 1 large or 2 medium sized tomatoes per person.):
*To Bake:* Wash and dry tomatoes. Cut in half across stalk. Place in a shallow fireproof dish. Brush with melted butter or margarine. Sprinkle lightly with salt and pepper. Bake half way down the oven, Regulo 3 or 150°C (300°F) for 15–20 mins. until just soft.
Serve as a vegetable with meat, or fish or baked cheese dishes.
*To Fry:* Wash and dry tomatoes. Cut in half across stalk. Melt 30 g butter or margarine in a frying pan without browning (or use fat after frying bacon).
Place tomatoes in fat, cut side up. Cook and serve as for fried mushrooms.
*To Grill:* Wash and dry tomatoes. Cut in half across stalk. Brush with melted fat and season lightly. Cook and serve as for grilled mushrooms.

**To Boil Rice** (Allow 80 g Patna long grain rice for 2 people.):
1. Wash rice in cold water.
2. Half fill a large saucepan with water. Bring to the boil; add 1 heaped tsp. salt and 2 tsp. lemon juice or white distilled vinegar.
3. Put rice into boiling water and boil fairly rapidly to keep the rice moving, do not cover pan. Cook until rice is just tender (10–15 mins.).
4. Drain well through a colander. Rinse through with boiling water from a kettle. Drain again.
5. Spread rice on a dish; cover and put in a warm place (such as the bottom of the oven) to dry off for about ½ hour. Fork over during drying.
Use as a vegetable in place of potatoes, or to accompany curry, etc.

**Stuffed Marrow** (serves 3)

    1 *medium sized marrow*
    Filling:   250 *g cooked minced meat (beef, pork, ham) or pork sausage meat*
               1 *small onion*
               50 *g white breadcrumbs*
               25 *g margarine*
               1 *level tsp. salt, 2–3 shakes pepper*
               1 *tomato, herbs, or other flavouring*
    To Bake: 25–40 *g dripping*

1. Wipe marrow, peel thickly. Either cut in rings 2–3 cm deep, or cut marrow in half lengthways. Scoop out seeds with a spoon.

2. Make fillings: Peel and chop onion finely. Melt margarine in a small saucepan and fry onion gently until golden brown. Remove from heat; add minced meat, breadcrumbs, seasoning and skinned chopped tomato, or chopped herbs.
3. Either fill marrow rings; or fill half the marrow, and place the second half on top.
4. Melt dripping in a baking tin. Place stuffed marrow in hot fat and baste well.
5. Cook half way down the oven, Regulo 4 or 180°C (350°F) for $\frac{3}{4}$–1 hour, or until marrow is soft when pierced with a skewer and golden brown.
6. Lift carefully on to a hot serving dish. Garnish with sliced tomato or parsley.
7. Serve with brown sauce, handed separately.

**Stuffed Tomatoes** (serves 2 or 4)

    4 *large tomatoes*
    Filling:  50 *g boiled ham or bacon, cut finely, or* 50 *g grated cheese*
                  1 *small onion*
                  15 *g margarine*
                  25 *g mushrooms*
                  50 *g white breadcrumbs or boiled rice*
                  *Salt and pepper*
    To Bake: 25 *g margarine*
    To Serve: 4 *croûtes of toast or fried bread the size of the tomatoes*

1. Wash and dry the tomatoes; cut a slice off each at the end away from the stalk. (Keep the slices for lids.)
2. Using a teaspoon handle, hollow out the tomatoes. Use the tomato pulp in the filling.
3. Make the filling: Peel and chop onion and mushrooms finely. Melt margarine in a small saucepan. Lightly fry onion, and bacon, if used; add mushrooms and fry without browning. Remove from heat; add finely cut ham, rice, tomato pulp and seasoning.
4. Pack filling into tomato cases. Put a lid on each.
5. Melt margarine in a baking dish. Place stuffed tomatoes in hot fat and baste.
6. Cook half way down oven, Regulo 3 or 150°C (300°F) for 15–25 mins. or until tomatoes are just soft.
7. Cut 4 round croûtes of bread, 5 mm thick and the size of the tomatoes. Toast or fry until golden brown.
8. Serve cooked tomatoes on croûtes of toasted or fried bread. Accompany with green salad.

## SALADS

Salads can be made from a great variety of vegetables, both raw and cooked; fruit, nuts and herbs can also be used to give flavour and colour

# VEGETABLES

Those made from raw vegetables are particularly valuable in the diet as they contain the maximum amount of nutrients. However careful you are in cooking some Vitamin C is always lost, especially from green vegetables, since it is soluble in water and is also destroyed by heat.

Salads can be served in summer or winter. They can be used to accompany hot and cold meat, fish or other savoury dishes; alternatively, a salad may form the main course of a meal. When served as a main dish, the salad must include some body building food such as meat, fish, egg or cheese, and be served with potatoes, or rolls and butter. All vegetables used in salads should be fresh and crisp and in good condition. Whenever possible, use vegetables which have just been gathered from the garden. If stored they lose Vitamin C very quickly, and also become limp and flavourless.

## Ingredients Suitable For Salads

*Raw Vegetables:* Lettuce, watercress, mustard and cress, chicory, cabbage heart, Brussels sprouts, cauliflower, cucumber, celery, onions, radishes, tomatoes, carrots, swede, etc.

*Cooked Vegetables:* Potatoes, beetroot, peas, beans, cauliflower, carrot, rice, etc.

*Fruit and Nuts:* Apple, orange, grapefruit, raisins, sultanas, walnuts, etc.

*Herbs:* Parsley, chives, mint. Herbs should be used carefully because of their definite flavour.

*Bodybuilding Foods:* Eggs: e.g. hard boiled, Scotch, Stuffed.

Cheese: grated, sliced, cut in cubes, or cream cheese.

Meat: such as boiled ham, tongue, cold sliced meat, chicken, etc.

Fish: e.g. tinned salmon, sardines, pilchards, soused herrings, etc.

## To Prepare Salad Ingredients

*Lettuce:* Discard discoloured outer leaves. Break off leaves and wash carefully in two or three lots of cold water, taking care not to bruise or damage them. Drain well on a dry cloth or in a colander.

*Watercress:* Discard any discoloured leaves. Gather together in a bunch. Cut off the long coarse stalks. Wash carefully in two or three lots of cold water. Drain well.

*Mustard and Cress:* Discard any wilted or discoloured leaves. Gather together in a bunch. Cut off stalks to about 3 cm length. Wash cress carefully in two or three lots of cold water, holding it together in a bunch and shaking it in the water to remove seeds. Drain well.

*Chicory:* Remove any coarse outer leaves. Cut in half lengthways and wash thoroughly under cold running water. Drain well.

*Cabbage heart, Brussels sprouts, Cauliflower:* Prepare and wash (see p. 82). Using a very sharp knife, slice or shred cabbage and Brussels sprouts very finely. For cauliflower, cut into very small flowerlets.

*Cucumber:* Wash and dry, or peel skin off thinly. Slice very thinly using a sharp knife.

*Celery:* Prepare and wash (see p. 88). Cut in to 1 cm cubes. Alternatively, cut in 5 cm lengths, cut almost through to form a tassel; place in cold water for ½ hour, until the celery curls. Small heart of celery can be served in whole sticks.

*Spring Onions:* Cut off root. Remove outer layer. Slice off coarse, dark green tops. Rinse in cold water.

*Radishes:* Wash to remove mud. Cut off root and leaves. Leave small radishes whole; slice large ones thinly. For 'roses', slit the radish down eight times almost to the root; leave in cold water to open out.

*Tomatoes:* Wash and dry. Slice very thinly, or cut in half. (Always cut across.)

*Carrot, Swede:* Wash and prepare (see p. 85). Grate very finely.

*Cooked Vegetables:* The vegetables should be boiled, then drained thoroughly. When cold, slice thinly or dice. Serve plain in a salad (e.g. peas, beans) or toss in salad dressing (e.g. potatoes). For beetroot, slice thinly and place in a dish. Cover with vinegar and allow to stand before use.

*Fruit:* Prepare fruit according to kind:

Apples: wash and dry, or peel. Quarter and remove core. Slice thinly, or cut in dice. Sprinkle with lemon juice to prevent browning.

Orange and Grapefruit: Peel and remove all pith. Separate into segments. Orange may be peeled, then sliced across into rings.

Sultanas and Raisins: Wash well and dry.

*Herbs:* Wash, dry, then chop finely.

Salad vegetables should be prepared just before they are needed. If they must be prepared beforehand, place in a polythene box or bag and put in the refrigerator or in a cool place.

## General Rules for Making Salads

1. Prepare all ingredients carefully; make sure they are all well drained and not served wet.
2. Blend the flavours of different ingredients carefully. Do not use too many different vegetables in a salad.
3. Choose a suitable dish for serving, either a bowl or a flat dish or individual plates.
4. Arrange the salad neatly. Take care that colours blend well so that the salad looks attractive.
5. Prepare salads carefully but quickly and avoid handling the vegetables too much. A salad can quickly look 'tired'.
6. Serve all salads with a suitable dressing (see p. 95). French Dressing should only be added immediately before serving.
7. If a salad has to be arranged before it is needed, slip the dish into

a large polythene bag and put it in the least cold part of the refrigerator.

**Summer Salad** (serves 3)

    1 *small lettuce*                 2–3 *tomatoes*
    *Watercress or mustard and cress*    1–2 *hard boiled eggs*
    *Cucumber*                    *Salad cream*

1. Hard boil eggs for 10 mins. (see p. 114). Cool. Slice thinly or cut in halves.
2. Prepare and wash salad vegetables.
3. Arrange salad in a bowl or flat dish. Use the coarser lettuce leaves to form a bed (they can be thinly sliced if liked); keep the small, crisper leaves for the top. Neatly arrange watercress in small bunches decorate with cucumber, tomato, and hard boiled egg.
4. Serve with cold meat, fish or cheese, also new potatoes or rolls and butter. Hand salad cream separately.

**Winter Salad** (serves 4)

    *Half a small white cabbage*     2–3 *sticks, or* 1 *heart celery*
    1–2 *medium sized carrots*       50 g *sultanas or raisins*
    1 *small cooked beetroot*         *Salad cream*

1. Prepare and wash salad ingredients. Wash sultanas.
2. Using a sharp knife, shred cabbage finely; grate carrot finely; cut cooked beetroot and celery in 1 cm dice.
3. Arrange a bed of shredded cabbage on a flat dish. Add other ingredients, arranging very neatly. (Take care to separate the carrot and beetroot colours.)
4. Serve as for Summer Salad, with cold meat, fish or cheese, and accompanied by boiled potatoes or rolls and butter. Hand salad cream separately.

**Green Salad** (serves 4)

    1 *medium sized lettuce*      *French dressing*
    1 *bunch watercress (if liked)*

1. Prepare and wash lettuce and watercress. Dry well. Put lettuce in a mixing bowl.
2. Make French dressing (see p. 95).
3. Sprinkle French dressing over lettuce; toss lightly using a spoon and fork until lettuce is well glazed with dressing.
4. Put into a wooden or glass bowl. Arrange watercress in neat bunches.
5. Serve immediately, to accompany roast poultry, grilled meat, omelets, cheese soufflé, etc.

**Orange Salad** (serves 4)

    1 medium sized lettuce          2 oranges
    1 bunch watercress              French dressing

1. Peel oranges; remove all pith.
2. Prepare green salad (see previous recipe). Toss in French dressing. Put in a bowl and decorate with bunches of watercress.
3. Slice oranges across in 5 mm slices.
4. Arrange orange on the green salad. Serve with roast duck, or cold meats.

**Celery and Apple Salad** (serves 4—6)

    1 heart of celery           Juice of 1 lemon, or French dressing
    2 thin slices onion            made with lemon juice
    3 crisp eating apples       Salt and pepper

1. Prepare and wash celery; cut into 1 cm cubes, and put in a mixing bowl.
2. Chop onion very finely and add to the celery.
3. Peel, quarter and core the apples. Cut into 1 cm cubes and add to other ingredients.
4. Sprinkle lightly with seasoning. Add lemon juice and toss the ingredients together.
5. Serve in a glass bowl, to accompany cold meats.

**Potato Salad** (serves 4)

    400 g cold boiled potatoes (new if possible)
    3-4 tablesp. salad cream or mayonnaise
    1 small lettuce
    1 tsp. finely chopped chives, or parsley

1. Prepare lettuce; wash and drain well.
2. Cut potatoes neatly in 1 cm dice, and put in a basin. Add salad cream and gently turn the potatoes with a spoon without breaking them until all are coated.
3. Arrange lettuce leaves round the edge of a glass bowl. Pile potatoes in the centre. Sprinkle the top with chopped chives or parsley. Serve to accompany cold meat, salads, etc.

**Tomato Salad** (serves 3-4)

    4 large, firm tomatoes
    1 thin slice of onion, or 2 tsp. chopped chives
    French dressing (see p. 95)

1. Wash and dry tomatoes. Slice thinly (across the stalk) and arrange on a fairly flat dish.

# VEGETABLES

2. Sprinkle with very finely chopped onion or chives.
3. Pour on the French dressing. Allow to stand ½ hour.

Serve to accompany meats, hot and cold fish dishes, cheese dishes, etc.

## SALAD DRESSINGS

### French Dressing

2 tablesp. olive oil or salad oil
1 tablesp. vinegar, or lemon juice
¼ tsp. salt, 1-2 shakes pepper
Pinch of dry mustard, if liked
¼ tsp. caster sugar

1. Put seasoning in a small basin; blend with vinegar or lemon juice.
2. Add olive oil.
3. Beat well with a fork until an emulsion is formed and the dressing appears cloudy.
4. Use immediately, as the oil and vinegar separate out again if allowed to stand.
5. Hand French dressing separately with salad; use it for tossing Green Salad.

### Salad Dressing

For white sauce:
150 ml milk
15 g margarine
15 g plain flour

10 g margarine
1 egg yolk
2 tablesp. vinegar
¼ tsp. salt, 2-3 shakes pepper
¼ tsp. made mustard

1. Make white sauce by the roux method (see p. 96).
2. Remove from heat; beat in margarine, then egg yolk.
3. Return to heat. Stirring all the time, cook very gently until the egg yolk no longer tastes raw (2-3 mins.). Do not boil the sauce.
4. Allow to cool, with a lid on the pan to prevent a skin forming.
5. Blend the seasonings with the vinegar.
6. Gradually whisk in the vinegar. Taste and correct seasoning if necessary.
7. Hand separately with salads, or use to make potato salad.

# 14. Sauces

A sauce may be served as an accompaniment to a dish; it may be used to coat food, or it may form part of a dish as, for example, in a stew or a curry. Whichever way it is served, a good sauce should complement the dish it is served with; it should help to bring out the flavour of the food, or add flavour and colour where it is lacking.

A sauce served with a meal helps to counteract dryness and so improves the texture of the food. When the sauce is made with milk or egg, it also improves the food value of the dish or meal.

**Classification:** There are several types of sauces which can be grouped according to the method of making:
1. Roux Sauces—white and brown
2. Simple Blended Sauces
3. Cooked Egg Sauces
4. Miscellaneous Sauces

### 1. ROUX SAUCES

**General Proportions:**

For a pouring sauce:
    30 g fat      30 g flour      500 ml liquid

For a coating sauce:
    50 g fat      50 g flour      500 ml liquid

For a panada:
    100 g fat      100 g flour      500 ml liquid

**Fat:** Butter gives the best flavour though margarine can be used successfully.
**Flour:** Plain flour must be used.
**Liquid:** All milk; or a mixture of half milk and half stock (meat, fish or vegetable depending on the dish the sauce is to accompany).

### BASIC RECIPE FOR PLAIN WHITE SAUCE

| POURING SAUCE | COATING SAUCE |
|---|---|
| 15 g butter or margarine | 25 g butter or margarine |
| 15 g plain flour | 25 g plain flour |
| 250 ml milk | 250 ml milk |
| 1 level tsp. salt | 1 level tsp. salt |
| 2–3 shakes pepper | 2–3 shakes pepper |

1. Melt fat in a small saucepan over a gentle heat. (Make sure the fat does not brown.)

# SAUCES

2. Add flour and stir in using a wooden spoon. Cook the roux gently for 1–2 minutes stirring all the time to prevent browning.
3. Remove pan from heat. Gradually add half the milk to the roux stirring briskly all the time. Beat well to remove any lumps and give a smooth glossy sauce. Stir in the remaining milk.
4. Return pan to the heat. Stirring well all the time, bring the sauce to boiling point and cook for 1–2 minutes.
5. Remove from heat. Add seasoning; taste.

*Consistency:*
A pouring sauce should pour or flow evenly when hot.
A coating sauce when hot should thickly and evenly coat the back of a wooden spoon.

*Amount of Sauce to Serve:*
Pouring sauce or gravy: allow 250–300 ml for 4–6 people.
Coating Sauce: allow 300 ml for 3–4 servings.

## VARIATIONS ON A BASIC WHITE SAUCE

**Anchovy Sauce**

    250 ml *white sauce (unseasoned)—pouring consistency*
    1 *tsp. lemon juice*
    2 *tsp. anchovy essence*

1. Make the white sauce but do not add seasoning.
2. Stir in the lemon juice and anchovy essence.
3. Taste and add seasoning if necessary.

**Cheese Sauce**

    250 ml *white sauce—pouring or coating consistency*
    40 g *finely grated cheese*

1. Make white sauce; season; taste.
2. Add cheese to the boiling sauce (off the heat) and beat in well until smooth. (The cheese should only be melted in the sauce and not cooked.)

When food is coated with cheese sauce, sprinkle evenly with 1 tablesp. fine white breadcrumbs mixed with one tablesp. finely grated cheese, and brown under the grill.

Examples: Eggs au Gratin; Cauliflower Cheese.

**Egg Sauce**

    250 ml *white sauce—pouring consistency*
    1 *hard boiled egg*

1. Make the white sauce. Season well and taste.
2. Stir in the hard boiled egg, chopped very finely, and reheat the sauce.

### Mushroom Sauce

    15 g *butter or margarine*      1 *level tsp. salt*
    15 g *plain flour*      2–3 *shakes pepper*
    250 *ml milk*      50 g *mushrooms*

1. Peel mushrooms; chop very finely.
2. Melt fat in a saucepan; fry the chopped mushrooms very gently for 5 minutes.
3. Add flour. Make the roux (do not remove mushrooms) and cook for 1–2 mins.
4. Add milk gradually and finish as for plain white sauce.
5. Season; taste.

### Mock Tartare Sauce

    250 *ml white sauce—pouring consistency*      2 *tsp. finely chopped gherkins*
    2 *tsp. lemon juice*      1 *tsp. finely chopped capers*

1. Make white sauce; season; taste.
2. Stir in lemon juice and finely chopped gherkins and capers.
3. Reheat if necessary but do not boil.

### Mustard Sauce

    250 *ml white sauce—pouring consistency*
    2 *level tsp. dry mustard*
    2 *tablesp. vinegar or cold water*

1. Mix mustard with vinegar or water.
2. Make white sauce; season; taste.
3. Remove from heat. Stir in mustard. Reheat.

### Onion Sauce

    250 *ml white sauce—pouring consistency*
    200 g *onions*

1. Prepare onions. Cook in boiling salted water until soft. Drain well and chop finely.
2. Make white sauce; season; taste.
3. Stir in the cooked onions. Reheat.

### Parsley Sauce

    250 *ml white sauce—pouring consistency*
    2 *tsp. finely chopped parsley*

1. Wash and dry parsley. Chop very finely.
2. Make white sauce; season; taste.

3. Add chopped parsley to the boiling sauce (off the heat) and stir in well. N.B. Parsley should not be cooked in the sauce.

## Shrimp Sauce

    250 ml *white sauce—pouring consistency*
    1 *tsp. lemon juice*
    50 *g peeled shrimps (or prawns)*

1. Chop the shrimps finely.
2. Make white sauce; season; taste.
3. Stir in the lemon juice and the shrimps. Reheat.

## Béchamel Sauce

| | |
|---|---|
| 15 *g butter or margarine* | Flavourings: 2–3 *slices carrot* |
| 15 *g plain flour* | ½ *small stick celery* |
| 250 *ml milk* | 1 *clove* |
| | 4 *black peppercorns* |
| | 1 *piece blade of mace* |
| | 1 *level tsp. salt* |

1. Put cold milk and flavourings into a saucepan and gradually bring to the boil. Remove from heat; cover pan and allow to stand until the milk has gone cold.
2. Strain the milk.
3. Prepare sauce by the roux method using the flavoured milk.
4. Season with salt; taste.

## BROWN SAUCE

| | |
|---|---|
| 15 *g dripping* | 1 *small carrot* |
| 15 *g plain flour* | 1 *tomato* |
| 300 *ml stock* | 1 *level tsp. salt* |
| 1 *small onion* | 2–3 *shakes pepper* |

1. Prepare and slice the vegetables.
2. Melt dripping in a saucepan; add onion and fry gently until golden brown.
3. Add flour to make a roux, cook very gently, stirring from time to time, until the roux is a rich golden brown.
4. Remove pan from heat; gradually add stock, stirring briskly all the time.
5. Return to the heat; bring the sauce to the boil stirring all the time.
6. Add remaining ingredients. Simmer gently for 20–30 mins.
7. Strain sauce; taste and correct seasoning if necessary.

**Gravy** (see Roasted Meat, p. 61).

## 2. SIMPLE BLENDED SAUCES

The blending method is usually used for making sweet sauces. The thickenings most commonly used for blended sauces are cornflour, custard powder or arrowroot. (Plain flour or semolina can also be used in some cases.)

**General Proportions:**
   For a pouring sauce:
      25 g *cornflour or* 15 g *arrowroot*, 25–40 g *sugar*, 500 *ml liquid.*
   For a coating sauce:
      40 g *cornflour or* 25 g *arrowroot*, 25–40 g *sugar*, 500 *ml liquid.*

*Liquid:* The liquid used may be milk, water or fruit juice.

*Type of thickening to use:* Use cornflour or custard powder when milk is used as the liquid. Use arrowroot when the liquid is water or fruit juice and a transparent sauce is required.

### BASIC RECIPE FOR A WHITE CORNFLOUR SAUCE

| POURING SAUCE | COATING SAUCE |
|---|---|
| 15 g *cornflour* | 20 g *cornflour* |
| 15 g *sugar* | 15 g *sugar* |
| 300 *ml milk* | 250 *ml milk* |
| 3–4 *drops vanilla essence* | 3–4 *drops vanilla essence* |

1. Put cornflour into a small basin; using a wooden spoon, blend to a smooth paste with 3 tablespoonfuls of cold milk.
2. Heat remaining milk and the sugar.
3. Stir paste; pour on the hot (not boiling) milk, stirring all the time.
4. Return the sauce to the pan. Stirring all the time, bring the sauce to the boil and cook for 1–2 mins.
5. Remove from heat. Add flavouring.

**Chocolate Sauce**

    15 g *cornflour*                             300 *ml milk*
    15 g *cocoa or drinking chocolate*   3–4 *drops vanilla essence*
    15 g *sugar*

1. Mix cornflour and cocoa together in a small basin.
2. Make as for white cornflour sauce.

**Custard**

| POURING SAUCE | COATING SAUCE |
|---|---|
| 15 g *custard powder* | 20 g *custard powder* |
| 15 g *sugar* | 15 g *sugar* |
| 300 *ml milk* | 250 *ml milk* |

Make as for white cornflour sauce. (N.B. If directions are given by the makers of the custard powder, follow them.)

## FRUIT AND JAM SAUCES

### Lemon Sauce

| 1 lemon | 40 g sugar |
| 1 level tsp. arrowroot | 200 ml water |

1. Thinly peel zest from half lemon. Put zest, 1 gill water and the sugar into a small saucepan and bring to the boil. Cover and allow to stand for 10 mins., then strain the liquid.
2. Put arrowroot in a small basin and blend to a smooth paste with ½ gill cold water.
3. Stir in the heated water; return to the pan. Stirring all the time, bring to the boil and cook for 1–2 mins.
4. Remove from heat and stir in the juice of the lemon.
5. Reheat if necessary, but do not boil.

### Orange Sauce

| 2 oranges | 40 g sugar |
| 1 level tsp. arrowroot | 150 ml water |

1. Thinly peel zest from 1 orange. Put zest and half of the water and the sugar into a small saucepan and bring to the boil. Continue as for lemon sauce.

### Jam Sauce

| 2 tablesp. raspberry jam | 15–25 g sugar |
| 1 level tsp. arrowroot | 2–3 tsp. lemon juice |
| 200 ml water | |

1. Put jam and 100 ml water into a small saucepan and bring to the boil.
2. Put arrowroot in a small basin and blend to a smooth paste with the remaining 100 ml cold water.
3. Add blended arrowroot to the hot jam and water. Stirring all the time, bring the sauce to the boil and cook for 1–2 mins.
4. Remove from heat. Add 15 g sugar and the lemon juice. Taste, then add more sugar if necessary.
5. Strain into a sauce boat.

### Marmalade Sauce

| 2 tablesp. marmalade | 15–25 g sugar |
| 1 level tsp. arrowroot | Juice of ½ lemon |
| 200 ml water | |

Make as for jam sauce, but do not strain before serving.

**Syrup Sauce**

    2 *tablesp. golden syrup*      200 *ml water*
    1 *level tsp. arrowroot*      2–3 *tsp. lemon juice*

Make as for jam sauce.

### 3. COOKED EGG SAUCES

**Custard Sauce**

    1 *whole egg or* 2 *yolks*      250 *ml milk*
    15 *g sugar*      3–4 *drops vanilla essence*

1. Beat egg (or yolks) and milk together until smooth.
2. Strain into a small saucepan (or double saucepan); add sugar.
3. Heat very gently, stirring all the time, until the sauce thinly coats the back of the wooden spoon, and the egg no longer tastes raw. The sauce must not boil.
4. Remove from heat; add vanilla essence.
5. Serve hot or cold.

### 4. MISCELLANEOUS SAUCES

**Apple Sauce** (serves 4)

    250 *g cooking apples*      10 *g butter*
    2 *tablesp. water*      15 *g sugar*
    2 cloves

1. Peel, quarter and core the apples; slice very thinly.
2. Put apples, cloves and water into a small saucepan and stew gently with the lid on the pan until the apples are soft.
3. Press cooked apples through a sieve to form a purée (or mash until smooth using a fork).
4. Add butter and sugar and reheat.

**Bread Sauce** (serves 4)

    2 *heaped tablesp. breadcrumbs*      1 *clove*
    150 *ml milk*      10 *g butter or margarine*
    ½ *small onion*      ¼ *tsp. salt*
    1 *piece blade of mace*      1–2 *shakes pepper*

1. Peel the onion and slice very thinly.
2. Put milk, sliced onion, mace, and clove in a small saucepan.
3. Bring the milk to the boil; remove from heat. Put a lid on the pan and allow to stand for ½ hour.
4. Strain the milk; rinse the pan.

5. Return strained milk to the saucepan. Add breadcrumbs, butter, salt and pepper; allow to stand for 15 mins.
6. Reheat; taste and correct seasoning if necessary before serving.

**Mint Sauce** (serves 3)

    1 tablesp. chopped mint      1 tablesp. boiling water
    1 tsp. caster sugar      1 tablesp. vinegar

1. Wash and dry the mint leaves; chop very finely.
2. Put mint and sugar into a small dish or sauce boat. Pour on boiling water. (This dissolves the sugar and helps to keep the mint green.)
3. Add vinegar.

**Parsley Butter (or Maître d'Hôtel Butter)** (serves 3)

    25 g butter      A pinch of salt
    2 heaped tsp. finely chopped parsley      A shake of pepper
    1 tsp. lemon juice

1. Wash parsley; chop very finely.
2. Using a knife, mash all the ingredients together on a plate.
3. Form parsley butter into a neat oblong and cut into six 1 cm squares.
4. Chill before serving.

**Curry Sauce** (serves 2–3)

    15 g butter or margarine      1 small cooking apple
    15 g plain flour      1 tomato
    15 g curry powder      25 g sultanas
    300 ml stock or water      1 tablesp. lemon juice
    1 level tsp. salt      2 tsp. sweet chutney
    1 small onion      1 tsp. black treacle

1. Peel onion and chop very finely. Peel and quarter the apple and grate coarsely. Peel tomato using boiling water; slice thinly.
2. Melt butter and fry onion lightly.
3. Add curry powder and flour and fry for 1 minute.
4. Add stock or water, grated apple, tomato, washed sultanas and salt. Bring to the boil, stirring all the time.
5. Allow to simmer gently for ½ hour.
6. Stir in the lemon juice, chutney and black treacle.

**Tomato Sauce**

    10 g butter or margarine      250–300 ml tomato juice
    25 g streaky bacon      2–3 drops Worcester sauce
    1 small onion      Seasoning
    15 g plain flour

1. Peel onion and slice thinly. Cut bacon into small pieces.
2. Melt butter in a small saucepan; add bacon and fry gently to draw out the fat. Add onion and fry slowly until limp, but not brown.
3. Add flour and stir in; cook the roux over a low heat for 1–2 mins. stirring all the time to prevent browning.
4. Remove pan from heat and blend in the tomato juice.
5. Return pan to the heat. Stirring well all the time, bring the sauce to boiling point and cook for 1–2 mins.
6. Remove from heat. Taste the sauce and season with salt and pepper if necessary.
7. Strain into a sauce boat.

# 15. Cheese

**Composition:** Cheese is made from milk. It is a very concentrated food, approx. ½ kg of Cheddar cheese being made from 4 litres of milk. Cheese is composed of roughly ⅓ fat; ⅓ protein; ⅓ water, though the amounts of the main constituents vary slightly according to the type of cheese. For example, a dry hard cheese contains less water than a soft cheese.

### Food Value
*1st class protein:* a very good source.
*Fat:* cheese is rich in fat.
*Carbohydrate:* cheese contains no carbohydrate.
*Vitamins:* good source of Vitamin A; also contains some Vitamin $B_2$ or riboflavin.
*Mineral elements:* very rich in calcium; also phosphorus.
*Water:* constitutes approx. ⅓ of the total weight of cheese.

Being very rich in protein, cheese is an excellent substitute for meat in vegetarian diets.

**Cheese For Cooking:** Cheese for cooking needs to be hard and fairly dry, and have a good flavour. Cheddar is very suitable and is usually less expensive than other varieties of cheese. Cheshire, Double Gloucester, Caerphilly and other plain English cheeses can be cooked, but they are mild in flavour and do not give such a well-flavoured dish. Gruyère cheese, if allowed to go hard, grates and flavours well.

Italian Parmesan cheese is undoubtedly the finest cheese for grating and cooking, but it is very expensive. Bought in small tins, ready grated, it is useful for flavouring or garnishing finished dishes. Blue vein and cream cheeses, also many processed cheeses, are not suitable for cooking.

**Digestibility:** Because of the large proportion of fat and the fact that it is such a highly concentrated food, some people find cheese hard to digest.

To make digestion easier, raw cheese can often be served grated or cut up in thin slices. When cooking cheese, to grate it finely and melt it in a sauce makes it more easily digestible. Always try to serve cheese with some form of carbohydrate food (e.g. bread, potatoes, macaroni, etc.) as the starch helps to absorb the large quantity of fat.

Because of its strong, distinctive flavour, cheese is often served as a savoury at the end of a meal. It stimulates the flow of digestive juices, making the meal more fully digested.

**Uses of Cheese:** Cheese can be used as a substitute for meat in main meals, or as a snack meal. It is also valuable in flavouring sauces, pastries and savoury fillings. It can be cooked by grilling, baking, frying, or simply melting in the heat of a sauce.

## RECIPES USING CHEESE

### Cheese and Potato Pie (serves 2-3)

500 g potatoes
15 g margarine
1 tablesp. top of milk
¼ tsp. salt

2-3 shakes pepper
60 g finely grated cheese
Garnish: 1-2 tomatoes
Parsley

1. Wash and peel potatoes; cut into even sized pieces.
2. Put potatoes in saucepan and cover with cold water; add 1 level tsp. salt. Put lid on pan.
3. Bring potatoes to boiling point; reduce heat and simmer gently until soft (15-20 mins.)
4. Drain potatoes and return them to the saucepan.
5. Mash the potatoes well.
6. Add margarine, milk and seasoning and cream the potatoes.
7. Beat in ¾ of the finely grated cheese.
8. Spread the potatoes in a greased fireproof dish. Sprinkle with the remaining grated cheese; garnish with thinly sliced tomato.
9. Grill until golden brown. Garnish with parsley.

### Stuffed Potatoes (serves 3)

3 large potatoes
15 g butter
¼ tsp. salt
2-3 shakes pepper

1 tablesp. top of milk
60 g cheese, grated finely
Garnish: Parsley

1. Scrub potatoes. Prick the skin in about six places, using a fork. Brush skins with melted lard.
2. Place potatoes on a flat baking sheet, or on the bars of the oven shelf, halfway down the oven.
3. Turn on the oven, Regulo 4 or 180°C (350°F) for 1-1½ hours, or until soft when tested with a skewer.
4. Cut potatoes in half lengthways. Scoop out centres, taking care not to break the skin.
5. Mash cooked potato; add margarine, seasoning, milk and 40 g grated cheese. Mix well.
6. Put cheese mixture back into potato cases. Smooth out evenly with a fork.

7. Sprinkle with remaining cheese and grill until golden brown. (Alternatively, reheat potatoes in oven, Regulo 7 or 220°C (425°F), for 15–20 mins., or until golden brown.)
8. Garnish with parsley. Serve on a heated dish with halved tomatoes, grilled or baked.

## Cheese on Toast (serves 2)

| | |
|---|---|
| 2 *slices bread*, 5 *mm thick* | 50 *g cheese* |
| *Butter* | Garnish: *Parsley* |

1. Slice cheese thinly, or grate finely.
2. Toast bread lightly on one side.
3. Spread untoasted side with butter.
4. Put cheese evenly over buttered side of toast.
5. Grill cheese until golden brown.
6. Trim off crusts if liked. Cut each slice in half and garnish with parsley. Serve immediately on a heated dish. Chutney can be handed separately.

## Welsh Rarebit (serves 2)

| | |
|---|---|
| 2 *slices bread*, 5 *mm thick* | ¼ *tsp. made mustard* |
| 25 *g butter* | 1 *tablesp. top of milk* |
| 50 *g cheese* | Garnish: *Parsley* |
| *Salt and pepper* | |

1. Grate cheese finely.
2. Make toast; butter it, using half the butter. Keep hot.
3. Melt remaining butter in a small pan; remove from heat. Add grated cheese, seasonings, and enough milk to give a stiff paste.
4. Spread the cheese paste on to the toast. Grill gently until golden brown.
5. Garnish with parsley; serve immediately on a heated dish.

## Bread and Cheese Pudding (serves 2)

| | |
|---|---|
| 4 *slices thin bread* | 2–3 *shakes pepper* |
| 25 *g butter or margarine* | 250 *ml milk* |
| 50 *g finely grated cheese* | 1 *egg* |
| ¼ *tsp. salt* | Garnish: *Parsley* |

1. Grease a 500 ml pie dish.
2. Spread bread with butter. Trim off crusts and cut each piece into four neat triangles.
3. Arrange a layer of bread and butter in the bottom of the dish; sprinkle on half of the cheese. Repeat with a second layer of bread, then cheese; finally arrange slices of bread neatly on top, butter side uppermost.

4. Beat egg in a basin until smooth; add milk and seasonings. Strain over pudding and allow to soak for 15 mins.
5. Bake half way down the oven, Regulo 4 or 180°C (350°F) for 30–40 mins. or until golden brown and set. Serve immediately, garnished with parsley.

## Cheese Pudding (serves 2)

| | |
|---|---|
| 125 ml stale white breadcrumbs | 15 g margarine |
| ¼ tsp. salt | 50 g finely grated cheese |
| 2–3 shakes pepper | 250 ml milk |
| ¼ tsp. dry mustard | 1 egg |

1. Grease a 500 ml pie dish.
2. Heat the milk.
3. Remove pan from heat; add breadcrumbs, seasonings, margarine. Cover the pan and allow to stand for ½ hour.
4. Stir in the egg yolk and the grated cheese.
5. Whisk the egg white stiffly and fold into the cheese mixture using a tablespoon.
6. Pour mixture into the greased dish. Bake a third of the way down the oven, Regulo 4 or 180°C (350°F) for 30–40 mins., until golden brown and well risen.
Serve immediately.

## Macaroni Cheese (serves 2)

| | |
|---|---|
| 60 g macaroni | Salt and pepper |
| 300 ml milk | 60 g finely grated cheese |
| 25 g margarine | Garnish: 2 thin slices bread toasted |
| 25 g plain flour | Parsley |

1. Grease a 500 ml pie dish.
2. Put macaroni into boiling salted water and cook for approx. 20 mins. until soft (or cook according to instructions on packet).
(Do not put a lid on the saucepan; cook the macaroni quickly enough to keep it 'moving' in the water.) Drain well when cooked.
3. Meanwhile make a white sauce by the roux method using the margarine, flour and milk. Season. Add two-thirds of the grated cheese and beat in well.
4. Add cooked macaroni to the sauce and pour the mixture into the greased gratin dish.
5. Sprinkle with remaining cheese. Grill until golden brown. (Or reheat in oven, Regulo 6 or 200°C (400°F) for 20 mins., or until golden brown.)
6. Place small triangular croûtes of toast round the edge of the dish. Garnish with parsley.

## Cauliflower au Gratin (serves 3)

| | |
|---|---|
| 1 medium sized cauliflower | Garnish: 1 tablesp. finely grated cheese |
| 400 ml cheese sauce, coating consistency | 1 tablesp. fine white breadcrumbs |
| | 2 thin slices bread, toasted |

1. Grease a gratin dish.
2. Prepare and cook cauliflower (see p. 83).
3. Prepare cheese sauce (see p. 97).
4. Put cooked cauliflower in greased gratin dish and coat with cheese sauce.
5. Mix together grated cheese and breadcrumbs, and sprinkle over sauce.
6. Grill until golden brown. Place small triangular croûtes of toast round the edge of the dish.

## Cheese Soufflé (serves 2)

| | |
|---|---|
| 25 g margarine | Salt and pepper |
| 25 g plain flour | 50 g finely grated cheese |
| 200 ml milk (1 teacup) | 2 eggs |

1. Grease a 750 ml soufflé dish.
2. Using margarine, flour and milk, make white sauce by the roux method. Season well. Beat in the finely grated cheese.
3. Separate the eggs. Beat yolks into sauce.
4. Whisk whites stiffly, and fold carefully into the sauce, using a tablespoon.
5. Pour mixture into the greased soufflé dish. Bake half way down the oven, Regulo 4 or 180°C (350°F), for 30–40 mins., until well risen, golden brown and firm to touch. Serve immediately.

## Cheese Straws

| | |
|---|---|
| 100 g plain flour | 50 g margarine |
| ¼ tsp. salt | 50 g finely grated cheese |
| ¼ tsp. dry mustard | 1 egg yolk |
| Pinch of cayenne pepper | Cold water |

1. Sieve the flour and seasonings into a mixing bowl.
2. Add margarine and rub in until the mixture resembles fine breadcrumbs.
3. Add finely grated cheese.
4. Mixing with a knife, add the egg yolk and enough cold water (about 2–3 tsp.) to give a stiff dry dough.
5. Turn dough on to a lightly floured board. Cut in half.
6. Roll out half the dough into a strip, 10 cm wide and approx. 3 mm thick. Trim ends and edges. Cut into straws 5 mm wide and place on a greased baking sheet.

7. Roll out remaining pastry to 3 mm. Cut into circles using a 5 cm cutter; remove centre of each circle with a 3–4 cm cutter to form rings. Reroll scraps of pastry to make more straws and rings.
8. Bake straws and rings a third of the way down oven, Regulo 6 or 200°C (400°F), for 5–8 mins., or until golden brown. Cool on a wire tray.
9. Put straws through rings. Arrange on a dish and garnish with parsley.

**Cheese Biscuits**

1. Make pastry as for cheese straws. Roll out to 3 mm thickness. Prick neatly with a fork.
2. Cut into biscuits using a 4 cm cutter, and place on a greased baking sheet.
3. Bake a third of the way down oven, Regulo 6 or 200°C (400°F) for 5–10 mins., or until golden brown. Cool on a wire tray.

**Cheese and Tomato Flan** (serves 4)

>  100 g shortcrust or cheese pastry       2–3 shakes pepper
>  Filling:  1 egg                         50 g finely grated cheese
>           150 ml milk                    Garnish: 1–2 tomatoes
>           ¼ tsp. salt                    Parsley

1. Make shortcrust or cheese pastry (see p. 139).
2. Turn on to a lightly floured board, and roll carefully to a round just large enough to line flan tin.
3. Line a 18 cm flan tin with pastry. Trim and decorate edges. Bake blind, a third of the way down the oven, Regulo 7 or 220°C (425°F) for 15–20 mins., or until pale golden brown.
4. Remove flan case from tin and place on a baking sheet or heat proof plate.
5. Beat egg and milk together in a small basin until smooth; add seasonings and finely grated cheese.
6. Pour cheese mixture into flan case. Bake half way down the oven, Regulo 3 or 150°C (300°F) until set but not brown (15–20 mins.).
7. Remove from oven. Garnish with thinly sliced tomato and return to oven to brown (10 mins.).
8. Garnish with parsley. Serve hot or cold.

**Cheese and Vegetable Flan** (serves 4)

>             100 g shortcrust or cheese pastry
>  Filling:   1 small pkt. frozen mixed vegetables
>              (or 1 small tin.)
>             250 ml cheese sauce (coating consistency)
>  Garnish: Parsley

1. Prepare pastry; line a 18 cm flan tin and bake **blind**, as for Cheese and Tomato flan above.

2. Remove flan case from tin and place on a heat proof plate.
3. Cook frozen mixed vegs., or heat canned mixed vegs., according to instructions.
4. Drain vegs. well and place in the flan case to half fill it. Keep hot.
5. Make cheese sauce (see p. 97). Coat the flan evenly.
6. Garnish with parsley. Serve hot or cold.

**Cheese and Onion Turnovers** (serves 4)

    100 g *flaky or rough puff pastry* (see pp. 141-3)
    Filling:  200 g onions
                60 g cheese
                ¼ *tsp. salt*
                2-3 *shakes pepper*

1. Make pastry (see pp. 141-3).
2. Peel onions; slice thinly. Cook in boiling salted water until soft (15-20 mins.). Drain very well, and allow to cool.
3. Grate cheese finely.
4. Roll pastry out to a 20 cm square. Turn pastry over. Trim edges. Cut to form four squares.
5. Mix onions and grated cheese together; add seasonings.
6. Place a quarter of the cheese mixture on each square.
7. Damp edges of each square; fold to form a triangular shape, pressing the edges well together; 'flake' the edges using a knife, then flute. Brush top of each turnover with milk.
8. Place on a floured baking sheet. Bake a third of the way down the oven Regulo 7 or 220°C (425°F) for 15-20 mins., or until golden brown and well risen.
9. Serve hot on a heated dish and garnish with parsley.

**Cheese d'Artois**

    100 g *flaky or rough puff pastry* (or 1 small pkt. frozen pastry)
    Filling:  50 g *finely grated cheese*    ¼ *tsp. salt*
                ½-1 *egg*                      2-3 *shakes pepper*
                15 g *butter or margarine*     ¼ *tsp. dry mustard*

1. Prepare pastry (see pp. 141-3).
2. Grate cheese finely; add seasonings.
3. Melt butter or margarine. Add to grated cheese, then enough beaten egg to give a soft paste.
4. Roll out pastry very thinly to form a rectangle 30 cm × 20 cm. Trim the edges; cut in half lengthways to give two strips 10 cm wide.
5. Spread the cheese mixture on half the pastry.
6. Put second piece of pastry on top and press well together. Brush with beaten egg.

7. Place on a greased baking sheet and cut through into fingers about 15 mm wide.
8. Bake a third of the way down the oven Regulo 7 or 220°C (425°F), for 15–20 mins., or until golden brown and well risen.
9. Separate the fingers after baking. Serve hot or cold, garnished with parsley.

   (Cheese d'Artois can be made using scraps of flaky or rough puff pastry.)

# 16. Eggs

Eggs have a very high food value. They form a valuable part of our diet, and also have many different uses in cookery.

## Food Value

*1st class protein:* a good source in both white and yolk.
*Fat:* found in the yolk only. It is in a finely emulsified form and it is easily digested.
*Carbohydrate:* eggs contain almost no carbohydrate.
*Vitamins:* Vitamins A and D are present in yolk, also Vitamin B. There is no Vitamin C.
*Mineral elements:* white and yolk contain sulphur. Yolk also contains iron, calcium, phosphorus.
*Water:* large proportion in egg white.
The shell is composed of calcium carbonate and is the only waste in the egg. The average weight of a hen's egg is 60 g.

**Digestibility:** Eggs are generally found easy to digest. They are most easily digested when lightly cooked (e.g. boiled, poached or scrambled). Hard boiled eggs are perhaps the most difficult to digest but these are made easier by mashing or chopping finely.

When heated, eggs harden, due to the protein present in both the yolk and the white. The longer and the more strongly egg white is heated, the tougher it becomes, and the less easy to digest. (For this reason, hard boiled eggs should not be boiled for longer than 10 mins.) Yolk never becomes tough because of the quantity of fat present. Hard boiled yolk can be sieved to form a powder.

**Properties of Eggs:** Protein in the form of albumen is found in eggs. (Yolk also contains the proteins vitellin and livetin.) When heated, albumen hardens. The yolk and white, however, do not harden at the same rate. The fat present in the yolk prevents it becoming tough. Albumen is soluble in water and other cold liquids. If heated in the liquid, the albumen will harden and thicken the liquid (e.g. in egg custard). If heated strongly, the albumen will harden too quickly and give a 'curdled' appearance. Egg white can be whisked or beaten to entrap air. When heated, the air will expand, the albumen harden and a firm risen mixture will result (e.g. cakes, soufflés, etc.).

All these properties are important when considering the uses of eggs in cookery.

## Uses of Eggs in Cookery

(a) *As a main dish:* Egg dishes can be substituted for meat or fish in a main meal. They are very useful in invalid or vegetarian diets; also for snack meals.

(b) *Raising agent:* Because air can be incorporated by beating or whisking eggs, they will act as a raising agent in cakes, soufflés, meringues, etc.

(c) *Thickening:* Liquids containing egg will thicken when heated gently (e.g. in egg custards, lemon curd, etc.).

(d) *Binding:* Egg can be used to bind dry ingredients together (e.g. in fish cakes, rissoles, stuffings, etc.).

(e) *Coating:* Beaten egg (with raspings) is often used to coat food to be fried. During frying, the heat hardens the coating, and so helps to keep the food together and prevent fats from entering.

(f) *Enriching:* Eggs can be added to pastries, puddings, etc., enriching the flavour and adding food value.

(g) *Glaze:* Pastry, etc., can be brushed with egg before baking to give a golden shiny surface.

(h) *Garnish:* Hard boiled egg, chopped or in rings can be used to garnish salads, flans, etc.

## RECIPES USING EGGS

**Boiled Egg** (Method 1)

1. Place egg (or eggs) in a small saucepan; cover with cold water (do not cover pan).
2. Bring water to the boil; reduce heat, and simmer for 3 minutes.
3. Drain off the boiling water. Place egg in egg cup.
4. Serve with thin bread and butter, or toast and butter.

**Boiled Egg** (Method 2)

1. Half fill a small saucepan with water and bring to the boil.
2. Using a tablespoon, carefully lower the eggs into the boiling water. (There should be enough water to cover the eggs.)
3. Boil for 4–4½ mins. (or 10 mins. for hard boiled eggs).

**Hard Boiled Eggs**

1. As for Boiled Egg (above). Simmer for 10 mins.
2. Drain off the boiling water.
3. If hard boiled eggs are to be used cold, cover with cold water and allow to cool quickly. (This avoids the black ring which sometimes develops around the yolk of a hard boiled egg.)

## Poached Egg (serves 1)

1 *egg*  
1 *slice of bread, 5 mm thick*  
*Butter*

1. Make toast, trim edges if liked, spread with butter and keep it hot.
2. Half fill a frying pan with water, bring to the boil, then reduce heat so that water is only simmering very gently.
3. Break the egg into a cup and slide it gently into the water. Cook for 2–3 mins., basting with water.
4. Remove from water and drain on a perforated fish slice.
5. Serve on hot buttered toast.

## Scrambled Egg (serves 2)

2 *eggs*  
15 *g butter*  
*Salt and pepper*  
2 *tablesp. top of milk*  
2 *slices bread, 5 mm thick; butter*

1. Make toast, trim edges if liked, spread with butter and keep it hot.
2. Break eggs into a basin; season lightly and add milk. Beat together using a fork.
3. Melt butter in a small saucepan. Add beaten egg and milk, and cook over a gentle heat, stirring all the time with a wooden spoon, until eggs are thick and creamy (1–2 mins.).
4. Serve immediately on buttered toast.

## Fried Egg

1. Break the egg into a cup.
2. Heat dripping or cooking fat in a frying pan, until very faintly hazing. The fat should be about 3 mm deep.
3. Tilt the pan. Slip the egg into the hot fat. Lower the pan as the egg white sets.
4. Using a metal spoon, baste the egg with hot fat until the yolk has a white veil over it, and the white is just firm.
5. Remove carefully with a fish slice and drain.

N.B. The fat for frying may have been produced after frying bacon, sausages, etc.

## Stuffed Eggs (serves 2)

2 *eggs*  
30 *g cream cheese*  
*Salt and pepper*  
1 *dessert sp. mayonnaise or salad cream*  
*Garnish: Parsley or paprika pepper*  
*Green salad for serving*

1. Hard boil eggs and allow to go cold (see p. 114).
2. Shell and cut eggs in half lengthways.

3. Place yolks in a small basin; mash with a fork, then add seasoning, cream cheese and enough mayonnaise to give a soft consistency.
4. Place mixture back in egg white cases using a teaspoon, or pipe in.
5. Sprinkle lightly with finely chopped parsley or paprika pepper.
6. Serve on a bed of green salad.

**Eggs au Gratin** (serves 3)

    3 *eggs*
    250–300 *ml cheese sauce, coating consistency*
    Garnish: 1 *tablesp. finely grated cheese*
              1 *tablesp. fine white breadcrumbs*
              2 *thin slices bread, toasted*
              *Parsley*

1. Grease a gratin dish.
2. Hard boil eggs (see p. 114). Shell the eggs when cooked; cut in half lengthways and place cut side down in the gratin dish.
3. Prepare cheese sauce (see p. 97).
4. Coat eggs with sauce. Finish as for Cauliflower au Gratin (p. 109). Garnish with parsley.

**Curried Eggs** (serves 2)

    2–3 *eggs*                       80 *g Patna rice*
    300 *ml curry sauce* (see p. 103)   Garnish: *Slices of lemon*
                                             *Parsley*

1. Prepare curry sauce (see p. 103).
2. Boil patna rice; rinse and put in a warm place to dry (see p. 89).
3. Hard boil eggs. Shell, cut in half lengthways and place in a gratin dish, cut side down.
4. Coat eggs with curry sauce.
5. Place rice round dish to form a border.
Garnish with slices of lemon and parsley.

**Scotch Eggs** (serves 2–4)

    2 *eggs*                         *Deep fat for frying*
    100–125 *g sausage meat*   Garnish: *Parsley*
    *Egg and raspings to coat*       *Watercress or green salad for serving*

1. Hard boil eggs and allow to cool; shell.
2. Divide sausage meat in two; place on a lightly floured board and press each piece out to a round about 7 cm wide. Take care not to get flour on upper side of sausage meat.
3. Coat eggs in sausage meat, keeping the floured side outside. Shape neatly.
4. Brush the coated eggs with beaten egg; toss in raspings. Reshape eggs if necessary.

5. Fry eggs gently in deep fat at hazing point, for 5-10 mins., until sausage meat is cooked.
6. Drain well on absorbent paper. Allow to cool.
7. Cut eggs in half lengthways, Garnish with parsley. Serve on a bed of watercress or green salad.

**Bacon and Egg Pie** (serves 4)

    200 g *shortcrust pastry*
    Filling: 100 g *lean rashers bacon*
            3-4 *eggs*
            1 *tsp. chopped chives or* 1 *tsp. finely chopped parsley*
            *Salt and pepper*

1. Make shortcrust pastry (see p. 139).
2. Using just over half the pastry, roll out thinly and line the base of a 18 cm flan tin. Roll out the remaining pastry to fit the top of the tin.
3. Trim rind from bacon. Cut bacon into 1 cm pieces. Mix the finely chopped herbs with the bacon.
4. Arrange bacon in a cross in the bottom of the flan, leaving 4 spaces for eggs.
5. Break an egg into each space. Sprinkle very lightly with seasoning.
6. Damp top edge of pastry. Put on pastry lid and press edges very well together. Decorate the edge.
7. Brush the top of pie with milk. Place half way down a hot oven, Regulo 7 or 220°C (425°F), for 10-15 mins., until pastry is brown; reduce heat to Regulo 3 or 150°C (300°F) and continue to cook for a further 30 mins. to set the eggs.
8. Serve hot with white or tomato sauce and vegetables, or cold with salad.

## OMELET

There are two main types of omelets:

(*a*) Plain or French omelets   (*b*) Soufflé omelets

**The Omelet Pan:** For making omelets it is essential to have a smooth, well 'proved' pan or the omelet will stick and break. If possible, keep a special omelet pan, which should be of good heavy quality; omelets can be made successfully in the frying pan, provided it is 'proved' before use.

**To Prove an Omelet Pan**

1. Warm the pan gently; sprinkle with salt and scour the pan well using a screw of greaseproof paper for rubbing.
2. Wipe out the salt, using a soft dry cloth.

3. Put a small piece of lard in the pan, about the size of a pea. Heat gently until the fat is at hazing point. Tip away the hot fat and wipe the pan clean with a piece of absorbent kitchen paper.
4. After use, wipe out the pan with absorbent paper. Only wash if really necessary, and then reprove before using again.

**Plain Omelet** (serves 1)

(use a 15–18 cm omelet pan)

  2 *eggs*         Filling: see below
  1 *tablesp. cold water*
  ¼ *tsp. salt; pinch of pepper*
  10 *g butter* (*unsalted if possible*)

1. Prepare filling for omelet. Heat serving dish.
2. Prepare the omelet pan.
3. Break eggs into a basin; add water and seasoning. Beat the eggs lightly with a fork until they are smooth but not frothy.
4. Heat the butter in the omelet pan over a medium heat; get it as hot as possible without browning. (Tilt the pan so that the fat covers the base.)
5. Pour the egg mixture into the pan. As it sets, draw the set part towards the centre of the pan with a palette knife and allow liquid egg to run on to the pan and set.
6. When the surface of the omelet is creamy and almost set, put the filling on half the omelet. Using a palette knife, fold the omelet over in half.
7. Keep the pan over the heat for another 20–30 secs. to brown the underneath. Total cooking time for the omelet should only be 1–2 mins.
8. Turn on to a heated dish. Garnish with a sprig of parsley. Serve immediately with green salad, new rolls and butter.

**Fillings for Plain Omelets**

(a) *Chopped herbs:* 1 tsp. finely chopped parsley; 1 tsp. finely chopped chives. Mix the herbs with the egg before making the omelet.
(b) *Grated cheese:* use 25 g finely grated cheese. Mix the cheese with the egg before making the omelet.
(c) *Mushroom:* use 25 g mushrooms.
 Skin; cut in half if large, or leave small ones whole. Melt 15 g butter in a small saucepan; add mushrooms. Put a lid on the pan and sauté the mushrooms very gently for 5 mins. Season lightly.

(d) *Tomato:* use 1–2 tomatoes.
Skin, using boiling water. Slice thinly. Sauté as for mushrooms.
(e) *Ham:* use 25 g boiled ham and 2 tsp. finely chopped onion.
Melt 15 g butter in a small sauce pan; fry onion gently until pale golden. Add ham, cut small, and heat with the onion. Season with salt and pepper.

## Soufflé Omelet

2 *eggs*  Filling: see below
1 *tsp. caster sugar*  *Sugared paper*
10 *g butter*

1. Preheat oven to Regulo 4 or 180°C (350°F). Prepare filling.
2. Prepare omelet pan.
3. Separate eggs, putting whites in one basin and yolks in a second basin.
4. Add caster sugar to egg yolks; beat together.
5. Whisk whites very stiffly until the mixture will hold peaks. Using a metal spoon, carefully fold the yolks into the whites.
6. Melt butter in the omelet pan. Add the egg mixture. Cook very gently for $\frac{1}{2}$ min. until the omelet is just firm underneath.
7. Put pan in a preheated oven, half way down and cook for 6–8 mins., until the omelet is firm to touch and golden brown.
8. Turn omelet out on to a piece of greaseproof paper, sprinkled lightly with caster sugar. Put filling on half and fold the omelet over. Serve immediately.

## Fillings for Soufflé Omelets

(a) *Jam:* use 1 tablesp. jam. Warm it in a basin standing over hot water.
(b) *Fruit:* use 1 tablesp. chopped tinned fruit, warmed in a little of the fruit syrup, then drained.

# 17. Puddings and Sweets

## MILK PUDDINGS

Whole grain or a cereal product is used to thicken the milk for milk puddings. The method of making a milk pudding depends on the size and type of grain used. There are three main types of grain:

- (*a*) Whole grain: rice; also large tapioca and sago and macaroni.
- (*b*) Medium or crushed grain: semolina, ground rice, flaked rice; also small sago.
- (*c*) Powdered cereal or fine grain: arrowroot, cornflour, custard powder.

**General Proportions for Milk Puddings:**
To 500 ml milk:

| | |
|---|---|
| 40 g whole grain, or | 25 g sugar |
| 40 g medium grain, or | Flavouring |
| 40 g powdered cereal | |

**Flavourings:** Suitable flavouring ingredients for milk puddings include nutmeg, a strip of zest of lemon or orange rind, vanilla essence, bay leaf, etc. Egg can be added to enrich the pudding.

**Rice Pudding** (serves 3)

| | |
|---|---|
| 40 g rice | 500 ml milk |
| 25 g sugar | 1 bay leaf or nutmeg |

Method for all whole grain puddings.

1. Grease a 650 ml pie dish.
2. Wash rice in cold water; drain well.
3. Put rice, sugar and bay leaf if used into the greased dish; add milk and stir well. (Sprinkle on a pinch of nutmeg if used.)
4. Bake half way down the oven, stirring occasionally, Regulo 3 or 150°C (300°F) for 1½–2 hours until the pudding is creamy and the skin golden brown.

**Semolina** (serves 3)

| | |
|---|---|
| 40 g semolina | 500 ml milk |
| 25 g sugar | 2–3 drops vanilla essence |

Method for all medium grain puddings.

## PUDDINGS AND SWEETS

1. Warm the milk. Remove from the heat.
2. Sprinkle the semolina into the milk, stirring well. Add sugar and vanilla essence.
3. Return pan to heat and bring to the boil, stirring all the time.
4. Reduce heat and allow the pudding to cook very gently for 15–20 mins., until thick and creamy. Stir occasionally.
5. Pour into a serving dish.

*Alternatively*
Follow Method Nos. 1, 2, 3 as above.
4. Pour semolina into a greased pie dish. Grate a little nutmeg on top.
5. Bake half way down the oven, Regulo 4 or 160°C (325°F) for 20–30 mins., until golden brown on top.

**Cornflour Mould** (serves 4)

40 g cornflour   *Strip of zest of lemon or orange rind*, or
25 g sugar       *3–4 drops vanilla essence*
500 ml milk

Method for all powdered cereal puddings.

1. Rinse mould in cold water.
2. Put cornflour into a small basin; using a wooden spoon, blend cornflour to a smooth paste using some of the cold milk.
3. Boil remaining milk with the sugar and lemon or orange rind.
4. Remove rind from milk; stir paste and add boiling milk, stirring all the time.
5. Rinse pan; return cornflour mixture to it; bring to the boil, stirring continuously and cook gently for 2–3 mins. (Add vanilla essence if used.)
6. Pour into wet mould. Allow to set.
7. Turn out on to a glass dish. Serve with stewed fruit, or jam sauce.

## EGG CUSTARD AND CUSTARD PUDDINGS

**Baked Egg Custard** (serves 3–4)

2–3 eggs         25 g sugar
500 ml milk      Nutmeg or 3–4 drops vanilla essence

1. Grease a 650 ml pie dish.
2. Break eggs into a basin and beat until smooth using a fork. (Add vanilla essence if used.)
3. Warm milk and sugar together to blood heat; make sure the sugar has dissolved.
4. Stir the warmed milk into the beaten egg.
5. Strain into the greased pie dish. Sprinkle lightly with nutmeg.
6. Bake two-thirds of the way down the oven, Regulo 3 or 150°C (300°F), for 40–50 mins., or until the custard is set.

### Bread and Butter Pudding (serves 3)

    4 *thin slices bread and butter*    15 *g sugar*
    50 *g sultanas*                             250 *ml milk*
    1 *egg*                                       *Nutmeg*

1. Grease a 500 ml pie dish. Wash sultanas.
2. Butter the bread. Trim off crusts and cut each piece into 4 neat triangles.
3. Arrange a layer of bread and butter in the bottom of the dish; sprinkle with half the sultanas. Repeat with a second layer of bread, then dried fruit. Arrange the remaining bread neatly on top, butter side uppermost.
4. Break egg into a basin; add sugar and beat well. Stir in milk.
5. Strain the egg and milk over the pudding; lightly grate nutmeg over the surface. Allow to soak 10 mins before baking.
6. Bake half way down the oven, Regulo 4 or 160°C (325°F), until firm and golden brown on top.

### Cabinet Pudding (serves 2–3)

    2–3 *small sponge cakes*      250 *ml milk*
    2 *eggs*                                3–4 *drops vanilla essence*
    15 *g sugar*

1. Grease a 500 ml basin.
2. Cut sponge cakes neatly into 1 cm pieces; put in basin.
3. Break eggs into a basin; add sugar and beat well. Stir in milk and vanilla essence.
4. Strain the eggs and milk over the sponge cake; allow to stand for 10 mins.
5. Cover basin with greased greaseproof paper and steam gently for 1 hour. When cooked, the pudding should be firm.
6. Turn on to a heated dish. Serve with jam sauce.

### Queen of Puddings (serves 3–4)

    125 *ml stale white breadcrumbs*    *Grated rind and juice of half a lemon*
    10 *g margarine*                         1–2 *tablesp. raspberry jam*
    15 *g sugar*                                Meringue: 2 *egg whites*
    2 *egg yolks*                                 75–100 *g caster sugar*
    250 *ml milk*

1. Grease a 500 ml pie dish.
2. Boil the milk; remove from heat and add margarine, sugar, grated lemon rind and breadcrumbs. Allow to stand for 15 mins.
3. Beat egg yolks into the bread and milk; pour into the greased pie dish. Bake half way down the oven, Regulo 4 or 160°C (325°F), for 20–30 mins., or until set.

4. Remove from oven; spread pudding carefully with jam, then sprinkle with lemon juice.
5. Make meringue using the egg whites and caster sugar (see p. 163). Pile meringue on top of the pudding. Sprinkle with 1 tsp. caster sugar.
6. Bake gently, low down in the oven, Regulo 1 or 120°C (250°F), for ½–1 hour until the meringue is firm to touch and pale fawn on the points.

## BATTERS

There are two main types of batters:
(a) Thin batter (used for Pancakes, Yorkshire pudding, etc.)
(b) Thick batter (used for coating food to be fried)
In making batters, plain flour is used. The main raising agent is the steam or water vapour which develops during baking from the liquid in the batter. Batters should be very well beaten, as the egg in the mixture and the air introduced during mixing also help to raise the batter.

### Basic Recipe for Thin Batter

100 g plain flour          1 egg
¼ tsp. salt                250 ml milk

1. Sieve flour and salt into a mixing bowl. Make a 'well' in the centre of the flour.
2. Break the egg into the 'well'.
3. Using a wooden spoon, stir the egg and draw in the flour from around the side.
4. Gradually add just enough milk to incorporate all the flour and make a thick paste.
5. Beat very well to remove all lumps and give a smooth mixture.
6. Stir in the remaining milk, a little at a time.
7. Beat (or whisk) the batter very thoroughly, until small air bubbles appear all over the surface (about 5 mins.).
8. Use batter as desired.

### Batter Pudding (serves 4)

250 ml thin batter
15–25 g cooking fat
To serve: Syrup, jam or butter and sugar

1. Prepare batter.
2. Put cooking fat in a baking tin, approx. 18 cm square. Place a third of the way down the oven, Regulo 7 or 220°C (425°F), and heat until the fat is at hazing point.

3. Pour batter into hot fat. Bake for 30–40 mins., until well risen, golden and firm to touch.
4. Serve immediately on a heated dish with syrup, jam, or butter and sugar, handed separately.

**For Yorkshire Pudding**

Prepare batter as above. Cook as for Batter Pudding, using 25 g dripping from the roasted joint. (Individual Yorkshire puddings can be made instead of one large one, using castle pudding tins, or small patty tins. It is necessary to have about 1 tsp. of melted dripping in each one.)

**Fruit in Batter** (serves 4)

> 250 ml thin batter
> 15 g cooking fat
>
> Either: 75 g *large raisins*
> Or: 2 *cooking apples*
> 50 g *sugar*

1. Peel, quarter, core and slice apples; or wash raisins.
2. Prepare batter.
3. Put cooking fat in a baking tin or fireproof dish. Place a third of the way down the oven, Regulo 7 or 220°C (425°F), and heat until the fat is at hazing point.
4. Put prepared fruit in the hot fat. If apples are used, sprinkle with sugar. Pour the batter over.
5. Bake as for Batter Pudding.
   Serve immediately. Hand custard separately.

**Pancakes** (makes approx. 8–10)

> 250 *ml thin batter*
> 25 g *white cooking fat*
>
> To serve: *Caster sugar*
> *Orange of lemon juice*
> Garnish: *Chunks of orange or lemon*

1. Prove the frying pan if necessary (see p. 117).
2. Prepare the batter.
3. Heat sufficient fat in the frying pan to only just cover the bottom.
4. Pour in batter, tilting the pan to give a thin layer over the base.
5. Cook gently until the underneath is golden and the top set (about 1 min.).
6. Turn with a palette knife or toss. Cook the second side until golden.
7. Turn on to a piece of sugared paper. Sprinkle with caster sugar and fruit juice. Roll up.
8. Place on a hot dish and garnish with orange or lemon. Serve pancakes immediately.

## Basic Recipe for Coating Batter

100 g plain flour  
¼ tsp. salt  
1 egg  
125–150 ml milk  

Make as for Thin Batter.

## Fruit Fritters (serves 3–4)

150 ml coating batter  
2 cooking apples  
2 bananas  
25 g caster sugar  
Deep fat for frying  

1. Make batter. (It should be thick enough to well coat the back of the wooden spoon.)
2. Peel cooking apples; remove core. Cut into 5–7 mm thick rings. Skin bananas; slice in half lengthways, then in half across to give 4 pieces each.
3. Coat the pieces of fruit in batter. Lower carefully into the hot fat which is just at hazing point.
4. Fry gently, about 2–3 mins.; turn the fritters and cook for a further 2–3 mins. (or the fritter may be cooked in deep fat). The fruit should be soft and the batter golden and crisp.
5. Remove the fritters using a perforated draining spoon; drain well on absorbent paper.
6. Pile on a heated dish; sprinkle well with caster sugar. Serve immediately.

## FRUIT

## Baked Apples (serves 4)

4 large cooking apples  
4 tsp. sugar  
25 g butter  
4 tsp. golden syrup  
} or 50 g raisins or chopped dates

1. Wipe and core apples. Lightly score round the centre of the apple, using a small knife, so that the skin does not split during cooking.
2. Place apples in a heatproof dish or tin.
3. Fill each core with 1 tsp. sugar, 1 tsp. syrup, and a small piece of butter (or with washed, dried fruit).
4. Put about 3 mm cold water in the bottom of the baking dish.
5. Bake half way down the oven, Regulo 4, or 180°C (350°F), for 30–40 mins., until apples are soft when tested with a skewer.
6. Lift on to a heated dish. Remove top half of skin if liked. Pour the syrup over the apples.
Serve immediately with custard or cream.

**Stewed Fruit** (serves 3-4)

> 500 g fruit (*apples, plums, gooseberries, rhubarb, etc.*)
> 125 ml water
> 50-80 g sugar (*depending on sweetness of fruit*)

1. Prepare fruit according to kind (see p. 196).
2. Put sugar and water in a saucepan (large enough so that the fruit will ⅔ fill the pan). Dissolve the sugar over a gentle heat, and boil for 3 mins.
3. Add the prepared fruit. Simmer gently with a lid on the saucepan until the fruit is soft.
4. Pour into a serving dish. Serve hot or cold, with custard or cream.

**Stewed Prunes** (serves 4-6)

> 500 g prunes
> 500 ml water
> 50 g brown sugar

1. Wash prunes. Place in a saucepan or casserole. Add water.
2. Soak fruit in the water overnight.
3. Add sugar. Stew fruit very gently until tender, either on top of the stove in a saucepan with a tightly fitting lid, or in a casserole in a moderate oven.
Serve hot or cold.

**Apple Charlotte** (serves 4)

> 500 g cooking apples
> 6 tablesp. breadcrumbs
> 2 tablesp. golden syrup
> 1 tablesp. brown sugar
>
> 25 g butter or margarine
> 2 tablesp. water
> Grated zest of half a lemon

1. Peel, quarter and core apples. Slice thinly into cold water.
2. Grease a 750 ml pie dish. Place half the apples in a layer in the bottom of the dish; cover with half the breadcrumbs. Repeat with the remaining apples, then finally a layer of breadcrumbs on top.
3. Heat the syrup, sugar, butter, water and grated lemon zest together in a small saucepan, until the sugar has dissolved and the butter melted.
4. Pour this mixture carefully over the pudding.
5. Bake half way down the oven, Regulo 4 or 180°C (350°F), for 40-50 mins., until the apples are soft and the pudding golden on top.
6. Serve hot with custard or cream.

## STEAMED PUDDINGS

(*a*) Steamed 'Sponge' puddings using Creaming Method.

## Basic Recipe for Steamed Sponge Pudding (serves 3)

50 g margarine  
50 g caster sugar  
1 standard egg  
100 g self raising flour  
1–2 tablesp. warm water or milk

1. Grease a 500 ml basin; prepare a piece of double greaseproof paper to cover the basin, and grease a circle in the centre where the paper touches the pudding.
2. Put on steamer.
3. Prepare mixture by creaming method (see p. 150).
4. Put mixture into the greased basin. Cover with the prepared paper. Tie down firmly with string.
5. Steam gently for 1–1¼ hours.
6. Turn on to a heated plate. Serve immediately.

### VARIATIONS ON THE BASIC RECIPE

### Jam Cap Pudding

Basic recipe. In addition: 1 tablesp. jam

Grease a 500 ml basin. Put jam in the bottom. Continue as for Steamed Sponge Pudding. Steam for 1–1¼ hours. Turn out on to a heated dish. Serve with jam sauce or custard.

### Castle Puddings

Make as for Jam Cap Pudding. Use 6 individual Castle Pudding tins, and put 1 small tsp. jam in each. Steam for ¾–1 hour.

### Syrup Pudding

Make as for Jam Cap Pudding, using 1 tablesp. golden syrup in place of jam.

### 'Spotted Dick'

Basic recipe. In addition: 50 g currants.

Wash and dry fruit. Make as for Steamed Sponge Pudding, stirring currants into the creamed mixture after the flour. Steam for 1–1¼ hours.
Turn out on to a heated dish.
Serve with custard.

### Chocolate Sponge Pudding

Basic recipe, using 85 g S.R. flour, and 15 g cocoa; instead of 100 g S.R. flour.
Prepare and cook as for Steamed Sponge Pudding.
Serve with custard or Chocolate sauce.

### Orange Sponge Pudding

Basic recipe. In addition grated zest of 1 orange.

Prepare and cook as for Steamed Sponge Pudding, adding finely grated zest after creaming fat and sugar.

Serve with custard or orange sauce.

### Lemon Sponge Pudding

Make as for Orange Sponge Pudding, using grated lemon zest in place of orange. Serve with custard or lemon sauce.

### Ginger Sponge Pudding

Basic recipe. In addition: 1 level tsp. ground ginger.

Prepare and cook as for Steamed Sponge Pudding, sieving ground ginger in with the flour.

Serve with custard or syrup sauce.

## STEAMED SUET PUDDINGS

### 'Boiled' Apple Pudding (serves 3–4)

150 g *suet crust pastry* (see p. 141)
500 g *cooking apples*
60–80 g *sugar*

1. Grease a 750 ml basin; prepare double greased greaseproof paper. Put on steamer.
2. Peel, quarter and core apples. Slice very thinly into cold water.
3. Make suet crust pastry (see p. 141).
4. Line the basin with ⅔ of the pastry. Roll remaining pastry to fit the top of the basin.
5. Drain apples. Put half the fruit in the basin; add sugar, then the rest of the fruit.
6. Damp top edge of pastry and press lid on.
7. Cover with greaseproof paper and tie down firmly.
8. Steam pudding gently for 2–2½ hours.
9. Turn out on to a heated dish. Sprinkle with caster sugar. Serve with custard.

### Fruit Layer Pudding

150 g *suet crust pastry* (see p. 141)
Filling: 1 *large cooking apple*
50 g *raisins*
25 g *brown sugar*
1 *tablesp. golden syrup*
*Pinch of mixed spice*

## PUDDINGS AND SWEETS

1. Grease a 750 ml basin; prepare greaseproof paper to cover the basin. Put on steamer.
2. Prepare filling: wash and chop raisins. Peel, quarter and core apple; grate coarsely, Add raisins, sugar, syrup, spice and mix together.
3. Make suet crust pastry. Divide into four pieces; one small piece, two medium, one large.
4. Press or roll out the small piece to fit the bottom of the basin; spread on a third of the filling. Repeat layers of pastry and filling, ending with a layer of pastry.
5. Cover the basin with greaseproof paper and tie down firmly.
6. Steam pudding gently for 2–2½ hours.
7. Turn out on to a heated dish. Serve with custard.
Alternative fillings: Jam or Mincemeat.

### Roly Poly Pudding

150 g suet crust pastry (see p. 141)
3 tablesp. jam or mincemeat or marmalade

1. Prepare steamer.
2. Make suet crust pastry. Roll out to a 20 cm square.
3. Spread jam or mincemeat over the pastry, leaving a margin of 2 cm all round without filling.
4. Damp side and top edges. Roll up and press ends together well.
5. Wrap the roll in greased greaseproof paper or cooking foil. Steam 2–2½ hours.
6. Unroll, and place on a heated dish. Serve with custard.

### Christmas Pudding

| | |
|---|---|
| 100 g sultanas | 100 g soft brown sugar |
| 100 g currants | 1 level tsp. mixed spice |
| 100 g raisins | Grated rind of 1 orange |
| 25 g mixed peel | 1 level tsp. salt |
| 100 g breadcrumbs | 2 eggs |
| 100 g plain flour | 1 tablesp. black treacle |
| 100 g suet | Milk or beer to mix |

1. Grease a 750 ml basin, also double greaseproof paper to cover the pudding. Prepare steamer.
2. Put all dry ingredients together. (The fruit should have been previously washed and dried.)
3. Beat egg; add to the dry ingredients. Add black treacle and enough milk to give a stiff dropping consistency. Mix well.
4. Place in the greased basin. Cover and tie down firmly.

5. Steam 8–10 hours.
   After this steaming, the pudding can be kept for some time. When needed, it should be steamed for 2–3 hours.
6. Turn out on to a heated dish. Stick a small sprig of washed holly in the top. Serve with White Cornflour Sauce (see p. 100) with 1 tablesp. rum added. Alternatively serve with 'Brandy Butter'.

**Brandy Butter** (Hard Sauce)

    50 *g butter*
    100 *g icing sugar*
    2 *tablesp. brandy*

Cream butter and icing sugar until very pale and fluffy. Very gradually, beat in the brandy. Pile the Brandy Butter on to a small glass dish.

## BAKED PUDDINGS

**Fruit Crumble** (serves 3–4)

    400 *g fruit* (apples, plums, rhubarb, gooseberries, etc.)
    25–60 *g sugar* (depending on sweetness of fruit)
    Crumble: 100 *g plain flour*
              50 *g margarine*
              50 *g sugar*

1. Grease a 750 ml pie dish.
2. Prepare fruit according to kind. Leave in water if necessary (e.g. apples) or pack into the greased pie dish. Sprinkle with sugar.
3. Make crumble: sieve flour, add margarine and sugar. Rub in with the fingertips until the mixture resembles fine breadcrumbs.
4. Spread the crumble over the fruit. Smooth the top with the back of a tablespoon.
5. Bake half way down the oven, Regulo 4 or 180°C (350°F), for 30–40 mins., until fruit is soft and crumble is golden brown.
   Serve with custard.

**Baked Sponge Pudding**: For Baked Sponge Pudding, the same recipes can be used as for 'Steamed Sponge Pudding'. Bake in a greased 500 ml pie dish. Place half way down the oven, Regulo 4 or 180°C (350°F), for 25–40 mins., until golden brown and firm to touch. Serve in the baking dish.

**Eve's Pudding** (serves 4)

    400 *g cooking apples*          Creamed mixture: 50 *g margarine*
      (or other fruit)                                 50 *g caster sugar*
    50 *g sugar*                                         1 *standard egg*
                                                      100 *g S.R. flour*
                                                      1–2 *tablesp. milk*

1. Grease a 750 ml pie dish.
2. Peel, quarter and core the apples. Slice thinly into cold water (or prepare other fruit according to kind).
3. Make creamed mixture.
4. Drain fruit well. Pack half in the dish; sprinkle with 2 oz sugar, then add remaining fruit.
5. Spread the creamed mixture evenly over the fruit.
6. Bake half way down the oven, Regulo 4 or 180°C (350°F), for 30–45 mins., until the apples are soft and the creamed mixture firm. Serve hot with custard.

**Baked Roly Poly Pudding:** Make as for Steamed Roly Poly Pudding (p. 129). Place roll on a greased baking tray. Bake for 30–40 mins., Regulo 6 or 200°C (400°F), until firm and golden brown. Serve with custard.

## PUDDINGS USING PASTRY

**Plate Jam Tart** (18–20 cm plate)

> 100 g *shortcrust pastry* (see p. 139)
> 2–3 *tablesp. jam*

1. Prepare and shortcrust pastry. Roll out on a lightly floured board to the shape and size of the plate.
2. Lift pastry on to the plate. Press on well. Trim and decorate edge.
3. Spread jam carefully over base of pastry, leaving edges free.
4. Bake a third of the way down the oven, Regulo 7 or 220°C (425°F), for 15–20 mins., until the pastry is pale fawn and firm. Serve hot or cold, with custard or cream.

**Syrup Tart** (18–20 cm plate)

> 100 g *shortcrust pastry* (see p. 139)    *Grated zest of ½ lemon*
> 3 *tablesp. breadcrumbs*                  2 *tablesp. golden syrup*

1. Prepare shortcrust pastry and line plate as for Jam Tart. Trim and decorate edges.
2. Spread breadcrumbs across base of plate.
3. Grate the zest of lemon rind finely over breadcrumbs.
4. Allow the syrup to run from a spoon as evenly as possible over the breadcrumbs.
5. Bake half way down the oven, Regulo 7 or 220°C (425°F), for 20–30 mins., until the pastry and filling are golden brown. Serve hot with custard, or cold.

### Egg Custard Flan

    100 g *shortcrust pastry* (see p. 139)
    Egg Custard: 250 *ml milk*    1 *egg*
       15 *g sugar*    Nutmeg

1. Make pastry. Roll out to line a 18 cm flan tin or pie plate.
2. Rinse flan tin or pie plate with cold water. Line with pastry. Trim and decorate edges.
3. Break egg into a basin; add sugar. Whisk lightly to break up the egg. Stir in the milk.
4. Strain the egg custard into the flan case.
5. Grate a little nutmeg over the surface.
6. Bake half way down the oven, Regulo 5 or 190°C (375°F), and cook until the custard has quite set.
Serve hot or cold.

*Alternative method:* Prepare flan case and bake blind. Continue as above method, Nos. 3–6.

### Jam Turnovers

    100 g *rough puff or flaky pastry* (see pp. 141, 143)
    3–4 *tablesp. jam*
    3 *tsp. caster sugar*

1. Make pastry (see pp. 141, 143). Shape as for Cheese & Onion Turnovers (see p. 111).
2. Brush turnovers with water and sprinkle lightly with caster sugar.
3. Place on a flat baking tray. Bake a third of the way down the oven, Regulo 7 or 220°C (425°F) for 15–20 mins., until risen, golden brown and crisp.
Serve hot or cold, with custard or cream.

*Alternative fillings:*
(*a*)   Fresh fruit, sprinkled with sugar;   (*b*)   Mincemeat.

### Fruit Pie (serves 4)

    Fruit to fill a 500 ml pie dish (approx. 500 g)
    50–100 *g sugar*
    100 g *shortcrust pastry* (see p. 139)
     (or rough puff or flaky pastry)

1. Make shortcrust pastry.
2. Prepare fruit according to kind.

3. Pack half the fruit into the pie dish; sprinkle with the sugar, then add the remaining fruit so that the dish is filled to just above the rim. Add 2 tablesp. water, unless the fruit is very juicy.
4. Roll out the prepared pastry to the shape of the dish, but 1 cm wider all round.
5. Cut a 1 cm strip of pastry from round the edge and use to line the rim of the pie dish. Damp the pastry rim.
6. Lift the pastry top on to the pie. Press damp edges together at the rim. Trim the edges with a knife.
7. Flake the edges of the pastry and decorate with small flutes. Loosen one corner of the pastry, to allow steam to escape. Bake half way down the oven, Regulo 7 or 220°C (425°F) for 15–20 mins., until pastry is lightly coloured. Reduce heat to Regulo 3 or 150°C (300°F) and continue to cook until fruit is soft when tested with a skewer.
8. Sprinkle lightly with caster sugar. Serve hot with custard or cream.

**Fruit Tart**

    200 g shortcrust pastry (see p. 139)
    400 g fruit (approx.)
    60–80 g sugar

1. Prepare shortcrust pastry. Divide in half.
2. Roll out one piece of pastry and line an 18–20 cm pie plate. Trim edges.
3. Roll remaining pastry to fit the top of the plate.
4. Prepare fruit according to kind. Pack carefully on to the lined plate and sprinkle with sugar.
5. Damp edges of pastry. Place top on and firm edges together. Trim; then flake and flute edges.
6. Bake as for Fruit Pie. Sprinkle with caster sugar and serve hot or cold with custard or cream.

**Apple Dumplings** (serves 2)

    2 cooking apples
    30 g demerara sugar
    100 g shortcrust pastry (see p. 139)

1. Make pastry. Divide in half and roll each piece out to a 15 cm circle.
2. Peel and core the apples. Stand an apple in the centre of each piece of pastry. Fill each 'core' with sugar.
3. Damp edges of pastry. Draw together carefully on top of the apple, and mould the pastry round to completely cover each apple.
4. Turn apples over with the joined edges of pastry underneath.
5. Place on a greased baking tray. Bake as for Fruit Pie.
6. Sprinkle lightly with caster sugar. Serve hot with custard or cream.

## COLD SWEETS

**Blancmange**

>A single packet of blancmange powder
>25 g sugar
>550 ml milk

1. Rinse mould inside with cold water. Do not dry.
2. Make as for White Cornflour Sauce, following Nos. 1-4 of the Method (see p. 100).
3. Pour blancmange into wet mould. Leave to set in a cool place.
4. When set, loosen blancmange and turn out on to a glass dish. Serve with cream, or with stewed fruit or jelly.

**Junket** (serves 3)

>550 ml milk
>1 heaped tsp. sugar
>1 tsp. essence of rennet (or quantity suggested by the maker)

1. Place milk and sugar in a saucepan. Warm to luke warm, stirring to make sure the sugar has dissolved.
2. Pour warm milk in to a glass dish. Carefully stir in the rennet, and leave in a warm place to set. Do not move the junket while setting.
3. The junket can be put in a cold place when set.
4. Sprinkle very lightly with grated nutmeg. Serve alone, or with cream, or to accompany stewed fruit.

**Milk Jelly**

>A packet of jelly
>Approx. 200 ml boiling water
>250 ml milk

1. Break up jelly cube. Place in a measuring jug. Add boiling water to come up to the 250 ml mark.
2. Stir well to dissolve the jelly cube.
3. Allow to go cold but not set.
4. Very gradually, stir in the cold milk.
5. Pour into a mould and put in a cool place to set.
6. Loosen jelly and turn out on to a glass dish. Serve alone, or with fruit and cream.

**Fruit in Jelly** (serves 4)

>250 g fresh fruit or 1 small tin of fruit
>A packet of jelly
>Juice of ½ lemon

## COLD SWEETS

1. Prepare fruit according to kind; cut up into neat even sized pieces. Place in serving dish, individual glasses, or a mould.
2. Make jelly, using syrup from tinned fruit, or water. (Follow maker's instructions for making jelly.)
3. Add lemon juice to jelly. Pour over fruit and allow to set.
4. If jelly was made in a mould, dip mould quickly into hot water and turn jelly out on to a glass dish.
Serve with cream, piped on neatly, or handed separately.

### Fresh Fruit Jelly

    2 *oranges*    80 *g sugar*
    1 *lemon*    15 *g powdered gelatine (bare measure)*
    *Water*

1. Wash fruit. Remove zest from one orange, using a potato peeler, and put in a saucepan.
2. Add fruit juice made up to 500 ml with water.
3. Add sugar, and finally gelatine.
4. Heat gently, stirring all the time, until the gelatine and sugar have dissolved. The mixture must not boil.
5. Remove from heat. Put a lid on the saucepan and allow the liquid to infuse for 15 mins.
6. Strain into a mould and allow to set in a cool place.
7. Warm mould in hot water. Turn jelly on to a glass dish. Serve with cream.

### Fresh Fruit Salad (serves 4)

500 g *fresh fruit* (use a selection: raspberries, strawberries, banana, orange, grapes, apricots, cherries, etc.)

    Syrup: 250 *ml water*
    80 *g sugar*
    *Juice of* 1 *lemon*

1. Try to choose a good selection of fruit to give variety in colour and texture.
Wash and prepare the fruit according to kind; cut into neat even sized pieces, and put into a mixing bowl.
2. Make syrup: put sugar and water together in a small saucepan. Dissolve slowly and allow to boil for 3 mins. Remove from heat; add lemon juice.
3. Pour hot syrup over fruit. Cover and leave to cool. Allow fruit to soak in syrup for 2–3 hours.
Serve in a glass dish, or individual sundae glasses. Hand cream separately.

### Gooseberry Fool (serves 4)

500 g gooseberries  
100 ml water  
60 g sugar  
Juice of ½ lemon  
250 ml custard (pouring consistency)  
150 ml evap. milk

1. Top and tail and wash gooseberries; stew gently in a covered saucepan with the water and sugar until soft.
2. Press through a sieve to form a purée.
3. Add lemon juice.
4. Make custard (see p. 100). Add to purée. Taste. Add more sugar if necessary.
5. Whisk evaporated milk until thick and creamy. Fold into fruit mixture.
6. Pour into a glass dish or individual sundae glasses. Chill before serving.

Serve with shortbread biscuits, handed separately.

### Trifle (serves 3-4)

1 small tin fruit  
2-3 sponge cakes or slices of plain stale cake  
2 tablesp. jam  
300-400 ml custard (coating consistency)  
Decoration: Fresh whipped cream  
Tinned fruit or glacé cherries and angelica

1. Cut sponge cakes in half; spread with jam and sandwich together. Cut sponge or cake into 2 cm pieces.
2. Drain juice from fruit; cut fruit into neat, even sized pieces.
3. Put fruit and sponge cake together in a glass dish. Add enough fruit juice to thoroughly moisten the cake. Allow to soak ½ hour.
4. Make custard (see p. 100).
5. Coat the trifle with hot custard. Allow to go cold.
6. Decorate neatly with piped whipped cream and small pieces of fruit, or glacé cherries and angelica leaves.

### Fruit Flan (serves 4-6)

100 g shortcrust pastry or flan pastry (see p. 139)  
Filling: 1 medium sized tin of fruit (or suitable fresh fruit)  
Glaze: 150 ml fruit syrup  
25 g sugar  
Juice of ½ lemon  
1 heaped tsp. arrowroot

1. Prepare pastry; line a 18 cm flan ring or tin. Bake blind, a third of the way down the oven, Regulo 7 or 220°C (425°F), for 15-20 mins., or until pale fawn.

# COLD SWEETS

2. Remove flan case from tin; cool. Place on a serving dish.
3. Arrange fruit in flan.
4. Make glaze: put arrowroot and sugar in a small saucepan and blend to a smooth paste with the fruit syrup. Stirring well, heat gently until the mixture boils and cook for ½ minute. Remove from heat and add lemon juice.
   Taste syrup; add more sugar if necessary.
5. Allow glaze to cool for 5–10 mins., with a lid on the saucepan. Coat the fruit in the flan.
   Serve with fresh cream, handed separately.

## Sponge Fruit Flan (serves 6)

Flan case: 2 *eggs*           Filling: *Tinned fruit or suitable fresh fruit*
        60 *g caster sugar*   Glaze: *½ packet of jelly, same flavour as fruit*
        60 *g S.R. flour*           *used*
        2–3 *drops vanilla*   Decoration: *100 ml double cream, whipped*
                                                     3 *glacé cherries; angelica*

1. Use jelly cube to make 250 ml jelly. (With tinned fruit, use fruit syrup; with fresh fruit, use water.) Put aside to partly set.
2. Thoroughly grease and flour a 20 cm sponge flan tin. Prepare mixture by whisking method (see p. 159). Pour into prepared flan tin. Bake half way down the oven, Regulo 7 or 220°C (425°F), for approx. 10 mins., or until golden brown and firm to touch.
3. Remove flan case from tin; cool on a wire tray.
4. Place flan case on serving dish. Arrange fruit neatly.
5. Coat with jelly (use when set enough to coat the back of a spoon thickly but evenly).
   Using a small rosette pipe, pipe whipped cream round the edge of the flan case. Decorate with small pieces of glacé cherry and angelica.

## Lemon Meringue Pie

100 *g shortcrust pastry*        Filling: 150 *ml cold water*
                                       25 *g cornflour*
                                       *Knob of butter or margarine*
                                       50 *g sugar*
Meringue: 2 *egg whites*        *Finely grated zest and juice of* 1 *lemon*
            100 *g caster sugar*     2 *egg yolks*

1. Make shortcrust pastry. Line an 18 cm flan ring or tin. Bake blind a third of the way down the oven, Regulo 7 or 220°C (425°F), for 15–20 mins., or until pale fawn. Remove flan case from tin and cool. Place on flat baking tin or heatproof serving dish.

2. Make filling: put cornflour in a small saucepan; blend carefully with the cold water. Stirring briskly all the time, bring to the boil and cook ½ min. Remove pan from heat; add butter and sugar and stir in, then grated zest and juice of lemon. Lastly, add egg yolks and stir in. Taste filling and add extra sugar if necessary.
3. Pour filling into prepared flan case.
4. Make meringue, using the egg whites and caster sugar (see p. 163). Pile meringue on top of filling. Sprinkle with 1 tsp. caster sugar.
5. Bake gently, low down in the oven, Regulo 1 or 120°C (250°F) until the meringue is firm to touch, and pale fawn on the points.
6. Decorate neatly with half glacé cherries and angelica leaves. Serve hot or cold.

# 18. Pastries

### Suitable Fat for Pastry Making

(i) All butter or all margarine
(ii) ½ margarine: ½ lard or white cooking fat
(iii) All lard or white cooking fat

**Flour:** Plain flour should be used for pastry making. Baking powder is added when the proportion of fat is less than half that of flour, e.g. suet crust pastry.

### General Rules for making Pastry

1. Keep everything as cool as possible—handle with finger tips only, mix with cold water using a metal knife, etc.
2. Introduce as much air as possible during sieving, rubbing in, mixing, rolling and folding, etc.
3. Mix to the correct consistency.
4. Handle lightly and as little as possible.
5. Roll out using as little flour as possible. Too much will give hard dry pastry with a floury appearance.
6. Roll lightly with short even strokes. Roll forwards only, quarter turning the pastry as necessary.
7. Pastry must not be stretched during rolling as this will cause it to shrink in cooking.
8. Allow pastry to 'relax' in a cool place before baking, if possible.
9. Bake in a hot oven.
10. After baking, cool away from a draught.

(N.B. Where a recipe requires pastry, e.g. 250 g shortcrust pastry, the quantity refers to the amount of flour to be used.)

## SHORTCRUST PASTRY

**General Proportion:**

½ fat to flour
2 level tsp. salt to 500 g flour
150 ml water (approx.) to 500 g flour

EXAMPLE:   250 g plain flour         125 g fat (½ lard; ½ margarine)
           1 level tsp. salt         75 ml water (approx.)

1. Sieve flour and salt into a mixing bowl.
2. Rub fat and flour together using the tips of the fingers until the mixture resembles fine breadcrumbs.
3. Mixing with a knife, add sufficient cold water to give a stiff dry dough. Knead lightly with finger tips.
4. Turn the dough on to a lightly floured board.
5. Roll out pastry to about 3–5 mm in thickness and use as required.
6. Bake in a hot oven until lightly browned. Regulo 7, 220°C (425°F). The temperature can then be reduced to cook any additional ingredients, e.g. pie fillings.

USES: Small tarts, plate tarts, pie coverings, flan cases, etc.

## VARIATIONS ON SHORTCRUST PASTRY

**Cheese Pastry:** To the rubbed in mixture for shortcrust pastry add: ¼ to equal quantities finely grated cheese to flour. All butter or all margarine is most suitable for this pastry.

EXAMPLE:  200 g plain flour          100 g finely grated cheese
          ¾ level tsp. salt          1 egg yolk and cold water to mix
          100 g margarine

1. Mix pastry with egg yolk and water to give a stiff dry dough.
2. Roll out and use as required.
3. Bake in a hot oven until lightly browned. Regulo 7; 220°C (425°F).

USES: Cheese savouries, savoury flan cases, cheese biscuits, canapés, etc.

**Oatmeal Pastry:** For this pastry use ¾ plain flour, ¼ fine oatmeal.

EXAMPLE:  150 g plain flour          100 g fat (50 g lard; 50 g
          50 g fine oatmeal               margarine)
          ¾ level tsp. salt          Water to mix

1. Sieve flour and salt; add oatmeal.
2. Continue as for shortcrust pastry.
3. Roll out and use as required.
4. Bake in a hot oven until lightly browned. Regulo 7; 220°C (425°F).

USES: Savoury flan cases; pie coverings.

**Flan Pastry:** To the rubbed in mixture for shortcrust pastry add: 50 g sugar to 500 g flour. All butter or all margarine is most suitable for this pastry.

EXAMPLE:  200 g plain flour          20 g caster sugar
          ¾ level tsp. salt          1 egg yolk and cold water to mix
          100 g margarine or butter

1. Mix pastry with egg yolk and water to give a stiff dry dough.
2. Roll out and use as required.
3. Bake in a hot oven until lightly browned. Regulo 7; 220°C (425°F).

USES: Fruit flans, individual fruit tartlets, etc.

## SUET CRUST PASTRY

**General Proportion**

$\frac{1}{3}$–$\frac{1}{2}$ suet to flour
2 level tsp. salt to 500 g flour
4 level tsp. baking powder to 500 g flour, or use self-raising flour
Approx. 300 ml water to 500 g flour.

EXAMPLE: 250 g plain flour    80 g suet
1 level tsp. salt    150 ml water (approx.)
2 level tsp. baking powder

1. Sieve flour, salt and baking powder.
2. Add shredded suet and mix in
3. Add water and mix to a soft but not sticky dough, using a knife.
4. Turn out on to a floured board and knead lightly with the finger tips.
5. Turn the smooth side up; roll out lightly and use as required.
6. Suet crust pastry can be boiled, steamed or baked in a hot oven. Regulo 7; 220°C (425°F).

USES: Boiled apple pudding, jam roly-poly, dumplings, steak and kidney pudding, etc.

*Suet:* Suet can be bought ready prepared; it is shredded and coated in starch to prevent it from forming lumps.

If suet is bought in a piece from the butcher prepare as follows: Remove skin and any particles of meat. Finely chop or grate the suet together with some of the total weight of flour which is to be used in the recipe. Beef suet taken from around the kidneys is best as it is softer and has a better flavour.

## ROUGH PUFF PASTRY

**General Proportion**

$\frac{2}{3}$–$\frac{3}{4}$ fat to flour
2 level teaspoonfuls salt to 500 g flour
300 ml water (approx.)
2 teaspoonfuls lemon juice } to 500 g flour

EXAMPLE: 200 g plain flour    150 g fat ($\frac{1}{2}$ lard; $\frac{1}{2}$ margarine)
1 level tsp. salt    125 ml water (approx.) with 1 tsp. lemon juice

1. Sieve flour and salt into a mixing bowl.
2. Add the fat cut into pieces the size of a walnut.
3. Lightly mix in the water and lemon juice to give a soft dough, taking care not to break down the lumps of fat.
4. Turn out on to a floured board and lightly press the pastry together, but do not knead it.
5. Roll out to an oblong keeping sides straight and ends square.
6. Fold the pastry in three, folding lower ⅓ up then top ⅓ down.

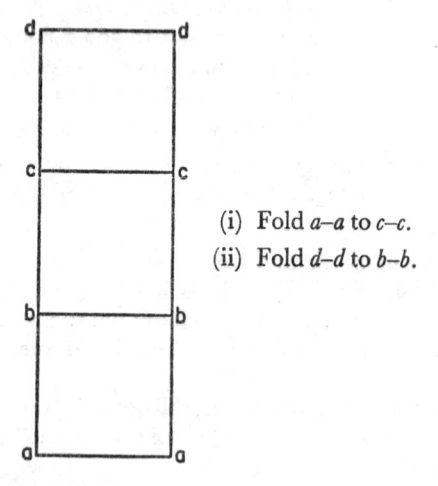

(i) Fold *a–a* to *c–c*.
(ii) Fold *d–d* to *b–b*.

7. Seal edges of pastry with the rolling pin.
8. Quarter turn the pastry (a) to bring the lower folded edge to the side (b). 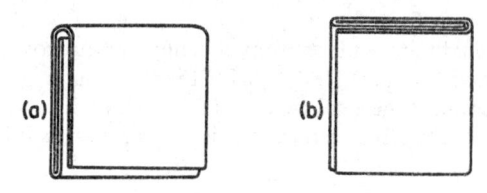
9. Roll out pastry to an oblong, fold in three and quarter turn again.
10. Repeat this process once more: set the pastry aside in a cool place (preferably in a refrigerator) to relax.
11. Re-roll and fold pastry twice more and allow to relax again if time permits.
12. Roll out pastry and use as required.
13. Bake in a hot oven, Regulo 7 or 220°C (425°F) until well risen and golden brown.

USES: Pie coverings, patties, fruit and savoury turnovers, etc.

## FLAKY PASTRY

**General Proportion:**

⅔–¾ fat to flour
2 level tsp. salt to 500 g flour
300 ml water (approx.)  }  to 500 g flour
2 tsp. lemon juice

EXAMPLE: 200 g *plain flour*
1 *level tsp. salt*
150 g *fat* (½ *lard;* ½ *margarine*)
125 *ml water* (*approx.*) *with* 1 *tsp. lemon juice*

1. Sieve flour and salt into a mixing bowl.
2. Mix fat on a plate. Divide into 4 equal parts.
3. Rub one quarter of fat into the flour.
4. Mix to a soft dough using water and lemon juice. (Try to add most of the liquid at once.)
5. Turn out on to a floured board and knead lightly.
6. Roll out to an oblong keeping sides straight and ends square.
7. Dot another quarter fat over top ⅔ of the pastry:

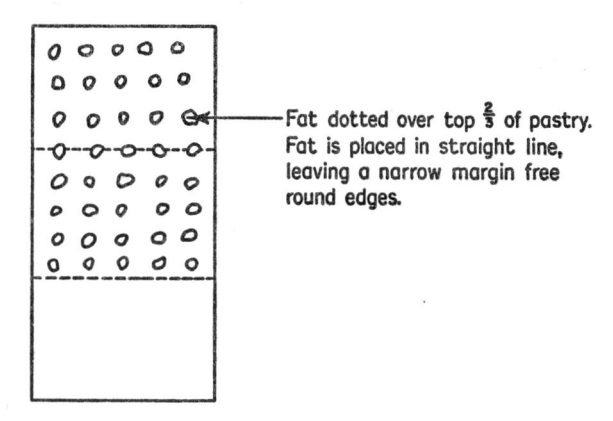

Fat dotted over top ⅔ of pastry. Fat is placed in straight line, leaving a narrow margin free round edges.

8. Fold the pastry in three, folding lower ⅓ up then top ⅓ down. Seal edges with rolling pin; quarter turn the pastry (as for rough Puff Pastry).
9. Re-roll pastry to an oblong. Repeat 7 and 8 twice more using the two remaining quarters of fat.
10. Roll and fold once more without any fat being enclosed.
11. Set the pastry aside in a cool place to relax.
12. Roll out and use as required.
13. Bake in a hot oven. Regulo 7; 220°C (425°F).

USES: Pie coverings, patties, turnovers, vol-au-vent, etc.

# 19. Scones

There are two main types of scones: baked scones which are cooked in a hot oven; and girdle and drop scones which are cooked on top of the stove on a heated iron 'girdle' or solid electric hotplate.

Scones should be very light in texture. As they contain little fat and are very plain, they should be eaten the day they are made, or better still, hot from the oven. They may be flavoured or plain; they can be made from plain or wholemeal flour.

The raising agents used in scone making may be
- (a) S.R. flour, or
- (b) plain flour with baking powder, or
- (c) plain flour with bicarbonate of soda and cream of tartar.

Fresh or sour milk can be used for mixing; usually better results are obtained when sour milk is used.

When making scones, the dough should be handled very quickly and lightly, and as little as possible. Scones must be baked in a hot oven, or cooked on a heated hotplate, as soon as they are made.

**Plain Oven Scones** (Basic Recipe) makes 10–12

250 g plain flour  }  or  250 g plain flour
1 level tsp. bicarbonate of soda  }       3 level tsp. baking powder
2 level tsp. cream of tartar  }  or  250 g S.R. flour
    1 level tsp. salt
    50 g margarine
    25 g caster sugar
    either   approx. 150 ml milk (fresh or sour)
    or   1 egg (optional) and enough fresh milk to make up to 150 ml liquid

1. Lightly grease a large baking tray.
2. Sieve flour, raising agent and salt into a mixing bowl. Add sugar.
3. Rub in margarine until very fine.
4. Make a 'well' in the centre of the flour mixture.
5. Pour in most of the liquid and using a knife, mix to a soft but not sticky dough adding remaining liquid as necessary.
6. Turn on to a floured board; knead lightly to give a smooth dough.
7. To shape either—
   - (a) Cut the mixture in half. Roll each piece out to a round, 15 mm in thickness. Cut each round into 6 triangles; or,
   - (b) Roll out dough to 15 mm thickness. Cut out scones using a 4–5 cm plain round cutter.

8. Brush the tops of the scones with milk if liked. Place on the greased baking tray.
9. Bake near the top of the oven, Regulo 8 or 230°C (450°F) for 10–15 mins. until well risen, firm and golden brown.
10. Cool on a wire tray or serve immediately.
Serve with butter and jam handed separately; alternatively, if served cold, they can be in halves, ready buttered.

### Fruit Scones

As for Plain Oven Scones. In addition: 50 g sultanas or raisins.

Wash and dry fruit. Make as for Plain Oven Scones, adding the prepared dried fruit after the margarine has been rubbed in.
Serve hot or cold with butter.

### Cheese Scones

As for Plain Oven Scones, leaving out the sugar but adding 50 g cheese.

1. Grate cheese finely.
2. Make as for Plain Oven Scones, adding the finely grated cheese after the margarine has been rubbed in.
3. Brush tops of scones with milk before baking.
Serve hot or cold with butter.

### Wholemeal Scones

As for Plain Oven Scones, but using $\frac{1}{2}$ white flour and $\frac{1}{2}$ wholemeal flour, instead of all white flour.

### Girdle Scones

Ingredients: As for Plain Oven Scones.

1. Sprinkle the girdle or hotplate lightly with salt; scour it using a screw of greaseproof paper. Wipe away salt with a soft cloth.
2. Make scone mixture as for Plain Oven Scones. Turn on to a floured board and knead lightly. Divide mixture in half. Roll out each piece into a round about 15 mm in thickness; but each round into 6 triangles.
3. Gently heat the girdle, or heat the hotplate on 'Low–Medium'. Grease lightly.
4. When the girdle is heated, put the scones on it carefully. Cook gently until the scones are brown underneath (about 5–7 mins.); turn and cook second side, until brown. The scones should be cooked for about 10–15 mins. altogether.
5. Serve Girdle scones hot on a folded table napkin. Hand butter separately.

**Scotch Pancakes** (Drop Scones) makes 12–15

        100 g *S.R. flour*  
or  100 g *plain flour and*  
      1 *level tsp. baking powder*

*Pinch of salt*

1 *heaped tsp. caster sugar*  
25 g *margarine*  
1 *tsp. golden syrup*  
1 *small egg*  
125 ml *milk*

1. Prepare girdle or hot plate as for Girdle Scones.
2. Sieve flour, raising agent and salt. Add sugar.
3. Rub in margarine. (Gently heat girdle or hotplate.)
4. Make a well in the flour mixture.
5. Add 1 tsp. golden syrup, the egg and a little of the milk. Using a wooden spoon, mix quickly to give a smooth paste.
6. Gradually add enough of the remaining milk to give a thick batter. (A trail left in the batter should just disappear when the bowl is shaken.)
7. Lightly wipe the heated girdle or hotplate with a small piece of lard held in greaseproof paper.
8. Drop the batter in teaspoonfuls on to the hotplate; the scones should spread out to about 5–7 cm across.
9. Cook gently until bubbles have risen to the surface, and underneath is golden brown (1–2 mins.). Turn carefully with a palette knife; cook the second side until brown.
10. Fold a clean teatowel on a wire cooling tray. Place the cooked drop scones between the teatowel until all are cooked.
11. Serve either hot or cold with butter.

# 20. Cakes

## Types of Cake Mixtures

There are four main types of cake mixtures which can be classified according to the method of making:

    (a) rubbed-in         (c) melted
    (b) creamed          (d) whisked

The higher the proportion of fat and eggs in a mixture, the richer the cake. In general, the rubbing-in method is used for plain cakes in which the proportion of fat to flour is half or less; the creaming method is used for richer cakes which contain more than half fat to flour.

## Main Ingredients Used in Cake Making

*Flour:* A good quality soft flour should be used. Self-raising flour can be used for plain cakes. For richer cakes which contain more than half fat to flour, plain flour with baking powder is often more suitable. In this way, the amount of raising agent can be varied; the more fat and eggs a mixture contains, the less baking powder should be used.

*Fat:* Butter gives the best flavour, though margarine is a good substitute.

*Sugar:* Caster sugar is best as it is finer than granulated sugar. For a darker cake and for fruit cakes, soft brown sugar is suitable. Demerara should not be used as it is too coarse.

*Eggs:* Eggs are important as they help to entrap air in a mixture. The more eggs in a cake, the smaller the amount of baking powder necessary. Eggs also increase the richness and food value of the cake, adding protein and fat.

*Liquid:* Milk or water can be added if necessary to give the correct consistency. Eggs also act as liquid.

*Flavourings:* These may include spices, essences, grated orange and lemon rind, fruit, nuts, etc. Dried fruit should be washed and thoroughly dried. Glacé cherries should be washed to remove syrup, dried and lightly dusted in flour.

**Preparation of Baking Tins:** The tins must be dry. Brush thoroughly with melted lard or white cooking fat. For small cakes, this preparation is sufficient.

*For sandwich cakes,* dredge the greased tin with flour and shake out any surplus.

*For large rich cakes* line the tin with double greaseproof paper; then grease the paper. When a very rich cake is to be baked a long time, the tin should be surrounded with three thicknesses of brown paper.

For a swiss roll, line the tin with greaseproof paper and grease the lining.

If a cake is to be baked in a wide shallow tin, e.g. gingerbread, it is advisable to line the base of the tin.

For consistency of mixtures and baking times and temperatures, see individual recipes.

In general, the smaller and plainer the cake, the higher the oven temperature.

**Testing Cakes when Cooked:** Cakes should be evenly brown and well risen. They should feel 'springy' when touched with a finger; they should not keep the impression of the finger. There should be no bubbling noise. When cooked, cakes shrink slightly away from the side of the tin. For a large or fruit cake, a fine skewer can be stuck into the centre of the cake; if the cake is cooked, the skewer will come out clean.

**Cooling after Baking:** Cakes should be removed from the baking tins as soon as possible and allowed to cool on a wire tray, away from all draughts. Any paper should also be removed to allow steam to escape.

For a large fruit cake, the cake can be allowed to cool partly in the tin; the paper should not be removed until the cake is to be used or iced.

## RUBBED-IN METHOD

**General Proportion:**

To 500 g flour : 125–250 g fat
125–250 g sugar
125–250 g fruit
1–4 eggs
150–300 ml milk
4–6 level tsp. baking powder

S.R. flour can be used instead of plain flour and baking powder.

**General Preparation:** Light oven, making sure the shelves are in the correct position. Prepare the baking tin. Prepare fruit according to kind. Weigh out ingredients.

**General Method**

1. Sieve dry ingredients (flour, baking powder, spice, etc.)
2. Rub in the fat until the mixture resembles fine breadcrumbs.
3. Mix in sugar and any additional ingredients, e.g. dried fruit, coconut, etc.

# CAKES

4. Stir in beaten egg, then any other liquid to give the required consistency.
5. Turn mixture into prepared tin and bake.

## RECIPES USING RUBBED-IN METHOD

### Fruit Loaf

| | |
|---|---|
| 150 g S.R. flour | 1 egg |
| 1 level tsp. mixed spice | 100 g mixed dried fruit |
| ½ level tsp. salt | 25 g candied peel |
| 75 g margarine | Milk to mix |
| 75 g caster sugar | |

1. Prepare cake by the rubbed-in method. Add sufficient milk to give a dropping consistency.
2. Put mixture in a greased and floured small loaf tin.
3. Bake half way down the oven, Regulo 4 or 180°C (350°F) for 1-1½ hours.

### Date and Raisin Cake

| | |
|---|---|
| 200 g S.R. flour | 50 g raisins |
| 100 g margarine | 50 g chopped dates |
| 100 g caster sugar | 1 egg |
| Grated zest of ½ lemon | Milk to mix |

1. Prepare cake by the rubbed-in method. Add sufficient milk to give a dropping consistency.
2. Place mixture in a greased and floured 15 cm round cake tin.
3. Bake half way down the oven, Regulo 4 or 180°C (350°F) for 1-1½ hours.

### Rock Buns (makes 8)

| | |
|---|---|
| 100 g S.R. flour | 50 g sugar |
| Pinch of mixed spice | 50 g currants or sultanas |
| 50 g margarine | 1 small egg |

1. Prepare cakes by rubbing in method.
2. Add sufficient beaten egg to give a stiff dry consistency.
3. Using a spoon and fork, place in rough heaps on a greased baking tray.
4. Bake a third of the way down oven, Regulo 7 or 220°C (425°F) for 10-15 minutes.

### Jam Buns (makes 8)

| | |
|---|---|
| 100 g S.R. flour | 1 small egg |
| 50 g margarine | 1-2 tablesp. jam |
| 50 g sugar | |

1. Prepare cakes by the rubbing-in method.
2. Add sufficient beaten egg to give a stiff dry consistency.
3. Form mixture into a roll on a lightly floured board. Divide into 8.
4. Lightly roll each piece into a ball and flatten slightly.
5. Make a hole in the top of each and put in ½ tsp. jam.
   Place cakes on a greased baking tray.
6. Bake a third of the way down, Regulo 7 or 220°C (425°F) for 10–15 mins.

**Coconut Buns** (makes 8)

    100 g S.R. flour         50 g desiccated coconut
    50 g margarine          1 small egg
    50 g sugar               Milk to mix

1. Prepare cakes by the rubbing-in method.
2. Add beaten egg, then sufficient milk to give a dropping consistency.
3. Put mixture in spoonfuls (use a dessertspoon) in greased bun tins or paper cases.
4. Bake a third of the way down the oven, Regulo 5 or 190°C (375°F) for 15–20 minutes.

## CREAMING METHOD

**General Proportion:**

    To 500 g flour: 250–500 g fat
                      250–500 g sugar
                      4–8 eggs
                      250 g–2 kg (2000 g) fruit
                      0–4 level tsp. baking powder

The more fat and eggs a recipe contains, the smaller the amount of baking powder necessary. Where a recipe contains equal quantities of flour, fat and eggs, no baking powder should be added.

**General Preparation:** Light oven, making sure the shelves are in the correct position. Prepare the baking tin. Prepare fruit according to kind. Weigh out all ingredients.

**General Method**

1. Using a wooden spoon, cream fat and sugar together until light in colour and fluffy in texture.
2. Beat in any flavouring essences or the grated zest of orange or lemon if used.
3. Beat in eggs one at a time, very thoroughly.
   (If the eggs used are very cold, or are not thoroughly beaten in, 'curdling' may occur. A tsp. of the flour for the mixture can be added with each egg and this will help to prevent curdling.)

# CAKES

4. Sieve half the flour into the mixture and fold in very lightly.
5. Sieve and fold in the remaining flour with sufficient additional liquid, if necessary, to give the correct consistency.
6. Stir in any fruit.
7. Turn into the prepared tin and bake.

## RECIPES USING THE CREAMING METHOD

### Queen Cakes (makes 16)

| | |
|---|---|
| 100 g margarine | 150 g S.R. flour |
| 100 g sugar | 50 g dried fruit |
| 2 eggs (standard) | 1-2 tablesp. warm water |

1. Prepare cakes by creaming method, adding warm water to give a dropping consistency.
2. Put mixture in dessertspoonfuls into greased patty tins or paper cases.
3. Bake a third of the way down oven, Regulo 5 or 190°C (375°F) for 15-20 mins.

### Cherry Buns (makes 16)

| | |
|---|---|
| 100 g margarine | 150 g S.R. flour |
| 100 g caster sugar | 50 g glacé cherries |
| 2 eggs (standard) | ¼ tsp. vanilla essence |
| | 1-2 tablesp. warm water |

1. Wash cherries to remove syrup, then dry. Dredge with flour. Cut in quarters.
2. Prepare cakes by creaming method. Continue as for Queen cakes.

### Ginger Buns (makes 16)

| | |
|---|---|
| 100 g margarine | 1-2 tablesp. warm water |
| 100 g caster sugar | 1 level tsp. ground ginger |
| 2 eggs (standard) | 25 g crystallized ginger (optional) |
| 150 g S.R. flour | |

1. Wash and dry the crystallized ginger to remove the sugar. Chop finely. Add ground ginger to the flour.
2. Prepare cakes by the creaming method. Continue as for Queen Cakes.

### Butterfly Cakes (makes 16)

| | |
|---|---|
| 100 g margarine | Filling: 40 g butter |
| 100 g caster sugar | 60-80 g icing sugar |
| 2 eggs (standard) | ¼ tsp. vanilla essence |
| 150 g S.R. flour | |
| ¼ tsp. vanilla essence | |
| 1-2 tablesp. warm water | |

1. Prepare cakes by the creaming method, adding warm water to give a dropping consistency.
2. Put mixture in dessertspoonfuls into paper cases.
3. Bake a third of the way down oven, Regulo 5 or 190°C (375°F) for 15–20 mins.
4. Make butter icing (see page 169).
5. When cakes are cool, slice off tops thinly and cut in half to form 'wings'. Place ½ teaspoonful (or pipe) butter icing on top of each cake. Stick two 'wings' into the butter icing on each cake. Dredge lightly with icing sugar.

**Madelenes** (makes 16)

100 g margarine
100 g caster sugar
2 eggs
150 g S.R. flour
¼ tsp. vanilla essence
1–2 tablesp. warm water

To decorate:
2–4 tablesp. raspberry jam
100 g desiccated coconut
9 glacé cherries

1. Grease and flour 16 Madelene tins or small castle pudding tins.
2. Prepare mixture by creaming method, adding warm water to give a dropping consistency.
3. Half fill the tins and stand them on a baking tray.
4. Bake a third of the way down the oven, Regulo 4 or 180°C (350°F) for 15–25 mins.
5. Allow cakes to cool; then trim top level, if necessary, so they stand up straight.
6. Put jam with 2 tablesp. water in a basin and allow to soften over hot water.
7. Put coconut on a piece of greaseproof paper.
8. Brush the cakes with warmed jam (it is easiest to hold the cakes on a skewer).
9. Roll each brushed cake in coconut.
10. Place cakes in paper cases. Put ½ glacé cherry on each.

**Small Fancy Cakes** (makes 16–20)

100 g margarine
100 g caster sugar
2 eggs

150 g S.R. flour
2 tablesp. warm water
¼ tsp. vanilla essence

1. Grease, then line the base of a Swiss Roll tin, size approx. 16 cm × 26 cm.
2. Prepare mixture by creaming method adding warm water to give a fairly soft dropping consistency. Spread the mixture evenly in the prepared tin.

# CAKES

3. Bake a third of the way down the oven, Regulo 5 or 190°C (375°F) for 15–25 mins.
4. Cool on a wire tray.
5. When cold, ice the large cake. Trim off edges. Cut into shapes, squares, oblongs, triangles or with a small round cutter.
6. Decorate the individual cakes. Place in paper cases.

**Decoration:** For icing the large cake, use 150 g icing sugar to make glacé icing (see p. 170). The flavour can be varied, e.g.

(*a*) Spread cake with orange icing; decorate with orange slices or angelica.
(*b*) Spread cake with lemon icing; decorate with lemon slices or pieces of glacé cherry.
(*c*) Spread the cake with chocolate icing; decorate with blanched almonds.
(*d*) Spread the cake with coffee icing; decorate with pieces of walnut.
(*e*) Spread the cake with butter icing; decorate with piped butter icing in a different flavour.
(*f*) Spread the cake with warmed raspberry jam; sprinkle with coconut and decorate with pieces of glacé cherry.

## Victoria Sandwich (see also p. 164)

| | |
|---|---|
| 100 g margarine | Filling: 2 *tablesp. jam* |
| 100 g caster sugar | Decoration: *Icing or caster sugar* |
| 2 eggs (*standard*) | |
| 100 g S.R. flour | |

1. Grease and flour two 15 cm sandwich tins (or one 18 cm tin).
2. Prepare cake by the creaming method. No additional liquid should be necessary to give a dropping consistency.
3. Divide the mixture evenly between the two tins and spread out evenly.
4. Bake a third of the way down oven, Regulo 5 or 180°–190°C (360°F) for 15–25 mins.
5. Cool on a wire tray.
6. When cold, sandwich the two cakes together with jam (sandwich the bases of the cakes together).
7. Dredge with icing or caster sugar.

## Chocolate Sandwich Cake

| | | |
|---|---|---|
| 100 g margarine | Filling: | 25 g *butter* |
| 100 g caster sugar | | 50 g *icing sugar* |
| 2 eggs (*standard*) | | 3 *drops vanilla essence* |
| 150 g S.R. flour | Icing: | 100 g *icing sugar* |
| 1–2 tablesp. chocolate liquid | | *Chocolate liquid* |
| | Decoration: | *Blanched split almonds* |

To make Chocolate Liquid: Put 20 g plain cocoa or drinking chocolate in a basin. Blend to a smooth liquid with 125 ml boiling water. Allow to cool. Use this chocolate liquid to add to the cake mixture and to mix the icing.

1. Grease and flour two 18 cm sandwich tins.
2. Prepare cake by creaming method. Add chocolate liquid to give a dropping consistency.
3. Divide the mixture between the two tins and spread out evenly.
4. Bake a third of the way down the oven, Regulo 5 or 180°-190°C (375°F) for 15-25 minutes.
5. Cool on a wire tray.
6. Make butter icing (see p. 169). Sandwich the cakes together with this filling.
7. Make chocolate glacé icing (see p. 170) and spread evenly over top of cake.
8. Decorate neatly with blanched split almonds arranged neatly round the edge of the cake.

**Coffee Sandwich Cake**

100 g margarine
100 g caster sugar
2 eggs (standard)
150 g S.R. flour
1-2 tablesp. coffee liquid

Filling: 25 g butter
50 g icing sugar
3 drops vanilla essence
Icing: 100 g icing sugar
coffee liquid
Decoration: Half walnuts

To make Coffee Liquid: Put 2 tsp. instant coffee powder in a basin. Add 100 ml almost boiling water. Allow to cool. Use this strong coffee add to the cake mixture and to mix the icing.
Prepare the cake as for Chocolate Sandwich Cake.

**Lemon Sandwich Cake**

100 g margarine
100 g caster sugar
2 eggs (standard)
150 g S.R. flour
1-2 tablesp. warm water
Finely grated zest of lemon

Filling: Lemon curd
Icing: 100 g icing sugar
Lemon juice
Decoration: Orange or lemon slices

1. Grease and flour two 18 cm sandwich tins.
2. Wash and dry the lemon. Finely grate the zest on to a plate.
3. Prepare the cake by the creaming method adding the finely grated zest to the creamed fat and sugar.
4. Continue and finish as for Chocolate Sandwich Cake.

## Orange Sandwich Cake

Prepare as for Lemon Sandwich Cake, using an orange in place of the lemon. For Filling, use butter icing, or orange jelly marmalade.

The recipes for these four sandwich cakes can be used to prepare small cakes.

## Sultana Cake

| 100 g margarine | Grated zest of ½ lemon |
| 100 g caster sugar | 100 g sultanas |
| 2 eggs (standard) | 3-4 tablesp. milk |
| 200 g S.R. flour | |

1. Grease and flour a 15 cm cake tin.
2. Wash and dry the fruit. Finely grate the zest of the lemon.
3. Prepare cake by the creaming method, adding enough milk to give a soft dropping consistency.
4. Turn the mixture into prepared tin. Bake half way down the oven, Regulo 4 or 180°C (350°F) for 1-1½ hours.

## Madeira Cake

| 150 g margarine | 1 level tsp. baking powder |
| 150 g caster sugar | 1-2 tablesp. milk |
| 3 eggs (standard) | Grated zest of ½ lemon |
| 200 g plain flour | Thin slice of citron peel |

1. Grease and line an 18 cm cake tin.
2. Sift the baking powder and flour together three times to make sure they are thoroughly and evenly mixed.
3. Prepare cake by the creaming method.
4. Turn mixture into the prepared tin. Smooth out and place the citron peel on top.
5. Bake half way down the oven, Regulo 3 or 150°C (300°F) for 1½-2 hours.

### BASIC RECIPE FOR LARGE CAKE

| 150 g margarine | 200 g plain flour |
| 150 g caster sugar | 1 level tsp. baking powder |
| 3 eggs (standard) | 1-2 tablesp. milk |

Prepare by creaming method adding enough milk to give a dropping consistency. Turn into a lined and greased tin.

Bake half way down the oven, Regulo 3 or 150°C (300°F) for 1½-2 hours.

### VARIATIONS ON THE BASIC RECIPE

## Cherry Cake

Add: 100 g glacé cherries and ¼ tsp. vanilla essence.

Add the essence to creamed fat and sugar. Stir in the prepared cherries after the flour.

## Dundee Cake

Add:
- 100 g *sultanas*
- 100 g *raisins*
- 100 g *currants*
- 50 g *candied peel*
- 50 g *glacé cherries*
- 50 g *ground, or chopped blanched almonds*
- Grated zest of ½ *lemon*

Decoration: 25 g *split blanched almonds*

Add grated zest of lemon to creamed fat and sugar. Stir in the prepared fruit, cherries and nuts after the flour.

Turn into a greased and lined 18–20 cm cake tin. Spread out evenly. Decorate the top with blanched split almonds before baking.

## Seed Cake

Add: 1 *level tablesp. caraway seeds.*
Add the seeds with the flour.

## Walnut Cake

Add: 50 g *chopped walnuts and* ¼ *tsp. vanilla essence.*

Add the essence to the creamed fat and sugar. Stir in the chopped walnuts with the flour. When baked, ice thinly with white glacé icing.

## Rich Chocolate Cake

- 150 g *margarine*
- 150 g *sugar*
- 3 *eggs (standard)*
- 200 g *plain flour*
- 1 *level tsp. baking powder*
- 100 g *plain chocolate*
- 60–70 ml *milk (bare measure)*

1. Grease and line an 18 cm cake tin.
2. Warm chocolate and milk together gently until the chocolate has dissolved. Allow to cool.
3. Prepare cake by creaming method. Add the chocolate dissolved in milk with the flour to give the correct consistency.
4. Bake half way down the oven, Regulo 3 or 150°C (300°F) for 1½–2 hours.

## Rich Christmas Cake

- 200 g *butter or margarine*
- 200 g *soft brown sugar*
- 4 *eggs (standard)*
- 200 g *plain flour*
- 1 *level tsp. mixed spice*
- 600 g *mixed dried fruit*
- 25 g *chopped candied peel*
- 25 g *glacé cherries*
- 25 g *ground almonds*
- 1 *tablesp. black treacle (good measure)*

1. Line and grease an 18 cm square or 20 cm round cake tin, and surround with double brown paper.
2. Prepare cake by the creaming method. Sift in mixed spice with the flour. Stir in the black treacle and the prepared fruit after the flour has been added. The mixture should be a dropping consistency.

CAKES 157

3. Turn the mixture into the prepared tin and smooth out. Make a hollow in the centre of the mixture to allow for rising. This will give a flatter cake after baking.
4. Bake 3–3½ hours, two-thirds of the way down the oven:
   1st hour:   Regulo 3 or 150°C (300°F)
   2nd „  :         „    2 or 140°C (275°F)
   3rd „  :         „    1 or 120°C (250°F)
   Any remaining time:  „   ½ or 110°C (225°F)

### Christmas Cake—II

150 g margarine               400 g mixed dried fruit
150 g soft brown sugar        25 g glacé cherries
3 eggs (standard)             25 g chopped candied peel
200 g plain flour             2 tablesp. milk
1 level tsp. baking powder    1 tablesp. black treacle
1 level tsp. mixed spice

1. Line and grease an 18 cm round cake tin.
2. Prepare as for Rich Christmas Cake.
3. Bake 2½–3 hours, half way down the oven at Regulo 3 or 150°C (300°F).

### Simnel Cake

Ingredients: As for Christmas Cake—II. Also almond paste, using 100 g ground almonds (p. 171).
Decoration: Almond paste using 100 g ground almonds.

1. Grease and line an 18 cm round cake tin.
2. Prepare the almond paste and roll out to fit the cake tin.
3. Prepare cake mixture.
4. Put half cake mixture in the tin, smooth out. Cover with the round of almond paste. Spread the remaining cake mixture on top.
5. Bake as for Christmas Cake—II
6. To decorate, make almond paste (p. 171). Brush the top of the cake with beaten egg white; roll out the almond paste to fit the top of the cake. Place almond paste on cake, firm on then roll lightly to make it smooth. Crimp or flute the edge neatly. Make a lattice design over the almond paste, pressing lightly with the back of a knife. Grill the top of the cake lightly to brown the almond paste.

## MELTING METHOD

**General Proportion:**

To 500 g flour: 125–250 g fat
125–250 g sugar
250–375 g syrup or treacle
0–4 eggs
2–4 level tsp. ground ginger
2 level tsp. bicarbonate of soda

In melted mixtures, plain flour is used, with bicarbonate of soda as the raising agent.

**General Preparation:** Light oven, making sure the shelves are in the correct position. Line and grease the baking tin. (If a wide shallow tin is used it may only be necessary to line the base.) Weigh out the ingredients.

### General Method

1. Sieve flour, ground ginger and bicarbonate of soda into the mixing bowl. Make a well in the centre of the dry ingredients.
2. Put fat, sugar and syrup into a small saucepan. Heat gently and stir until the fat has just melted; the mixture must not boil.
3. Beat the eggs thoroughly in a basin.
4. Add the melted mixture to the dry ingredients, together with any beaten egg and mix in thoroughly. Add any additional liquid to give a smooth thick batter.
5. Pour into the prepared tin.
6. Bake in a slow oven, half or two-thirds of the way down, at Regulo 3 or 150°C (300°F).

### Gingerbread

200 g *plain flour*  
1 *level tsp. bicarbonate of soda*  
1-2 *level tsp. ground ginger*  
50 g *sugar*  
150 g *syrup or black treacle*  
100 g *margarine*  
1 *egg*  
50-100 ml *milk (approx.)*

1. Line and grease a large loaf tin.
2. Prepare cake by the melting method. Turn mixture into the prepared tin.
3. Bake half way down the oven, Regulo 3 or 150°C (300°F) for 1-1½ hours.

Instead of a loaf tin, the cake can be baked in a square tin approx. 18 cm × 18 cm, then cut in squares.

### Fruit Gingerbread

To the recipe for Gingerbread, add:

75 g *chopped sultanas*  
25 g *chopped candied peel*, or 1 *tablesp. marmalade*.

Prepare and bake as for Gingerbread. Add fruit to the sieved dry ingredients.

### Ginger Parkin

100 g *medium oatmeal*  
100 g *plain flour*  
1 *level tsp. bicarbonate of soda*  
1 *level tsp. ground ginger*  
75 g *golden syrup*  
75 g *black treacle*  
50 g *margarine*  
25 g *sugar*  
*Milk to mix*

## CAKES

1. Grease and line the base of a shallow rectangular tin, approx. 15 cm × 25 cm.
2. Sieve flour, ginger and bicarbonate of soda. Add oatmeal.
3. Prepare cake by melting method, adding milk if necessary to give the consistency of a thick batter.
4. Pour into the prepared tin.
5. Bake half way down the oven, Regulo 3 or 150°C (300°F) for approx. ¾–1 hour.
6. Allow to cool in the tin. When almost cold, cut in squares and remove from tin.

Gingerbreads are improved by being kept in a tin for 2–3 days before using.

### WHISKING METHOD

**Basic Recipe**

3 eggs  90 g plain flour
90 g caster sugar  ¼ tsp. vanilla essence

**General Preparation:** Light oven, making sure the shelves are in the correct position. Line and grease the baking tin. Weigh out all ingredients and sieve flour on to a plate.

**General Method**

1. Break eggs into a mixing bowl and add sugar and vanilla essence.
2. Whisk until the mixture is thick and creamy and the whisk will leave a trail lasting 1–2 seconds on the surface of the mixture.
3. Sieve in the flour in two halves and fold in quickly and lightly using a tablespoon. Stop folding as soon as the flour is evenly mixed in.
4. Pour mixture into the prepared tin and allow to run into the shape of the tin. Do not spread out with a knife.
5. Bake straight away.

(N.B. Eggs and sugar can be whisked together over hot water which will speed up their thickening. Remove from heat and whisk until cool before adding flour.)

**Sponge Cake:** Use basic recipe.

1. Line and grease a 15 cm cake tin.
2. Prepare mixture by the whisking method.
3. Pour into the prepared tin. Sprinkle lightly with caster sugar.
4. Bake half way down the oven, Regulo 3 or 150°C (300°F) for 40–50 mins.

**Sponge Sandwich:** Use basic recipe.

1. Grease, then line the base of two 18 cm sandwich tins.
2. Prepare the mixture as for Sponge Cake and pour into the prepared tin.

3. Bake a third of the way down oven, Regulo 4 or 180°C (350°F) for 20–30 mins.
4. Cool on a wire tray.
5. When cold, sandwich together with jam or cream and lightly dredge the top with icing sugar.

## Swiss Roll

Using basic recipe but using S.R. flour instead of plain flour.

In addition: 1–2 *tablesp. raspberry jam*
           15 g caster sugar

1. Grease and line a rectangular tin, 18 cm × 28 cm.
2. Prepare as for Sponge Cake. Pour into the prepared tin and allow the mixture to run evenly over the tin.
3. Bake a third of the way down the oven, Regulo 7 or 220°C (425°F) for 9–10 mins. until just firm to touch.
4. While the cake is in the oven, put jam to warm in a basin standing over hot water. Prepare a piece of greaseproof paper, approx. 5 cm larger all round than the cake. Sprinkle with 15 g caster sugar.
5. Turn the cake out on to the sugared paper. Remove lining paper.
6. Spread the cake with warmed jam, leaving a 2 cm margin all round the edges with no jam. (As the cake is rolled, jam spreads to the edges.)
7. Using a knife, make a groove in the cake, an inch in from the edge nearest to you.
8. Tuck this grooved end in firmly to form a firm start to the roll.
9. Roll the cake up tightly with the aid of the paper.
10. Cool the cake on a wire tray.
11. Trim ends when the cake is cold.

## Chocolate Swiss Roll

3 *eggs*
90 g *caster sugar*
75 g *S.R. flour*
15 g *cocoa*

Filling: *Double cream, whipped,*
*or Butter cream:*
40 g *butter*
60–80 g *icing sugar*
¼ tsp. *vanilla essence*

1. Sieve together the flour and cocoa.
2. Prepare and bake as for plain Swiss Roll.
3. When cake is cooked, roll up using a piece of greaseproof paper the same size as the cake for the 'filling'.
4. Allow cake to go cold.
5. Carefully unroll, spread in the cream, then roll up again.

## CAKES MADE WITH PASTRIES

**Jam Tarts** (makes approx. 12)

    100 g *shortcrust pastry* (see p. 139)
    *Jam or lemon curd*

1. Prepare pastry (see p. 139); roll out to 3 mm thickness.
2. Cut pastry out in rounds, using a fluted cutter 5 mm larger than the top of the patty tins. Reroll any scraps of pastry and cut out more rounds.
3. Line patty tins with pastry. Put 1 tsp. jam in each tart.
4. Bake a third of the way down the oven, Regulo 7 or 220°C (425°F), for 10–15 mins. until the pastry is pale golden. Cool on a wire tray.

**Mince Pies** (makes 10)

    150 g *shortcrust pastry* (see p. 139)
    *Mincemeat*
    *Icing sugar or caster sugar to sprinkle*

1. Prepare pastry (see p. 139); roll out to 3 mm thickness.
2. Cut pastry out as for jam tarts, also cutting an equal number of rounds, slightly smaller, for lids.
3. Line patty tins with pastry. Put 1–2 tsp. mincemeat in each case.
4. Damp the edge of each lid and press on to the pies.
5. Make a small hole in the centre of each lid.
6. Bake for 15–20 mins. as for jam tarts.
7. When cooked, sprinkle lightly with caster or icing sugar. Serve hot or cold.

**Welsh Cheesecakes** (makes 12)

| | |
|---|---|
| 100 g *shortcrust pastry* (see p. 139) | Creamed mixture: |
| | 50 g *margarine* |
| | 50 g *caster sugar* |
| 1–2 tablesp. *raspberry jam* | 1 *egg (standard)* |
| | 75 g *S.R. flour* |
| *Icing sugar to sprinkle* | 1 tablesp. *warm water* |

1. Prepare shortcrust pastry. Roll out to 3 mm in thickness. Cut out and line patty tins as for jam tarts. Put ¼ tsp. jam in each tart.
2. Make creamed mixture. (Use General Creaming Method, p. 150.)
3. Put a tsp. of the mixture in each case, making sure the jam is covered.
4. Bake half way down the oven, Regulo 5 or 190°C (375°F), for 15–20 mins. until the cakes are pale golden, and the creamed mixture is springy to touch.
5. Cool on a wire tray. Sprinkle lightly with icing sugar before using.

### Jam Puffs (makes 8–10)

150 g rough puff or flaky pastry (see pp. 141, 143)  Cream (optional)
Raspberry jam or lemon curd                          Icing sugar for sprinkling

#### To make Patty Cases

1. Make rough puff or flaky pastry (see pp. 141, 143). Roll out to 5 mm in thickness.
2. Cut pastry into rounds using a 5 cm plain cutter. From half the rounds remove the centre with a 2 cm plain cutter to form rings. Re-roll and use scraps of pastry to make additional rounds and rings.
3. Damp the edge of the rounds; press a ring on top of each. Using a knife, 'knock up' the edges to hide the join.
4. Place pastry cases on a flat baking sheet. Bake a third of the way down the oven, Regulo 7 or 220°C (425°F), for 15–20 mins., until well risen, golden and firm to touch. Cool on a wire tray. (When the patty cases have baked for 10–12 mins., and the pastry is just firm and beginning to colour, remove patties from oven. Using the handle of teaspoon carefully but quickly scoop the soft pastry from the centre of each case. Put patty cases back in oven to dry off.)
5. When patty cases are cold, put 1–2 tsp. jam in each. Fresh or mock cream can be piped on top of the jam if liked. Sprinkle lightly with icing sugar before serving.

(N.B. For savoury patties, e.g. mushroom, shrimp, etc., the small circle cut from the centre of the pastry rounds is baked separately to form a lid for the patties. Sweet patties are usually served without lids.)

### Cream Slices (makes 8)

150 g rough puff or flaky pastry      Mock cream (see p. 169)
Raspberry jam                          or 125 ml fresh whipped cream
                                       100 g icing sugar

1. Prepare rough puff or flaky pastry. Roll out to a rectangle 30 cm long and 20 cm wide. Trim edges.
2. Cut pastry in half lengthways, to give two 10 cm strips. Cut each strip across into eight equal pieces.
3. Place the pieces of pastry carefully on a flat baking sheet. Bake a third of the way down the oven, Regulo 6 or 200°C (400°F), for 10–15 mins. or until well risen and golden brown. Cool on a wire tray.
4. When pastry is cold, sandwich the slices together in twos with jam and cream (spreading the filling on the bases of the slices).
5. Make white glacé icing (see p. 170) and coat each slice (or dredge thickly with icing sugar).

## Cream Horns (makes 6)

*100 g rough puff or flaky pastry*
*Raspberry jam*
*Mock cream (see p. 169) or 125 ml fresh whipped cream*
*Icing sugar for sprinkling*

1. Make pastry (see pp. 141, 143). Roll out to a rectangle 30 cm long and approx. 12 cm wide. Trim edges.
2. Cut pastry into narrow strips, 30 cm long and 2 cm wide.
3. Lightly brush one edge of each strip with water.
4. Carefully wind strips on to cream horn shapes, starting at the bottom, and overlapping each layer of pastry slightly. The pastry must be placed so that the damped edge is always overlapping the previous pastry. Place on a baking sheet.
5. Bake a third of the way down the oven, Regulo 7 or 220°C (425°F), for 15–20 mins., until pale golden. Carefully remove the tins and cool the horns on a wire tray.
6. When the horns are cold, put 1–2 tsp. jam in each and pipe mock or fresh cream in the top. Dredge horns with icing sugar.

## MISCELLANEOUS RECIPES

### Meringues

*2 egg whites (standard)*
*100 g caster sugar*
*125 ml fresh whipped cream*

1. Lightly grease 2–3 flat baking sheets. Prepare a forcing bag with a 15 mm plain or star meringue pipe.
2. Separate egg whites carefully; place in a mixing bowl. Weigh out caster sugar.
3. Whisk whites stiffly until they will stand up in peaks.
4. Add 2 tsp. of the caster sugar, and whisk again until extremely stiff. Remove the whisk.
5. Using a tablespoon, carefully and quickly fold in half the sugar then the remaining sugar.
6. Put the mixture into the forcing bag. Pipe in small stars or pyramids on to the baking sheets. Sprinkle very lightly with caster sugar to keep the surface of the meringues crisp.
7. Bake low down the oven, Regulo ½–1 or 110°–120°C (200°F), until firm (1–3 hours). The meringues should be white or only very faintly coloured.
8. Remove carefully from the baking sheets, and cool on a wire tray.
9. Sandwich together in twos, with fresh cream, just before they are needed.

(N.B. If meringues are to be stored 1–2 days, do not put in cream. Keep them in an airtight tin, lined with greaseproof paper, and separate each layer of meringues with greaseproof paper.)

## Éclairs (makes 8–10)

Choux pastry:  50 g margarine ⎫
                Pinch of salt ⎪
                125 ml water ⎬ Panada
                50 g plain flour ⎪
                2 eggs (standard) ⎭
Filling: 125 ml fresh whipped cream or mock cream
        100 g icing sugar

1. Grease a flat baking sheet. Prepare a forcing bag with a 15 mm plain meringue pipe.
2. *Make choux pastry:*
   Sieve the flour on to a piece of greaseproof paper. Put margarine, salt and water into a small saucepan and bring to the boil. Remove from heat; add all the flour at once and beat over a gentle heat using a wooden spoon, until the mixture is smooth.
   Allow to cool slightly. Beat in eggs very thoroughly, one at a time.
3. Place mixture in the forcing bag. Pipe in 7 cm lengths on to the greased baking sheet.
4. Bake half way down the oven, Regulo 6 or 200°C (400°F), for 20–30 mins., until golden brown and firm to touch.
5. Remove from oven; split each éclair carefully along one side using a sharp pointed knife. Using the handle of a teaspoon, scoop out any soft mixture if necessary, and put back in the oven for 2–3 mins. to dry off. Cool on a wire tray.
6. When éclairs are cold, fill with cream, using a forcing bag.
7. Make glacé icing, either chocolate or coffee flavoured (see p. 170). Ice the top by carefully dipping the éclairs into the mixing bowl. Place on a wire tray until the icing has set.

## Victoria Sandwich—'Quick Mix'

100 g margarine (a soft variety)    Filling: 2 *tablesp. jam*
100 g caster sugar                           Decoration: *Icing or caster sugar*
2 eggs (standard)
100 g S.R. flour
1 level tsp. baking powder

1. Grease and flour two 15 cm sandwich tins.
2. Put all ingredients together in a mixing bowl.
3. Beat ingredients for 1–2 minutes to give a dropping consistency.
4. Continue as for Victoria Sandwich (Method Nos. 3–7) on p. 153.

# 21. Biscuits

## RUBBED IN METHOD

**Lemon Biscuits** (makes 12—15)

    100 g plain flour      Finely grated zest of 1 lemon
    50 g margarine      1 egg yolk
    50 g caster sugar      Caster sugar for sprinkling

**General Method for Making Biscuits by the Rubbed-in Method**

1. Lightly grease a baking tray.
2. Sieve flour; add sugar.
3. Rub in fat until mixture resembles fine breadcrumbs. Add finely grated zest of lemon rind.
4. Add egg yolk. Using a knife, mix to a stiff dry dough, adding a little water if necessary.
5. Turn mixture on to a floured board; knead lightly. (Cut dough in two, and shape half at a time.)
6. Roll biscuit dough to 3–5 mm in thickness. Prick neatly.
7. Cut out using a 4 cm plain round cutter. Place on the baking tray. Re-roll and cut out any scraps of dough.
8. Bake a third to half the way down the oven, Regulo 3–4 or 160°C (325°F), for 10–20 mins. until pale straw coloured and firm to touch.
9. Using a palette knife, lift off baking tray very carefully and cool on a wire tray. Sprinkle lightly with caster sugar if liked.

**Shortbread Biscuits**

    100 g plain flour      25 g caster sugar
    50 g butter      1 egg yolk

1. Prepare as for lemon biscuits.
2. To shape, either cut out using a 4 cm plain round cutter; or roll out the biscuit dough to a strip 10 cm wide. Trim edges. Prick neatly. Cut biscuits in fingers 3 cm wide.
3. Bake as for lemon biscuits.

**Shortbread**

    100 g plain flour      50 g caster sugar
    50 g semolina      Pinch of salt
    100 g butter

1. Grease an 18 cm sandwich tin, or a baking tray and an 18 cm plain flan ring.
2. Sieve flour and salt. Add semolina and sugar.
3. Rub in butter, then knead with the hand until the mixture binds together into a smooth dough.
4. Turn on to a lightly floured board.
    *Either:* Carefully press shortbread into the greased sandwich tin with the knuckles. (It must fit the tin well and reach straight to the edge.) Decorate the edge with a spoon handle. Prick neatly all over. Cut through into 8 equal pieces.
    *Or:* Carefully roll the dough to an 18 cm round using the flan ring as a guide. Make sure no cracks develop round the edges. Lift carefully on to the baking tray. Place flan ring round shortbread. Decorate and finish as above.
5. Bake half way down the oven, Regulo 3 or 150°C (300°F), for 40–50 mins., until a pale fawn and firm to touch.
6. Sprinkle very lightly with caster sugar while still hot. Allow to cool before removing from baking tin.

## CREAMING METHOD

**Plain Biscuits** (Basic Recipe) (makes approx. 15)

> 100 g plain flour  50 g caster sugar
> 50 g margarine  ½ egg (or 1 yolk)

### General Method

1. Grease a baking tray.
2. Sieve the flour on to a plate. Beat the egg in a basin.
3. Cream the margarine and sugar until pale in colour and fluffy in texture.
4. Beat in the egg.
5. Using a wooden spoon, gradually stir in the sieved flour to give a smooth, firm dough.
6. Turn the dough on to a floured board and knead lightly. Roll, cut and bake as for Lemon Biscuits. (see p. 165).

**Jam Ring Biscuits** (makes about 12)

Ingredients: As for Plain Biscuits. In addition, 2 tablesp. raspberry jam, 1–2 tsp. icing sugar.

1. Prepare mixture by General Method.
2. Roll to 3 mm in thickness. Cut out using a 5 cm fluted cutter. From half the biscuits, remove the centre, using a 2 cm or small fancy cutter.

3. Bake rounds and rings.
4. Cool on a wire tray.
5. Spread the underside of the rounds thinly with jam. Dredge the rings with icing sugar. Sandwich the biscuits together.

## Shrewsbury Biscuits

Ingredients: As for Plain Biscuits. In addition, $\frac{1}{4}$ tsp. cinnamon.

1. Add cinnamon to flour.
2. Make and bake by the General Method.

## MELTING METHOD

### Oatcake

| | |
|---|---|
| 160 g rolled oats | 1 large tablesp. golden syrup |
| 80 g margarine | 1 tablesp. water |
| 80 g brown sugar | |

1. Grease a 20 cm sandwich tin, or a shallow 18 cm square tin.
2. Put margarine, sugar, golden syrup and water into a saucepan. Heat very gently, stirring all the time, until fat has melted and the sugar dissolved. The mixture should not boil.
3. Add rolled oats and mix well.
4. Pour into the greased tin and smooth out.
5. Bake half way down the oven, Regulo 3 or 150°C (300°F), for 40–50 mins., until golden brown.
6. Allow to cool for 5 mins. Mark into 8–12 slices with a pointed knife.
7. Cool in the tin. Separate the pieces when cold.

### Ginger Biscuits (makes 12–15)

| | |
|---|---|
| 100 g plain flour | 50 g margarine |
| $\frac{1}{2}$ level tsp. bicarbonate of soda | 50 g golden syrup |
| 1 level tsp. ground ginger | 50 g sugar |

1. Grease a baking tray.
2. Sieve flour, bicarbonate of soda and ginger into a mixing bowl.
3. Put margarine, golden syrup and sugar into a small saucepan. Stirring all the time, heat gently until the margarine has melted and sugar dissolved.
4. Pour melted mixture into the sieved dry ingredients and mix to a fairly stiff dough.
5. Take the mixture in teaspoonfuls and gently roll into a ball between the hands.
6. Place well apart on the greased baking tray; flatten slightly with the hand.

7. Bake a third of the way down the oven, Regulo 3 or 150°C (300°F), for 15–20 mins., until a rich golden brown.
8. Allow to set for 2–3 mins before removing carefully from the tin with a palette knife. Cool on a wire tray.

### Chocolate Crispy Cakes (makes 12)

| | |
|---|---|
| 15 g butter | 1 tablesp. cocoa |
| 50 g brown sugar | 8 tablesp. rice crispies or |
| 2 tablesp. golden syrup | cornflakes |

1. Prepare 12 small paper cake cases.
2. Put butter, sugar, golden syrup and cocoa into a small saucepan. Heat very gently, stirring all the time, until the fat has melted and the sugar dissolved. The mixture should not boil. Remove from heat.
3. Add half the rice crispies or cornflakes and stir in gently; stir in the remainder until all the cereals are lightly coated with chocolate mixture.
4. Using a spoon and fork, carefully put the mixture into the paper cases. Allow to set.

## 'WHISKING' METHOD

### Almond Macaroons (makes 12)

| | |
|---|---|
| 2 egg whites (standard) | 125 g caster sugar |
| 100 g ground almonds | 12 halves blanched almonds |
| 2 tsp. semolina | For baking: Rice paper |

1. Cover a baking tray with rice paper.
2. Whisk egg whites until very stiff.
3. Gently fold in the ground almonds, semolina and caster sugar, using a tablespoon.
4. Take the mixture in teaspoonfuls and lightly roll into a ball between the hands.
5. Place the macaroons 5–7 cm apart on the rice paper. Put half a blanched almond on top of each.
6. Bake a third of the way down the oven, Regulo 3 or 150°C (300°F), for 30–40 mins., until pale golden and firm. Cool on a wire tray.

# 22. Fillings and Icings

## FILLINGS

**Butter Icing**

This can be used for fillings in sandwich cakes, butterfly cakes, etc. Make and flavour as on page 170.

**Softer Butter Icing**

    50 g butter                2 tsp. boiling water
    100 g icing sugar         2 tsp. top of milk
    2–4 drops vanilla essence

1. Prepare butter icing (see p. 170).
2. Very gradually beat in the boiling water, then the cold top of milk. Take care when adding the milk; stop adding it if the butter icing begins to look 'curdled'.

This filling can be used plain, or add:
    25 g chopped walnuts, or
    25 g chopped raisins and glacé cherries, or
    25 g grated chocolate

**Mock Cream**

    1 level tablesp. cornflour     50 g butter or margarine
    150 ml water                  50 g caster sugar
                                         2–4 drops vanilla essence

1. Make a thick sauce using the cornflour and water (method as for Custard, see p. 100).
2. Cover saucepan and allow the cooked sauce to go completely cold.
3. Cream butter and sugar until white and fluffy; add vanilla essence.
4. Beat the sauce until very smooth; add it, a tsp. at a time, to the creamed fat and sugar and beat it very thoroughly after each addition. The cornflour sauce must be added carefully otherwise the mock cream can get a 'curdled' appearance.

## ICINGS

**Butter Icing**

    50 g butter
    100 g icing sugar
    2–4 drops vanilla essence

1. Using a small wooden spoon, cream the butter and vanilla essence until soft.
2. Sieve icing sugar and stir it gradually into the butter. Beat well until the butter icing is almost white and fluffy in texture.

FLAVOURING: Make butter icing as above, adding only 2 drops of vanilla essence. (The essence masks the fatty flavour.)
(a) *Coffee:* Put 2 level teaspoons of powdered instant coffee into a cup; blend with 2–3 teaspoons boiling water. Allow liquid to go cold. Beat this strong coffee very gradually into the prepared butter icing.
(b) *Chocolate:* Put 2 level teaspoon of cocoa or drinking chocolate into a cup; blend with 2–3 teaspoons boiling water. Allow liquid to go cold. Beat very gradually into the prepared butter icing.
(c) *Orange or lemon:* Wash the orange or lemon and dry it. Beat the very finely grated zest of half the orange or lemon rind into the prepared butter icing.

COLOURING: Butter icing can be coloured by adding a few drops of food colouring, such as cochineal or green colouring. This should be spotted in carefully off the point of a skewer.

Use butter icing for sandwiching together cakes and biscuits, or for decorating cakes. It can be piped successfully.

## Glacé Icing

Quantity sufficient to coat an 18 cm round sandwich cake.

> 100 g *icing sugar*
> 1 *tsp. lemon juice* (*approx.*)
> 1 *tablesp. cold water* (*approx.*)

1. Sieve icing sugar into a mixing bowl; add lemon juice.
2. Gradually add the water, beating well to obtain a smooth consistency. The icing should coat the back of the wooden spoon thickly.
3. Use straight away to coat cakes or biscuits. Pour it on to the cake and spread evenly and quickly with a palette knife.
4. Decorate as necessary. Leave to set.

Glacé Icing can be coloured as for Butter Icing.

FLAVOURING
(a) *Coffee, Chocolate:* Prepare as for plain white glacé icing, leaving out the lemon juice. Mix the icing sugar with coffee or chocolate liquid, made as for flavouring butter icing in place of the cold water.
(b) *Orange, Lemon:* Prepare as above, mixing the icing sugar with orange or lemon juice.

## Marzipan or Almond Paste

Quantity sufficient to coat an 18 cm–20 cm cake, top only.

100 g ground almonds   1–2 tsp. *lemon juice*
50–100 g *icing sugar*   2–3 drops *vanilla essence*
50–100 g *caster sugar*   1–2 tsp. *sherry (if liked)*
1 *egg*

1. Sieve icing sugar into a mixing bowl; add caster sugar, ground almonds and mix together.
2. Add lemon juice, vanilla essence and sherry to the dry ingredients.
3. Beat egg well in a small basin. Gradually add the beaten egg to the dry ingredients, mixing well with a wooden spoon. When the ingredients are beginning to cling together, knead lightly with the hand to form a firm paste.
4. Turn the marzipan on to a board lightly sprinkled with icing sugar and knead until smooth.
5. Use as required.

*Quantity of Sugar in Marzipan:* From equal quantities to double the amount of sugar to ground almonds can be used for the marzipan. The sugar can be all icing sugar, all caster sugar, or a mixture of these.

### To Cover a Cake with Marzipan

When covering a cake with marzipan, it is necessary to brush the cake with either: egg white, or 'apricot glaze' (warmed sieved apricot jam) in order to stick the marzipan firmly on the cake.

*Method for Top only*

1. Stand the cake on a table or pastry board. Look at the cake carefully; if it has risen slightly, it will be necessary to 'build up' the edge. Brush edges with egg white; put on a roll of marzipan. Firm and shape it on the edge of the cake to give a good flat surface. Brush any cracks on top of the cake with egg white and fill in with marzipan.
2. Brush the whole top of the cake, including any marzipan on the edges, with egg white.
3. Roll out the marzipan to the size of the top of the cake, taking care to keep it a good shape and making sure the edges do not crack.
4. Place marzipan on top of the cake; firm and roll it on with a rolling pin, making sure the surface is really flat. Keep the edges straight and neat.

*Method for Top and Sides*

1. Build up the edges and fill in any cracks on top of the cake as above.
2. Brush the whole cake thoroughly with egg white.

3. Roll marzipan out to the shape of the cake and large enough to cover the top and down the sides of the cake. Lift marzipan on to the top of the cake.
4. Gently firm the marzipan on to the cake, moulding it on with the hands.
5. Flatten top by rolling with the rolling pin; straighten sides by rolling a straight sided tin or jar round the cake. Use a palette knife to shape the top edge. Great care must be taken to make the marzipan a good shape.

**Royal Icing**

Quantity sufficient to cover an 18–20 cm Christmas Cake, top only.

250 *g icing sugar*
1–2 *egg whites*
2 *tsp. lemon juice (may be omitted)*

1. Sieve icing sugar into a mixing bowl; add lemon juice if used.
2. Lightly beat the egg whites in a small basin.
3. Gradually add the egg white to the icing sugar, working it well in with a wooden spoon. Continue to add egg white until the icing will coat the back of the wooden spoon thickly. The consistency should be one where a trail left in the icing will just disappear when the bowl is shaken.
4. Beat the icing very vigorously to whiten it and make it glossy.
5. Remove wooden spoon. Wring out a teatowel in cold water; fold it and cover the mixing bowl.
6. Set the bowl of icing aside in a cool place for 1–2 hours so that air bubbles can rise to the surface.
7. Just before using the icing, draw the back of a tablespoon carefully across the surface of the icing to break air bubbles.

**To Flat Ice a Cake:** Stand the marzipanned cake on an upturned plate. Pour the prepared royal icing on top. Work it quickly over the surface with a palette knife. Gently bump the plate down on a folded cloth on the table. The icing will shake down and find its own level.

If flat icing the cake all over, work the icing out to the edges of the cake using a palette knife. Let the icing roll down the sides of the cake. Sweep the palette knife round the sides to smooth the icing. Gently bump the plate down on a folded cloth as above, to level the top. If necessary, smooth the sides again.

*Royal Icing for Piping:* The icing must be stiff enough to stand up in peaks.

*Royal Icing for Rough Icing:* The icing must be stiff enough to hold peaks which just curl over at the point.

*Additions to Royal Icing:*

(a) Lemon Juice: this tends to make the icing hard if it has to be kept for a long time, though it does give the icing a good flavour.
(b) Glycerine: this can be added to icing to help keep it soft. Use 2 tsp. glycerine to 500 g icing sugar, and omit the lemon juice. Glycerine should never be added to icing for piping.

# 23. Bread and Yeast Mixtures

## MAIN INGREDIENTS USED

**Yeast:** The raising agent used in bread mixtures is yeast. It is a single-celled, living organism; it belongs to the fungi group, and is classed as a non-green plant. There are many varieties of yeasts; the one mainly used in bread making is called compressed or German yeast, and is produced as a by-product in the process of brewing beer.

Under suitable conditions, yeast can produce enzymes which convert starch to sugar, and sugar to alcohol and carbon dioxide. It is the carbon dioxide produced during this 'fermentation' which raises bread-dough. As yeast is a living thing, it requires food, moisture and warmth if it is to grow and reproduce. In bread making, the 'food' is provided by a small quantity of sugar, or by the flour; moisture by water or milk; warmth during making, rising and proving.

Compressed yeast used in bread making must be very fresh. It should be pale creamy fawn, crumbly and have a pleasant smell. Stale yeast is brown, dry and hard and should not be used. Dried yeast is often used now; it needs to be soaked for 10–15 mins in the lukewarm liquid before use. For quantities, follow makers' instructions.

**Flour:** Wheat flour contains the protein 'gluten'. When flour is mixed with water, gluten forms a sticky elastic substance, and helps to trap air or gases in its meshes.

For breadmaking, a 'strong' flour containing a high proportion of gluten should be used. Softer household flours are not as satisfactory for breadmaking. The flour may be brown or white. Plain flour *must* be used; self raising flour is unsuitable.

**Salt:** Bread made without salt is flavourless. Use 2 level tsp. salt to 500 g flour. Salt also slightly retards the growth of yeast.

**Sugar:** Often 1 teaspoonful sugar is added to the yeast to 'cream' it. (This helps to provide 'food' for the yeast.)

**Liquid:** Either water or milk or a mixture of these is used. The liquid is usually used at 'blood' heat.

### The Process of Bread-making

(a) Yeast and a small amount of sugar are 'creamed' together until liquid. The sugar provides food material for the yeast.

# BREAD AND YEAST MIXTURES

(b) Yeast and warmed liquid are added to the flour and mixed to form a dough.

(c) Kneading helps to distribute the yeast and liquid evenly throughout the dough. It also helps to 'develop' the gluten and makes the dough more elastic.

(d) Rising: the dough is set aside in a warm place. The yeast multiplies; carbon dioxide is formed which raises the dough to double its size. The gas is trapped in the meshes of the gluten.

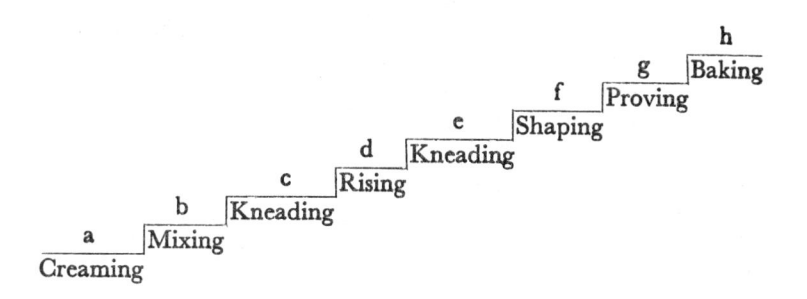

```
                                                 h
                                          g   Baking
                                    f   Proving
                              e   Shaping
                        d   Kneading
                  c   Rising
            b   Kneading
      a   Mixing
  Creaming
```

(e) Kneading: this helps to distribute the carbon dioxide throughout the dough to give an even texture. In the process, some of the carbon dioxide is knocked out.

(f) Shaping: the dough is formed into rolls, loaves, etc.

(g) Proving: the shaped dough is put in a warm place again until more carbon dioxide has been produced, and the dough is allowed to almost double in size. Care must be taken not to 'overprove' or the bread will be a poor open texture.

(h) Baking: yeast mixtures are baked in a hot oven, Regulo 7, or 220°C (425°F). When they first go in the oven there is a rapid 'oven spring' and the dough rises very quickly. The heat of the oven kills the yeast so the dough cannot rise any more. The heat also hardens the gluten and sets the shape of the bread. The typical smell of bread baking is given by the alcohol formed being driven off by the oven heat.

(N.B. It is most important that the liquid added to yeast and bread dough is only at 'blood' heat; also that dough is only put in a gently warm place to rise. Too strong heat at these stages can kill the yeast making it inactive. Cold conditions retard the growth of the yeast but do not kill it.)

It is possible to put dough to prove in a refrigerator, and it will rise very gradually overnight.

## Quick Method of Bread-making

The number of processes can be cut down to

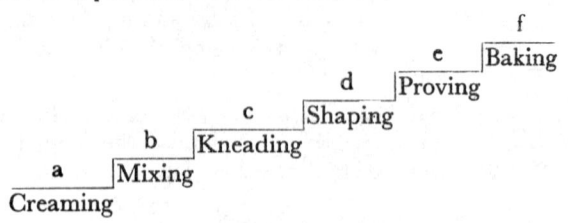

```
                                    f  |Baking
                              e  |Proving
                        d  |Shaping
                  c  |Kneading
            b  |Mixing
       a  |Creaming
```

This quick method is more satisfactory when used for small buns than for large loaves, where it may give a poor texture.

*Quantity of Yeast to Use:* For bread and very plain mixtures, use 15 g yeast to 500 g flour; 25 g yeast to 500 g–1½ kg (1500 g) flour. More yeast is used for richer fruit breads, where there is a greater weight of ingredients to raise.

### RECIPES USING YEAST

**White Bread** (1 large loaf)

| | |
|---|---|
| 500 g *plain flour* | 15 g *yeast* |
| 2 *level tsp. salt* | 1 *tsp. caster sugar* |
| 25 g *lard (optional)* | 300 *ml warm water (approx.)* |

1. Sieve flour into a warmed bowl; add salt. Rub in lard.
2. Put yeast and sugar in a small basin. Using a teaspoon, cream together until liquid. Add most of the lukewarm water.
3. Make a well in the centre of the flour. Mixing with the hand, add yeast liquid and enough of the remaining warm water to the flour to form a soft dough. Beat well, until the dough is smooth and leaves the sides of the bowl clean.
4. Turn on to a floured board; knead the dough well.
5. Put the dough in the bowl and cover with a slightly damp teacloth; set in a warm place to rise until the dough is twice the size (½–1 hour).
6. Knead the dough lightly; shape, then press the dough into a greased and floured large loaf tin. (Dough should half fill the tin.)
7. Put in a warm place to prove until dough just reaches the top of the tin.
8. Brush the top of loaf with water. Bake half way down the oven, Regulo 7, or 220°C (425°F) for 20–30 mins. until brown. Reduce heat to Regulo 4 or 180°C (350°F) and continue to bake for a further 20–30 mins. When cooked, the bread will be crisp and firm, and sound hollow when tapped underneath. (To brown the sides, the loaf can be removed from the tin when firm, and placed on the bars of the oven shelf.)

## Brown Bread (1 large loaf)

Ingredients: As for white bread, replacing 500 g plain flour with

either: 500 g wholemeal flour
or: 250 g wholemeal flour }
250 g plain flour }

Make as for white bread, except that wholemeal flour must not be sieved.

## Splits (makes 6–8)

| | |
|---|---|
| 250 g plain flour | 15 g yeast (bare weight) |
| 1 level tsp. salt | 1 tsp. sugar |
| 25 g margarine | 150 ml warm milk (approx.) |

1. Sieve flour and salt into a warmed bowl. Rub in margarine.
2. Cream yeast and sugar; add warmed milk.
3. Make a well in the flour; add the yeast and liquid and mix to give a soft dough. Beat well until the dough is smooth.
4. Cover bowl with a damp cloth; set in a warm place until the dough has doubled in size ($\frac{1}{2}$–$\frac{3}{4}$ hour).
5. Turn on to a floured board; knead lightly.
6. Divide dough into 6 or 8 equal pieces. Knead each one to form a neat round shape. (Turn over, so that smooth side is uppermost.)
7. Put splits 5 cm apart on a floured baking tray. Prove until almost double in size.
8. Brush tops with milk; bake a third of the way down the oven, Regulo 7, or 220°C (425°F), for 15–20 mins. until well risen, golden and rolls sound hollow when tapped underneath. Cool on a wire tray.

## Bread 'Shapes'

The above dough can be divided into eight pieces, then shaped in rolls, plaits, twists, etc. Bake as above.

## Chelsea Buns (makes 9)

Ingredients: As for Splits. In addition:

| | |
|---|---|
| 25–50 g dried fruit | Pinch of mixed spice |
| 15 g mixed peel (if liked) | 25 g margarine |
| 25 g sugar | |

1. Prepare dough as for splits. Allow to rise in a warm place until double in size.
2. Wash dried fruit and allow to drain well.
3. Turn dough on to a floured board; knead lightly. Roll out to a 30 cm square.

4. Sprinkle dough with dried fruit and mixed peel; then sugar and spice.
5. Melt margarine in a small saucepan and sprinkle over the dough.
6. Roll up loosely; cut into 9 even sized pieces. Place buns about 2 cm apart, cut edge up, in a shallow 18 cm square greased baking tin so that they rise against each other.
7. Prove.
8. Bake a third of the way down the oven, Regulo 7, or 220°C (425°F), for 15–20 mins. until firm and brown on top, and the baking tin sounds hollow when tapped underneath. Turn on to a wire tray. Break apart when cool.
Serve cold with butter.

## Lardy Cake

Dough: 250 g *plain flour*
1 *level tsp. salt*
15 g *lard*
15 g *yeast*
1 *tsp. sugar*
150 *ml warm water* (*approx.*)

Filling: 50 g *lard*
50 g *currants*
50 g *sugar*

1. Make dough and allow to rise (as for white bread).
2. Turn on to a floured board; knead lightly. Roll to an oblong.
3. Dab half the lard over the top ⅔ of the dough; sprinkle on half the sugar and dried fruit.
4. Fold up lower ⅓ of dough, top ⅓ down (as for Flaky Pastry, p. 143). Seal edges; quarter turn the dough. Re-roll and repeat with remaining lard, sugar and fruit, then fold again.
5. Roll lardy cake to 18 cm square (should be about 2 cm thick).
6. Place in a shallow 18 cm square tin which has been greased and floured. Prove.
7. Brush top with water. Sprinkle lightly with caster sugar.
8. Bake a third of the way down the oven, Regulo 7, or 220°C (425°F), for 20–30 mins. until golden brown and hollow sounding when tapped underneath. Cool on a wire tray.
Serve with butter.

## Quick Teacakes (makes 8)

200 g *plain flour*
1 *level tsp. salt*
25 g *margarine*
15 g *yeast*
15 g *sugar*

1 *egg, beaten*
75 *ml milk* (*approx.*)
50 g *sultanas or currants*
Pinch of *mixed spice*

1. Wash dried fruit; drain well.
2. Sieve flour, salt and spice into a warm bowl. Rub in margarine. Add dried fruit and all except 1 tsp. sugar.
3. Cream yeast and 1 tsp. sugar. Add warm milk.
4. Add yeast and liquid to the dry ingredients; then beaten egg, and mix well to give a soft dough.
5. Knead lightly on a floured board. Divide and shape into 8 small teacakes, or 2 large ones.
6. Prove on a lightly floured tin.
7. Bake (as for splits).
Serve hot or cold with butter.

## 24. Reheated Dishes

However carefully shopping is planned so that the right amounts of food are bought, most housewives find that they sometimes have food left over. For economy, this food should be used up whenever possible. It should be noted that reheated foods are not always very digestible and should not, therefore, be given to children, invalids, or old people who find digestion difficult.

### Examples of Common Left-over Foods and Uses

*Stale bread:* Bread and butter pudding, queen of puddings, bread and cheese pudding, raspings.
*Stale plain cake:* Trifle, cabinet pudding.
*Cold roast meat:* Shepherd's pie, rissoles, hash, curry, etc.
*Boiled potatoes:* Used on top of Shepherd's pie, fish pie, fish cakes, fried, potato cakes, etc.
*Green vegetables:* Mixed with cooked potato and made into 'bubble and squeak.'
*Stewed fruit:* Trifle, fruit fool, fruit tartlets (depending on variety).
*Cold custard:* Fruit fool.

### Rules to Follow when Making 'Reheated Dishes'

1. All food used must be very fresh.
2. Foods which have been once cooked tend to be dry if reheated, so they should be served either in, or with a sauce, e.g. rissoles with tomato sauce, curry of cold meat, etc.
3. Try to divide up food to be reheated very finely (by mincing or chopping) so that heat can penetrate quickly. Reheated dishes should only be reheated, not recooked, and so all flavourings and additions to the recipe must also be cooked, e.g. cooked onion added to flavour Shepherd's pie.
4. Reheated dishes tend to be flavourless and need careful seasoning.
5. Some food value, especially Vitamin C is destroyed when once cooked foods are reheated. Try to serve reheated dishes with other foods which will add any missing nutrients, e.g. fish cakes, served with grilled tomatoes or a fresh green vegetable.
6. Try to make a completely different dish from the 'left-over' food; the reheated dish should not resemble the once cooked food.
   Reheating is usually done rapidly in a very hot oven, or often by deep fat frying.

# RECIPES FOR USING LEFT-OVER FOODS

**Shepherd's Pie**

    250 g *lean cooked meat*      15 g *dripping*
    1 *level tsp. salt*, 2–3 *shakes pepper*      100–125 ml *gravy or stock*
    1 *small onion*      500 g *potatoes, creamed*
    (see p. 86)

1. Grease a 500 ml pie dish.
2. Prepare and boil potatoes (see p. 86).
3. Skin onion; chop very finely. Melt dripping in a frying pan and fry the onion lightly until golden brown. Drain well.
4. Trim any fat, gristle, skin from the meat. Mince meat finely.
5. Add seasoning and cooked onion to the meat, and place in a pie dish. Add enough gravy or stock to moisten the meat.
6. Drain potatoes well when soft, and cream them (see p. 86). Spread evenly over the meat and fork the top to give a neat pattern. (If liked, put on a few very thin pieces of butter to help brown potatoes.)
7. Reheat near the top of the oven, Regulo 7 or 220°C (425°F), for approx. 30 mins. Garnish with parsley.

**Rissoles** (makes 4)

    250 g *lean cooked meat*      *Salt and pepper*
    1 *small onion*      1 *tsp. Worcester sauce*
    15 g *dripping* ⎫
    15 g *plain flour* ⎬ Panada      To coat: *Beaten egg and raspings*
    75 ml *stock* ⎭      For frying: *Dripping or deep fat*

1. Trim, then mince the meat finely.
2. Skin onion and chop finely. Melt the dripping in a small saucepan and fry the onion gently until golden brown. Stir in flour to make a roux, and cook over a gentle heat until brown.
3. Add stock, and bring to the boil, stirring all the time. Cook for 1–2 mins.
4. Remove pan from heat; add minced meat, Worcester sauce and seasoning. Taste and correct seasoning if necessary. (There should be just enough sauce to bind the meat into the mixture.)
5. Turn mixture on to a lightly floured board, and divide in 4. Shape each piece into a flat cake, 2 cm thick, using the hand and a palette knife.
6. Coat in beaten egg, then in raspings. Replace on the board. Reshape if necessary with the palette knife, and pat the raspings on firmly.
7. Fry in shallow or deep fat which has just reached hazing point, for 3–5 mins., or until golden all over. (The rissoles must be turned if using shallow fat.) Drain well.

8. Serve on a hot dish; Garnish with parsley and grilled tomatoes (see p. 89) or peas. Hand brown or tomato sauce separately.

### Curry of Cold Meat (serves 3)

    250 g *lean cooked meat*     100–120 g *Patna rice*
    300 ml *curry sauce*     Garnish: *Parsley*

1. Prepare curry sauce (see p. 103). Simmer for ½ hour.
2. Trim off any fat or skin from the meat. Cut meat in 2 cm cubes. Add to curry and simmer for a further ½ hour.
3. Boil and dry rice (see p. 89).
4. Serve curried meat, with a border or rice. Garnish with parsley.

### Potato Cakes (makes 4–6)

    250 g *cooked potato*     For frying: 25 g *dripping*
    *Salt and pepper*     or *white cooking fat*
    1 *tablesp. plain flour*     Garnish: *Small pieces of butter*

1. Mash the potatoes well; add salt and pepper and work the flour in.
2. Turn the mixture on to a floured board; divide into 4–6 even sized pieces. Using a palette knife, form each piece into a flattened cake, about 1 cm thick.
3. Heat fat in a frying pan until at hazing point. Fry potato cakes until golden brown, 3–4 mins. on each side.
4. Serve on a heated dish, with a small piece of butter on each.

### 'Bubble and Squeak'

    Cold cooked potatoes and green vegetables (*cabbage, sprouts, etc.*)
    *Salt and pepper*
    For frying: 25 g *dripping*

1. Mash potatoes; chop up green vegetables, then mix the two together.
2. Season well.
3. Heat dripping in a frying pan; fry bubble and squeak until golden underneath; turn and fry the second side.
4. Serve with bacon, cold meat and chutney, sausage, etc.

### Raspings

    Cut stale bread into 1 cm thick slices. Place on a baking tray. When the oven is on, put low down in oven. Bake very gently until pale fawn, crisp, and the bread is thoroughly dried out.

    Put baked bread between greaseproof paper; roll firmly to break it up. Sieve the raspings and store in an airtight jar or tin.

# 25. Beverages

## TEA

**Proportions:** Allow 2–3 rounded teaspoonfuls tea to 500 ml boiling water, depending on the strength liked, or 1 level tsp. per person plus 1 for the pot. Make the tea with freshly boiled water.

1. Throw away any 'once-boiled' water in the kettle. Use freshly drawn cold water; bring to the boil.
2. When the water is almost boiling, 'scald' the teapot with some of the hot water, then empty it.
3. Put the tea into the heated pot.
4. As soon as the water boils, pour it on the tea. (Take the teapot to the kettle, not the kettle to the teapot.)
5. Allow to stand and infuse for 3–5 minutes. (Fine tea will need less time to infuse than one with coarse leaves.)
6. Stir the tea before pouring; strain it into the cups.

Serve the tea with cold milk and granulated sugar handed separately. When first cups have been poured, add boiling water to the pot, ready for second cups. Some people like tea without milk, sometimes with a slice of lemon added instead. In this case, the tea should be served fairly weak.

## COFFEE

The fine flavour of coffee depends on the aroma of the ground coffee, and this is quickly lost if the coffee is stored too long before use. Freshly ground coffee should be bought in small quantities only, so that it is used up quickly. If the coffee was bought in a vacuum sealed tin, store it in that; if bought loose, keep it in an airtight tin or polythene container. The best flavour is obtained if you can buy the roasted coffee beans and grind them freshly at home just before using.

Coffee should be freshly made for each meal; if reheated, it loses flavour and often tastes bitter.

Coffee may be served either white, with hot but not boiling milk; or black, either alone or with cream. Hand demerara, or coffee sugar, separately with both types.

**Proportions:** For making coffee, allow 3–4 heaped tablesp. (40–50 g) ground coffee to 500 ml water.

**Quantity of Coffee to Make**

Served black: 500 ml coffee will give 3 teacups full.
Served white: 500 ml coffee with 250–300 ml hot milk will give 4–5 teacups full.

There are numerous ways of making coffee, though the following are perhaps the commonest.

## THE JUG METHOD

40–50 g ground coffee        250–300 ml hot milk
500 ml boiling water         To serve: *Demerara or coffee sugar*

1. Choose a heavy stoneware jug.
2. Use freshly drawn cold water; bring to the boil.
3. Just before the water boils, heat the jug with some of the nearly boiling water, then empty it.
4. Put the coffee into the heated pot.
5. As soon as the water boils, pour it on to the coffee. Stir well.
6. Cover jug, and allow the coffee to infuse for 5 mins. in a warm place.
7. Strain the coffee through a fine strainer into a heated coffee pot.
8. Heat the milk, but do not boil it. Serve in a separate jug. Hand sugar separately.

## COFFEE MADE IN A PERCOLATOR

Use the same quantities as for coffee made by the jug method.

1. Measure the coffee, and place it in the perforated metal container from the percolator. Put the container lid on. (The ground coffee should not more than two-thirds fill the container.)
2. Put the measured cold water in the percolator jug. Put in the coffee container then close the percolator lid.
3. Heat the percolator gently until the water is boiling. When boiling the water will rise up the central tube, hit the glass lid, and spray down through the coffee container.
4. Continue to percolate very gently for 10 mins.

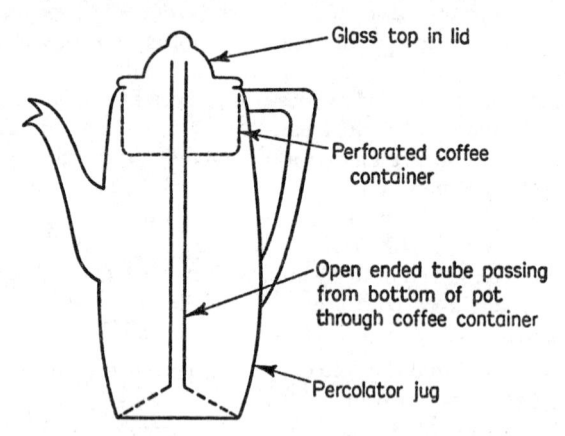

BEVERAGES

5. To Serve: either remove the coffee container, and serve the coffee from the percolator jug, or pour the coffee into a heated pot. Serve the coffee with hot milk in a separate jug, and hand sugar separately.

## COCOA

2 *level tsp. cocoa*
1–2 *tsp. sugar, according to taste*
1 *cupful* (250 *ml*) *milk, or milk and water*

### Method 1

1. Blend cocoa (and sugar) to a smooth paste with a little of the cold milk.
2. Heat the remaining milk in a small saucepan; add hot milk to the blended cocoa.
3. Rinse pan; pour in cocoa. Heat the cocoa gently, stirring at the same time until it boils. Allow the cocoa to cook gently for ½–1 mins., otherwise it may taste powdery due to the starch present in cocoa.
4. Pour straight into the cup, or into a serving jug.
5. Sugar (granulated) can be put in when making, or can be handed separately.

### Method 2

1. Mix the sugar and cocoa together.
2. Warm the milk in a small saucepan.
3. Sprinkle the cocoa and sugar on to the warm milk and gently beat in with a fork until the cocoa boils. Allow to cook for ½–min.
4. Serve as in above method.

For 'Drinking Chocolate' or 'Flaked Chocolate Powder', follow makers' instructions on the tin.

## FRESH LEMONADE

(makes 2 tumblerfuls)

1 *lemon*       25 g *sugar*       400 *ml water*

1. Wash and dry the lemon. Using a potato peeler, thinly remove the zest from ½ the lemon.
2. Put zest and sugar in a jug. Boil and add 150 ml of the water.
3. Stir until sugar has dissolved. Cover jug and allow to infuse until the water is quite cold.
4. Add remaining 250 ml cold water, and finally the lemon juice.
5. Strain into a glass jug and serve chilled if possible.

Whenever possible add lemon juice to the drink just before serving. Vitamin C is lost if the drink stands for too long.

**Lemonade to Drink with a Meal:** Make sure to prepare the lemonade in good time so that it is really cold when needed.

**As an 'Invalid' Drink:** The lemonade can be made entirely with boiling water and served hot.

## ORANGEADE
(makes 2 tumblerfuls)

    2 *oranges*      30 *g sugar*      400 *ml water*

Prepare and serve as for lemonade.

## EGG FLIP

    1 *egg*      1 *drop vanilla essence,*
    1–2 *tsp. sugar*      *or* 1 *tsp. brandy, if liked*
    150 *ml milk*

1. Break egg into a small basin. Add sugar, and whisk or beat to break the egg up thoroughly.
2. Add milk, chilled if possible, and vanilla essence or brandy. Stir well.
3. Strain into a glass to serve.

# 26. Invalid Cookery

Whatever illness a patient may be suffering from, it is most important that he or she should be properly and carefully fed. In the case of some illnesses, especially those concerned with digestive, circulatory and metabolic disorders of the body (e.g. gastric and duodenal ulcers, anaemia, diabetes, etc.) the doctor will prescribe a special diet and this must be strictly followed.

In more general cases of illness such as the more common children's ailments, influenza, bronchitis and similar diseases, the doctor will probably suggest first a 'liquid' or 'semi-liquid' diet, followed by a 'light' diet.

**Food Requirements in Illness:** During any illness, there is bound to be some wasting of body tissues; because of this it is essential to provide the patient with adequate protein for rebuilding the body. Protective foods must be given, to make sure that the diet is not lacking in Vitamins and mineral elements.

If in bed, the patient will not be using up so much energy, and will require less of the energy giving foods; quantities of foods containing sugar and starch should be reduced. All food given to the patient should be easily digestible. Fat is difficult to digest, so only small amounts of the more easily digested ones such as butter and cream should be given. No food should be served fried or baked in fat.

**Diet in Different Stages of Illness:** Many illnesses begin with a rise in temperature, and the patient is said to be 'feverish'. While the fever lasts, a 'liquid' diet should be given. A liquid diet is easy to digest and also helps to reduce fever and quench the thirst.

**Liquid Diet:** Suitable foods are:

Milk and milk drinks; egg in milk
Freshly squeezed orange juice
Orange and lemonade made from fresh fruit
Blackcurrant juice; rosehip syrup
Barley water
Thin gruel made with fine oatmeal
Strained or puréed soups if allowed
Glucose or honey are easily digested and can be used to sweeten fruit drinks instead of granulated sugar
Beef tea' used to be regarded as a 'must' in invalid cookery. Like stock, it has almost no nutritional value.

Once the temperature has returned to normal, small quantities of more solid food can be given. All the food must be very easily digestible. As the condition of the patient improves and appetite returns, quantities can be gradually increased.

During convalescence, the light diet should be continued and the patient put back very gradually on to a normal diet.

**Light Diet:** Suitable foods include:

Eggs, lightly cooked (scrambled, poached, boiled)
Milk, and dishes made with milk (milk pudding, milk jelly, junket, egg custard)
White meats such as chicken, veal, rabbit, tripe, sweetbread
Liver (casseroled or grilled)
Very lean beef (casseroled or roasted)
Soups
Butter; cream; ice cream
Fresh vegetables, carefully cooked
Salads
Fresh and stewed fruits
Brown and white breads; toast
Cereals
Plain sponge cakes; plain biscuits
Steamed or baked 'sponge' puddings
Drinks made from milk; also fruit drinks rich in Vitamin C

The light diet should be continued when the patient becomes convalescent, towards the end of convalescence, the patient should be put back on to a normal diet very gradually.

**Foods to be Avoided During Illness**

| | |
|---|---|
| All fried foods | Very new bread |
| Pastry | Suet puddings |
| Rich cakes and biscuits | Reheated foods |
| Pork, bacon, ham | Strong tea and coffee |
| Mutton | Highly seasoned foods, such |
| Oily fish | as curry, pickles, etc. |
| Cheese | |

**Suggestions for a Day's Meals for a Convalescent**

*Breakfast:* ½ grapefruit. Lightly boiled egg. Thin bread and butter. Thin crisp toast with butter and marmalade. Weak tea to drink.

*Mid-morning:* Fresh lemonade, or weak milky coffee. Plain biscuits.

*Lunch:* Fresh fruit juice. Grilled liver and tomatoes. Gravy. Runner beans. Creamed potatoes. Stewed fruit and custard.

*Tea:* Thin bread and butter with honey or jam. Milk jelly and cream. Sponge cake. Weak tea to drink.

# INVALID COOKERY

*Snack before bedtime:* Milk drink, such as cocoa or malted milk. Plain biscuits, or thin buttered toast, if needed.

**Considerations when Serving Food to an Invalid:** Do everything possible to tempt the patient's appetite. Prepare and season all food carefully and make it attractive by using colourful garnishes and decoration where necessary. Serve the food in individual portions on pretty china or glass dishes. Make everything look as fresh and bright as possible, with a crisp clean cloth on the tray and well polished cutlery.

Try to make all meals 'easy to manage'. Where a patient is in bed, food can be cut up for him, or unnecessary skin, bones or fat removed. Only give small helpings of food at a time; it is easy to be 'put off' by too large a portion. Have 'second helpings' available in case they are needed. Cover hot food while carrying it to the sick room, so it is still hot when the patient gets it.

Try not to discuss the coming meals with the patient; an element of surprise may help to tempt the appetite. Avoid all foods you know the patient does not like and where possible try to give any foods which are especially liked and asked for.

If a patient is suffering from an infectious disease, dishes and cutlery should be kept separate and should be washed up separately (not with the rest of the family's things). Scald if possible. Any food given to the patient but not eaten should be thrown away.

# 27. Vegetarian Cookery

People may be vegetarians for several reasons: they may be forced to be vegetarian because of their religious beliefs; some consider it cruel to have to kill animals to provide food; they may think animals and animal products 'unclean', and that to eat animal food is unhealthy.

Vegetarians are of two types: there are those who are 'strict' vegetarians and refuse to eat any food derived from an animal source; and there are others who are termed 'lacto-vegetarians'. Lacto-vegetarians make full use of eggs, milk, cream and cheese, all products which can be obtained from an animal, without its having to be killed. They will eat no form of flesh (meat, poultry, or fish).

**Strict Vegetarians:** Like all other people, strict vegetarians need a balanced diet if they are going to remain healthy, but it is difficult to provide this when foods are limited purely to those of vegetable origin.

Protein must be obtained from pulses, cereals and nuts, and the small amount found in some vegetables. Since the proteins from these sources are 'incomplete' (see p. 1), it is essential that a variety of foods is eaten to try to provide all the 'essential amino acids' (see p. 1); also the quantity of protein contained in vegetable foods is nearly always less than in the same weight of animal food, so a vegetable diet is necessarily more bulky.

Fats must be obtained from nuts and other vegetable sources, such as olive oil, cotton seed oil, etc. Vegetarian margarine is also made. Carbohydrates, fortunately, are all of plant origin. Vitamins B and C are found in the fresh fruit, vegetables and cereals included in the diet. Vitamin A has to be obtained from carotene, the orange-yellow colouring in vegetables, and converted in the body to Vitamin A. (However, 3 parts of carotene only convert to 1 part of Vitamin A, so more must be taken.) Vitamin D can only be produced by the action of sunlight on the body (see p. 4). An adequate supply of calcium, phosphorus, sulphur and iron is found in vegetables, cereals, dried fruits and black treacle.

The diet of a strict vegetarian is bound to be more bulky if all essential nutrients are to be obtained from often relatively poor sources.

**Lacto-vegetarians:** It is much simpler to provide well balanced meals for lacto-vegetarians. They use eggs, milk and cheese freely and these are all rich sources of first class protein, as well as Vitamin A and some Vitamin D. These vitamins are also obtained from vitaminized margarine.

**Preparing Food for Vegetarians:** Most vegetables, pulses, nuts and cereals tend to be insipid and it is necessary to flavour these vegetable dishes very carefully to make them stimulating and palatable. Herbs, curry powder and spices, seasonings, strongly flavoured vegetables such as onions and garlic are all used to add flavour.

Different methods of cooking, such as frying or baking, boiling and steaming, will help to give varying texture to the food. Crispness can also be given by the use of raw fruit and vegetables. Particularly when cooking for lacto-vegetarians, many ordinary recipes can be adapted. In this case, foods of animal origin must be exchanged for vegetable products. For example, use vegetable stock, water or milk instead of meat stock for soups, sauces and gravies; white cooking fat instead of lard for pastry; yeast extract instead of meat extract in gravies; agar agar instead of gelatine; 'nut meat' in place of ordinary meat, and peanut butter in place of ordinary butter.

## LACTO-VEGETARIANS

**Suggestions for a Day's Meals**

*Breakfast:* Half a grapefruit; poached egg on toast; toast with butter and marmalade; coffee.
*Mid-morning:* Coffee and biscuits.
*Dinner:* Onion soup; 'nut meat' rissoles; tomato sauce; spring greens; creamed potatoes; fruit flan and cream; coffee.
*High Tea:* Mixed salad, with nuts and raisins and grated cheese; rolls and butter; chocolate mousse; fruit cake; tea to drink.
*Before Bed:* Milk drink; sweet biscuits or biscuits and cheese.

*RECIPES SUITABLE FOR LACTO-VEGETARIANS*
See also Recipes for 'Eggs', 'Cheese' and 'Vegetables'.

**Vegetarian Pie** (serves 2)

> *Mixed diced vegetables to fill a* 500 *ml pie dish. (carrot, onion, turnip, cauliflower, celery, beans, peas, baked beans, etc.)*
> 1 *tsp. yeast extract*
> 150 *ml water*
> *Seasoning*
> 100 *g cheese pastry* (see p. 140)

1. Make pastry (see p. 140).
2. Prepare vegetables according to kind (see pp. 82–8). Dice into 1 cm dice; leave peas whole.
3. Put prepared vegetables in pie dish so that it is filled to just above the rim; season very lightly with salt and pepper.
4. Dissolve the yeast extract in warm water and add to the vegetables.

5. Line rim of dish, then cover pie with pastry (as for fruit pie, see p. 132). Flake and flute edges. Brush with milk, and make a small hole in the centre of the pie crust.
6. Bake half way down the oven, Regulo 7 or 220°C (425°F) for 15–20 mins., until the pastry is just brown. Reduce heat to Regulo 3 or 150°C (300°F), for a further ½–¾ hour until the vegetables are cooked. (Test with skewer to see if they are soft.)

## Vegetable Curry (serves 2)

> 400 ml mixed diced vegetables (as for Vegetarian Pie)
> 300 ml *curry sauce* (see p. 103)
> 80 g *Patna rice*
> Garnish: *Parsley*

1. Make curry sauce (see p. 103)
2. Prepare vegetables and cut into 1 cm dice. Cut enough to fill a 400 ml measure.
3. Add raw vegetables to curry sauce, and cook gently for ½–¾ hour. (Add root vegetables first, and later any vegetables such as peas which cook more quickly.)
4. Cook and dry the Patna rice (see p. 89).
5. Serve curried vegetables in a heated dish; arrange the boiled rice in a border around the edge. Garnish neatly with parsley.

## Egg Cutlets (serves 2)

> 2 or 3 *hard boiled eggs* (see p. 114)     For coating: ½ *egg, beaten*
> Panada: 125 ml *milk*                                     *Raspings*
>    25 g *plain flour*                      *Oil for frying*
>    25 g *butter*                     Garnish: *Parsley*
>    *Seasoning*                            *Grilled tomatoes*

1. Remove shells from eggs. Mash eggs very finely.
2. Make a panada with the milk, flour and butter (see p. 96).
3. Add hard boiled egg. Season with salt and pepper. Taste and correct seasoning if necessary.
4. Spread the mixture into an oblong shape, 15 mm thick on a plate. Divide in half diagonally. Chill the mixture if possible, or leave to harden in a cool place.
5. When firm, put mixture on a lightly floured board; shape to form 2 'cutlets'. Coat with beaten egg, then raspings.
6. Fry cutlets in deep or shallow oil which is just at hazing point 4–5 mins. (or 2–3 mins. each side) until golden brown. Drain well; arrange on a heated dish. Garnish with parsley and grilled tomato.

**Nut Cutlets** (serves 2)

*Panada, coating and garnish as for Egg Cutlets*
80 *g chopped nuts in place of* 2 *hard boiled eggs*
1 *small onion*

1. Chop nuts very finely.
2. Skin onion; chop very finely.
3. Prepare panada; melt butter in a small saucepan and lightly fry the onion until just soft. Add flour to make roux.
   Continue as for 'Egg Cutlets'.

# 28. Preserving Fruit and Vegetables at Home

Fruit and vegetables are preserved when they are 'in season' so that they may be kept and used at a time of the year when they are not normally available.

**Principles Underlying Preservation:** Although a few fruits and vegetables will keep fairly well in a fresh state, most have to be preserved in some way if they are to be kept for any length of time. Unless preserved, the fruit or vegetables will 'go bad'. This decay or spoilage may be due to one or more of the following factors:

*Enzyme Action:* Enzymes are chemical substances present in all fruit and vegetables and are responsible for ripening, over-ripening and finally decay. The browning of an apple or pear after peeling, for example, is due to enzymes. Enzyme action is increased by warmth, but slowed down or stopped completely by cold. Heat destroys enzymes. In preserving it is essential that enzyme action is stopped.

As well as enzyme activity which occurs inside the fruit or vegetable, the food may also be attacked from outside by micro-organisms which are present in the air. These include yeasts, moulds and bacteria.

*Yeasts:* These are minute single celled organisms which are able to reproduce very rapidly by 'budding'. Yeasts are able to ferment fruit juices, syrup and jam, spoiling the food; they are, however, usefully employed in wine and bread making.

Yeasts are quickly destroyed by heat. In extremely cold conditions, they form spores and remain dormant though are not killed. For growth yeasts need moisture. They can thrive in acid conditions.

*Moulds:* These also cause food spoilage and harm the flavour of the food. Like yeasts, moulds need moisture for growth. They are usually destroyed by heat and are either destroyed or made inactive by very low temperatures. Moulds can develop on foods containing a large proportion of sugar (e.g. on top of jam).

*Bacteria:* These are single-celled micro-organisms which under suitable conditions will multiply very rapidly. Most bacteria are destroyed by heating to boiling point of water (100°C) especially when in an acid medium (e.g. fruit acid). A few are more resistant and need temperatures of up to 120°C before they are destroyed. (For this reason, when bottling vegetables which are non-acid the higher temperature of a pressure cooker is needed for processing.)

Bacteria can survive at very low temperatures but will not grow and develop. Some bacteria if not destroyed can produce harmful toxins in non-acid foods (e.g. meat, vegetables) which may cause severe food poisoning.

**Aims in Preserving:** In preserving food, it is essential that all agents of spoilage are either destroyed or made inactive; also that they are prevented from re-entering the preserved food. Care must be taken to seal vacuum jars and cans, and cover down jams and chutneys properly.

| | Principle | Method | Uses |
|---|---|---|---|
| (a) | By heating and exclusion of air | Bottling; canning | Fruit, vegetables, etc. |
| (b) | By freezing | Deep freezing | Fruit, vegetables, meat, etc. |
| (c) | Removal of moisture | Drying | Fruits, vegetables, herbs, etc. |
| (d) | High concentration of sugar | Jam and jelly making; crystallizing | Jams, jellies, fruits |
| (e) | High concentration of salt | Salting | Beans, etc. |
| (f) | Addition of vinegar | Pickling; chutney making | Pickles and chutneys |
| (g) | Formation of alcohol | Wine making | Wines, etc. |

Several methods of preserving incorporate more than one principle. For example, in jam making, the fruit is preserved by heating and by the addition of a high concentration of sugar.

## BOTTLING

This method of preserving is especially suitable for fruit. Bacteria are rarely found in fruits as they do not develop in an acid medium. The normal temperatures used for bottling are sufficient to destroy yeasts, moulds and most enzymes. Vegetables are not acid and if bottled should be processed in a pressure cooker, where higher temperatures can be reached. Once processed, the bottles must be sealed to prevent the re-entry of micro-organisms.

**Types of Bottles to Use.** Jars for bottling may have: (a) glass (or lacquered metal) lid, rubber ring and a screw band; or (b) lacquered metal lid, rubber ring and a clip top.

The jars may be specially made for bottling; alternatively, rubber rings, metal lids and clip tops can be bought to fit most ordinary jam jars.

**Examination of Jars and Rings:** There must be no chips in the rim of the jar or in the glass lid as these would prevent sealing. Rubber rings must not be perished or the jars will not seal. (If perished, they will not return to their proper shape if stretched; when held up to the light, small holes can be seen in a perished ring.) It is as well to use new rubber rings for each lot of bottling.

**Preparation of Jars, Lids and Rings**
1. Wash in hot soapy water.
2. Rinse in clear water; leave to drain.
3. Hold jars in a teatowel; allow steam from a boiling kettle to flow in for a few seconds.
4. Put lids, rubber rings, screws or clips in a bowl and scald with boiling water.

### FRUIT FOR BOTTLING

Choose good quality firm fruit which is not blemished.

**Preparation of Fruit**

*Apples:* peel, core and slice thinly or cut in 7 mm rings. Place in a bowl of cold water as prepared, adding 1 level tablesp. salt to 1 litre cold water; this prevents browning. Rinse in fresh cold water before packing into bottles.

*Apricots, Cherries, Damsons, Plums* (whole): remove stalks; rinse fruit in cold water.

*Apricots, Plums* (halved): remove stalks; rinse fruit in cold water. Slit round the fruit, beginning at the stalk end. Twist the halves to separate. Discard the stones.

With apricots, it is usual to crack some of the stones and add a few kernels to the bottled fruit.

*Blackberries, loganberries, raspberries:* discard any soft or damaged fruit. Remove stalks, etc. Rinse fruit very carefully in cold water if necessary.

*Black and Red Currants:* strip off from stems; cut off blossom end if liked. Rinse carefully in cold water.

*Gooseberries:* top and tail the fruit; rinse in cold water.

*Pears:* choose good quality dessert pears. Peel very thinly; cut in half lengthways. Scoop out the core with a teaspoon. Remove fibres and blossom end with a small vegetable knife. As prepared, put into salted water as for apples.

*Strawberries:* choose medium sized berries. Discard any soft fruit. Remove the hulls. Rinse fruit carefully in cold water.

*Tomatoes:* place tomatoes in a colander or piece of muslin. Plunge into boiling water for 20–30 seconds. Remove from boiling and plunge into cold water. Skin tomatoes. Leave whole or cut through in half.

## Syrup for Bottling

250 g *sugar*          500 ml *water*

Put sugar and water in a saucepan; bring to the boil. Skim if necessary. Boil for 1 minute. Less sugar can be used for a lighter syrup or when bottling very sweet fruit. Fruit can be bottled in water and sweetened when used, but the flavour and colour of the finished product is not as good as when syrup is used.

## General Method for Bottling Fruit

1. Heat oven, Regulo 3 or 150°C (300°F).
2. Prepare jars, lids and rubber rings (see p. 196).
3. Prepare fruit according to kind (see p. 196).
4. Make syrup.
5. Pack fruit as tightly as possible into jars filling to 1 cm above the rim.
6. Half fill jars with *boiling* syrup. Give jars a quick half turn to shake out air bubbles. Fill to overflowing with boiling syrup. (Stand each jar on a plate while filling with syrup.)
7. Put on rubber ring and glass or metal lid. Put on the screw band *loosely*; or place metal clip on.
8. Stand jars 5 cm apart in a baking tray padded with several thicknesses of newspaper. Put 2 cm hot water into the tin.
9. Place half way down the oven. The time for processing depends on the variety of fruit:

|  |  |
|---|---|
| Apple slices | |
| Blackberries, loganberries, raspberries | |
| Black and red currants | 30—40 mins |
| Gooseberries | |
| Strawberries | |
| Apricots—whole | |
| Plums—whole | 40—50 mins |
| Damsons | |
| Cherries | |
| Apricots—halved | 50—60 mins |
| Plums—halved | |
| Pears | 60—70 mins |
| Tomatoes—solid pack | 70—80 mins |

The above times are for 500 g and 1 kg jars.

10. When jars have been processed, remove carefully from the oven and stand on a wooden board. Tighten screw bands as much as possible straight away, so that a vacuum can form as the jar cools down. Clip tops need no attention.
    Leave overnight.
11. Next day, test for seal.

(a) Screw band type: remove band and carefully lift the jar by the glass lid. The lid should not come off.
(b) Clip type: remove clip. Carefully invert the jar. The lid should stay in position.
12. Wash and wipe jars and screw bands. Label with date when processed and store in a cool dark place.
(N.B. If jars have not sealed tip off syrup. Fill up jar with extra fruit. Fill with boiling syrup, and re-process. This is not always worth doing however as the fruit becomes very soft and overcooked.)

**Bottled Tomatoes** (Ingredients for a small 'Kilner' jar)

    Approx. 500 g tomatoes    1 *level tsp. salt*    1 *level tsp. sugar*

1. Prepare jar, lid and ring. Preheat oven.
2. Scald and skin tomatoes; cut in half.
3. Pack tomatoes tightly, cut side downwards, to half fill the jar. Add salt and sugar. Pack in more tomatoes to fill the jar.
4. Put on rubber ring and lid, then the screw band *loosely*.
5. Process as for General Method for Bottling (see p. 197).

## JAM MAKING

Jam making is perhaps the commonest method of preserving used at home. Good jam should have a clear and bright colour and a full fruity flavour. It should be well set but not too stiff. If properly made, jam will keep well for at least a year.

**Choice of Fruit:** The fruit must be dry and in good fresh condition. Choose fruit which is slightly under-ripe, though not so under-ripe that the flavour has not fully developed. A mixture of ripe and under-ripe fruit can also be used. Jam made from over-ripe fruit will not set properly.

**Pectin:** All fruit contains a gum-like substance called pectin in its cell walls, and it is this which enables a jam to set or form a 'gel'. Pectin is released from the fruit when it is stewed (before the sugar is added in jam making). Pectin is most easily released from fruit which is under-ripe; in over-ripe fruit the pectin is converted to pectic acid and this has no setting qualities. The presence of acid in the fruit also helps in the extraction of pectin. Not all fruits contain the same amount of pectin or acid.

    Fruits of good setting quality (rich in pectin and acid) include cooking apples, black and red currants, damsons, gooseberries.
    Fruits of fairly good setting quality (fairly rich in pectin and acid) include apricots, plums, raspberries.
    Fruits of poor setting quality (low in pectin and acid): cherries, strawberries, blackberries.

**Addition of Acid:** Where a fruit is poor in acid, the following can be added before the fruit is cooked: 1 tablespoon lemon juice to 1 kg fruit; or ½ level tsp. citric acid to 1 kg fruit.

**Addition of Pectin:** To improve the setting qualities of jam made from fruit poor in pectin:
(a) Mix the fruit with one rich in pectin (e.g. strawberry and gooseberry, blackberry and apple), or
(b) Add a fruit juice rich in pectin (e.g. red currant juice added to strawberry jam), or
(c) Add commercially prepared pectin extract.

**Sugar:** Use either granulated, preserving or cube sugar in jam making. The amount of sugar added to jam is important. If too much sugar is used the jam will be too sweet, will not set properly and may crystallize; if too little is added the jam will be very stiff and may ferment when kept.

In general:

for fruit rich in pectin and acid:     *add 600 g sugar to 500 g fruit*
for fruit fairly rich in pectin and acid:     *add 500 g sugar to 500 g fruit*
for fruit poor in pectin and acid:     *add 400 g sugar to 500 g fruit*

If jam is to keep well, there should be 60% concentration of sugar.

**Amount of Water to Add:** No water is added to very soft fruits which are poor in pectin. Up to 150 ml water to 500 g fruit is added to those rich in pectin.

**Jam Pans:** Choose a large saucepan or preserving pan, big enough so that it is not more than half full when fruit and sugar are in, and so that the jam has room to boil vigorously.

Aluminium, stainless steel, or heavy enamelled iron pans are the most suitable. Enamelled pans must not be used if chipped. If a copper or brass pan is used, it must be very clean and free from verdigris which is poisonous.

**Jam Jars:** These must not be chipped or cracked. Jars must be thoroughly washed, rinsed and dried. The remains of the old labels should be removed.

**Covers:** All jam should have a waxed disc placed immediately on the surface of the jam. The jars should be covered with cellophane or parchment covers. Secure cellophane with a rubber band and parchment with thin string.

**To Calculate the Amount of Jam Made:** Amount of sugar added × 5/3 = quantity of finished jam.

e.g. $\dfrac{3^1}{1} \text{ kg} \times \dfrac{5}{3_1} = 5 \text{ kg jam.}$

## General Method for Making Jam

1. Select fruit; discard any very soft and bruised parts. Remove stalks and leaves, etc. Weigh the fruit.
2. Prepare fruit as for bottling (see p. 196).
   Wash carefully in cold water and drain well. (For soft fruits, wash by placing in a colander and dipping in cold water.)
3. Put fruit and any water or acid in preserving pan. Heat gradually, then simmer very gently until fruit is broken down to a pulp and skins are completely soft (20–40 mins., depending on to the type of fruit and the quantity). For large whole fruit, e.g. plums and apricots, which will take longer to cook, try to cover the pan to prevent undue evaporation.
4. While fruit is cooking, wash and dry jam jars. Place on a baking tray in a very cool oven or put in a warm place to get dry and hot.
5. Add sugar to the fruit and dissolve slowly over a gentle heat, stirring all the time with a wooden spoon.
6. Increase heat and boil rapidly until setting point is reached. Stir from time to time.

### To Test for Setting Point

(a) The jam boils 'lower down' in the jam pan.
(b) Flake Test: dip a clean dry wooden spoon in the jam, lift out and twirl it round. If the jam runs off quickly as in (i), it has not

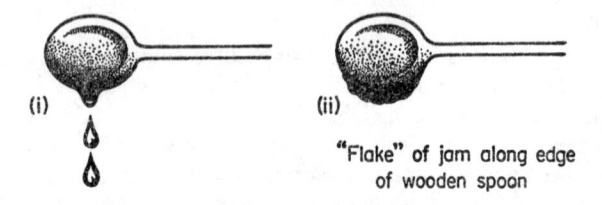

(i)    (ii)

"Flake" of jam along edge of wooden spoon

reached setting point; if it forms a thick flake along the edge of the wooden spoon, it has reached setting point as in (ii).
(c) Saucer Test: put a small amount of jam on a cold dry saucer and allow to cool. Run the little finger very gently across the surface. If the jam has reached setting point, a very thin skin will wrinkle up.

(N.B. Remove the jam pan from the heat while testing for setting point.)

7. Using a metal spoon, carefully skim off any scum. (If the jam is stirred from time to time as it comes up to setting point, scum can usually be dispersed.)

# PRESERVING FRUIT AND VEGETABLES AT HOME 201

8. Bottle jam immediately it has reached setting point (except for strawberry jam which should be allowed to cool for 10 mins before bottling). Place the tray of heated jars next to the preserving pan. Scoop out the hot jam with a small jug or cup, holding a saucer underneath to catch drips. Fill jars to within 3 mm of the rim.
9. Place a waxed disc down on the surface of the jam in each jar. Wipe the rim of the jar if necessary with a clean muslin wrung out in hot water.
10. Dip one side of cellophane or parchment covers in cold water; place dry side down on each jar, stretch across and secure with a rubber band or thin string.
11. Wipe jars with a cloth wrung out in hot water, to remove any sticky patches.
12. Allow jam to go cold. Label neatly with type of jam and date when made. Store in a cool dry place, preferably in the dark.

## RECIPES FOR JAMS

In all cases, follow 'General Method' for making jam. All recipes given make 2½ kg jam (approx.).

### Apricot

1½ kg fresh apricots          300–400 ml water
1½ kg sugar

Halve apricots; split some stones and add the kernels to the fruit while stewing.

### Blackberry

1½ kg blackberries            80 ml water
1½ kg sugar                   2 tablesp. lemon juice

### Blackberry and Apple

1 kg blackberries             1½ kg sugar
½ kg cooking apples           150 ml water

Prepare blackberries; stew gently in half the water until soft. Peel, core and slice the apples. Stew in the remaining water in a separate pan. Combine the two lots of fruit pulp. Continue as for General Method.

### Blackcurrant

1 kg blackcurrants            850 ml water
1¼ kg sugar

This fruit needs long simmering to soften the skins.

### Damson

| | |
|---|---|
| 1¼ kg damsons | 400–450 ml water |
| 1½ kg sugar | |

Remove stones as they rise to the surface during cooking.

### Gooseberry

| | |
|---|---|
| 1¼ kg gooseberries | 450 ml water |
| 1½ kg sugar | |

### Plum

| | |
|---|---|
| 1½ kg plums | 300 ml water |
| 1½ kg sugar | |

### Raspberry

| | |
|---|---|
| 1½ kg raspberries | No water |
| 1½ kg sugar | |

### Strawberry

| | |
|---|---|
| 1¾ kg strawberries | Juice of 1 lemon |
| 1½ kg sugar | |

## *MARMALADE*

Marmalade is made from citrus fruits, oranges, lemons, grapefruit and limes. It may be made from one single variety of fruit, or from a mixture. The oranges most frequently used are bitter oranges such as Sevilles, though sweet ones and tangerines can also be used.

The making of marmalade is very similar to jam-making. All marmalade recipes contain a very large amount of water; as the tough skins of the citrus fruits need long cooking, the quantity of water allows for evaporation.

Citrus fruits are rich in pectin but most of it is contained in the pith and pips so these should be simmered (tied in muslin) with the fruit. Additional acid is often added to marmalade in the form of lemon juice. Though citrus fruits are very acidic, the large quantity of water added dilutes the acid greatly.

### Seville Orange Marmalade

| | |
|---|---|
| ¾ kg Seville oranges | 1½ kg sugar |
| 1¾ litre water | Juice of 1 lemon |

1. Scrub the oranges; cut in half and squeeze out the juice.
2. Tie pips in muslin; slice the peel very finely (or mince).

3. Put orange juice, lemon juice, sliced peel and pips in preserving pan; add water.
4. Bring to the boil and simmer very gently for 1½–2 hours, until the peel is very soft. Remove muslin bag of pips, squeeze out and discard.
5. Add sugar. Continue as for General Method of jam making.

**Mixed Fruit Marmalade**

| 1 *grapefruit* | 1¾ *litre water* |
| 2 *sweet oranges* | 1½ *kg sugar* |
| 2 *lemons* | |

Make as for Seville Orange Marmalade.

### CHUTNEY

Chutneys are made from a mixture of fruits and vegetables flavoured with sugar, seasonings and spices, and cooked with vinegar. Chutney should be cooked very slowly throughout to give a good smooth texture. It is best made in an aluminium or enamelled pan; copper and brass pans give an unpleasant flavour. It should be bottled as soon as it is made, in clean hot jars. The jars should be covered with lacquered screw lids which have a layer of waxed cardboard inside; or with 'plastic skin' covers. Cellophane covers allow chutney to evaporate and shrink during storage. The flavour of chutney improves with keeping.

**Apple Chutney** (makes approx. 1½–2 kg)

| 1½ *kg cooking apples* | 1 *tablesp. salt* |
| ½ *kg onions* | 2 *level tsp. ground ginger* |
| ½ *kg raisins* | 2 *level tsp. cinnamon* |
| ½ *kg demerara sugar* | ½ *level tsp. cayenne pepper* |
| 550 *ml vinegar* | |

1. Peel, quarter and core the apples; skin onions and cut in quarters. Wash raisins.
2. Mince apples, onions and raisins. Put in a preserving pan with salt, spices and half the vinegar.
3. Simmer gently for ½–1 hour until ingredients are soft.
4. Add remaining vinegar and simmer until thick, smooth consistency is obtained. Stir from time to time to prevent burning.
5. Bottle and cover; label with variety, and date when made.

**Tomato Chutney** (makes approx. 1½ kg)

| 1 *kg tomatoes (green or red)* | 250 *g brown sugar* |
| 250 *g cooking apples* | 2 *tsp. salt* |
| 250 *g onions* | 6 *red chillis* |
| 250 *g raisins* | 2 *pieces whole ginger* |
| | 550 *ml vinegar* |

1. Cut up tomatoes (skin red ones first in boiling water).
2. Peel apples and onions and cut in quarters; wash raisins.
3. Mince all fruit and put in preserving pan.
4. Add brown sugar, salt and vinegar.
5. Bruise spices; tie in muslin and add to the other ingredients.
6. Bring to the boil; simmer very gently until the correct consistency is reached.
7. Bottle, cover and label.

## PICKLES

Many fruits and vegetables can be preserved at home by pickling in vinegar which is often flavoured with spices. Before pickling the vegetables are usually soaked in strong brine or sprinkled with salt and left to stand overnight. The bring or salt withdraws water from the vegetables, and this water is discarded. If fresh vegetables were put in vinegar, the water contained in them would dilute the vinegar.

### To Make Spiced Vinegar

1 litre vinegar
1 level tsp. cloves
1 level tsp. mace
1 level tsp. black peppercorns
A 3 cm piece stick cinnamon
2 pieces whole ginger, bruised

Whole spices are used; powdered ones would make the vinegar cloudy.

Put spices and vinegar in a saucepan and cover with a lid. Bring the vinegar slowly to the boil. Strain and allow to cool.

### Pickled Onions

1½ kg small even sized onions ('silver skins' are best)
500 ml spiced vinegar
For brine: 100 g salt to 500 ml water

1. Prepare brine: dissolve 100 g salt in 500 ml cold water.
2. Skin onions; place in brine and leave for 24 hours.
3. Drain onions. Pack in clean jars.
4. Cover with cold spiced vinegar. Cover the jars. Keep 1-2 months before using.

### Piccalilli

1 kg prepared vegetables
 (marrow, cucumber, cauliflower, beans, onions, etc.)
100 g salt
1 litre water
100 g sugar
500 ml vinegar
15 g plain flour
½ level tablesp. mustard
2 level tsp. turmeric
1 level tsp. ground ginger

1. Prepare brine, using the salt and water.
2. Prepare vegetables, cutting in 1-2 cm pieces. Place in brine. Cover and leave overnight.
3. Drain vegetables. Put vegetables, sugar and 400 ml of the vinegar in a saucepan, bring to the boil and cook for 15 minutes.
4. Put plain flour, mustard, turmeric and ground ginger in a small basin; blend with remaining vinegar.
5. Add blended mixture to the cooked vegetables. Stirring all the time, bring to the boil and cook for 1 minute.
6. Bottle in hot jars. Cover (as for chutney).

## ADDITIONAL RECIPES

### Mincemeat

| | |
|---|---|
| 250 g cooking apples | 250 g shredded beef suet |
| 250 g raisins | 25 g mixed peel |
| 250 g sultanas | Grated zest and juice of 1 orange |
| 250 g currants | 1 level tsp. mixed spice |
| 250 g soft brown sugar | 75 ml brandy (optional) |

1. Wash all dried fruit and drain well.
2. Peel, quarter and core cooking apples.
3. Mince or finely chop apples and dried fruit and put into a mixing bowl.
4. Add sugar, suet, finely chopped mixed peel, zest and juice of the orange, mixed spice and brady. Mix all ingredients together well.
5. Pack the mincemeat into clean dry jam jars, only filling to within 2 cm of the top rim. (Syrup often forms on top of the mincemeat and can run over if jars are filled.)
6. Cover jars with cellophane or parchment covers.

The flavour of mincemeat improves if it is kept for a short time before using.

### Lemon Curd

| | |
|---|---|
| 2 eggs (large) | 70 g butter |
| 2 lemons | 140 g cube sugar |

1. Wash and dry lemons. Rub about 10 pieces of cube sugar over the lemon skins to extract the flavour.
2. Squeeze out lemon juice. Break eggs into a basin and beat up lightly, until they will run smoothly off the fork.
3. Place butter in a double saucepan and heat gently until melted.
4. Add lemon juice, eggs and sugar. Stirring all the time, cook the mixture very gently until the lemon curd coats the back of the wooden spoon and all the sugar has dissolved.
5. Pour into a clean dry warm jar. Cover down as for jam.

# 29. Convenience Foods

The term 'convenience' foods includes a very wide variety of pre-packed and ready prepared foods which are available in all shops nowadays.

## Types of Convenience Foods Available

(a) *Frozen Foods:* almost all types of food can now be obtained 'deep frozen' from cakes and pastries to fruit and vegetables, fish and meat, and even complete meals. These foods are ready prepared and of very high quality, though they do tend to lack some of the flavour of the fresh article. Most can be stored in the freezing compartment of the domestic refrigerator for 2–3 days, or much longer in a 'deep freeze' cabinet. Care must be taken, however, that once thawed these foods are not re-frozen (see p. 21).

(b) *Canned Foods:* fruit and vegetables, soup, meat and fish, ready prepared dishes, and many other foods can be bought in tins. Some of these foods can be eaten cold; others only require a very short time for reheating. Tins are very convenient to store and are an excellent 'stand-by'.

(c) *Dehydrated Foods:* packet soups, vegetables, complete meals, milk and many other foods are obtainable 'dried'. These products can be stored for long periods at home, and take up little space. They are easy to cook and give good results.

(d) *Packet Cake Mixtures:* these can be made up quickly, often with the addition of egg and fat and liquid. Most give a satisfactory finished product.

(e) *Miscellaneous 'Convenience' Products:* including the use of S.R. flour in place of plain flour and baking powder; ready prepared custard and blancmange powders instead of using cornflour and having to colour and flavour it; ready prepared jelly cubes; stock cubes, in place of the lengthy method of making stock at home; instant tea, coffee and cocoa; the use of ready creamed or 'whipped up' fats for cakes and pastries, etc.

**Food Value:** In many cases, the food value of convenience foods is almost equal to that of the fresh article. This is particularly true of 'deep frozen foods'. In tinned foods, some Vitamin C is lost from fruit and vegetables since it is easily destroyed by heat during the canning process.

**Advantages of using Convenience Foods:** Undoubtedly the main advantage of using convenience foods is the time they can save; this is a particularly important consideration for the housewife who also goes out to work. With most convenience foods, no preparation time is involved and many cook more quickly than the same food used fresh (e.g. frozen peas cook in 5–7 mins., while fresh ones take 15 mins.).

By using frozen and canned fruit and vegetables, these foods can be used when they are not normally 'in season' and so add variety and colour to the diet.

Many convenience foods take up less space than fresh food would, so shopping and storage in the larder are made easier.

To keep a selection of packet or tinned foods in the store cupboard is valuable in case of emergencies, such as the unexpected visitor arriving, or being able to avoid shopping in bad weather.

Some convenience foods seem expensive. It should be remembered though, that any slight extra cost may be offset by the facts that there is no waste in the food and less preparation time is involved.

Whenever possible convenience foods should only be incorporated in meals which are prepared from fresh foods. These 'quick to use' foods have many obvious advantages and great value, but give a 'sameness' and uniformity of flavour and colour which can become monotonous. For variety of flavour, richness and also for nutritive value, it is advisable to use as much really fresh food as possible.

# 30. Time and Labour Saving Devices

Nowadays there are many appliances on the market which are designed to save the housewife both time and effort in her kitchen. Though one can think of many examples, perhaps two of the commonest and most important are the automatic timing device now fitted to many electric and some gas ovens, and also the power food mixer.

## TIME CONTROLLED OVENS

Many ovens, both electric and gas are now fitted with either an electric or a clockwork timing device. This is very useful for the housewife who has to be out for part of the day; ready prepared food can be put into the oven and the thermostat set to the correct temperature; at the same time, the clock is set so that it will switch on the oven automatically at the desired time. In this way, it is possible to come home to a hot meal, ready to eat.

When planning meals to be cooked in a time controlled oven, it is necessary to consider the following points:

(a) All the dishes chosen must require approximately the same cooking temperatures and time. Slight variation in cooking temperature can be achieved by packing the oven carefully, putting those dishes which need the highest temperatures at the top of the oven, and those which need slower baking lower down.

(b) The types of food or dishes most suitable for cooking in an automatically timed oven are those which can be successfully cooked from cold. These include stews, roast meats, fruits and root vegetables cooked in casseroles, milk puddings, shortcrust pastry, rubbed in or creamed cake mixtures. Some dishes are not successful if placed in a cold oven: these include rich flaky pastries, yeast mixtures, meringues and whisked cake mixtures. Foods requiring only a short cooking time are not suitable for cooking in automatically timed ovens.

(c) Some foods, especially fruit and vegetables may discolour if left to stand in a cold oven for some time after preparation. Fruit such as apples, can be lightly sprinkled with lemon juice; vegetables can be brushed with melted fat to prevent discoloration.

(d) Take care, with foods left standing in a cold oven, that no strong smelling foods can pass flavour on to other dishes—e.g. onions placed round meat to bake, passing flavour into a milk pudding.

**Timing:** For meals cooked in a time controlled oven, allow ¼ hour longer than the dishes usually take to cook, as the oven has to heat up from cold.

## Suggestions for Meals cooked in Time Controlled Ovens

1.  Liver Casserole (see p. 72)   Apple Crumble (see p. 130)
    Braised Carrots               Custard
    Jacket Potatoes

    *Special Points:* Carrots—prepare and cut into rings; lay in a covered casserole with seasoning, 15 g butter and 150 ml water.
    Potatoes—choose medium sized potatoes so that they will cook in time.
    *Arrangement in the oven:* Place casserole and potatoes a third of the way down the oven; crumble and carrots two thirds of the way down the oven.
    *Cooking Temperature:* Regulo 4 or 180°C (350°F).
    *Cooking Time:* 1½ hours.

2.  Roast Loin of Pork (approx. 6 chops)
    Apple Sauce
    Braised mixed vegetables (carrots, parsnips, turnips)
    Roast potatoes
    Gravy
    Rice Pudding

    *Special Points:* Cover the meat tin with foil (or use a covered meat tin) so that potatoes can 'baste themselves'.
    For apple sauce, place all ingredients in a small covered dish. Prepare vegetables and slice in 5 mm slices. Place in a covered casserole with seasoning, 15 g butter and 150 ml water. Gravy made at end of meal.
    *Arrangement in the oven:* Meat and braised vegetables half way down the oven. Potatoes placed round the meat. Milk pudding and apples on the lowest shelf in the oven.
    *Cooking Temperature:* Regulo 5 or 190°C (375°F).
    *Cooking Time:* 2 hours.

3.  Lamb Chops                Gravy
    Grilled tomatoes
    Frozen Peas               Eve's Pudding (see p. 130)
    Boiled Potatoes           Custard

    *Special Points:* Potatoes, peeled and brushed with melted margarine, can be placed in a covered casserole with seasoning and 150 ml water.
    Gravy and custard will have to be made when the meal is cooked. Frozen peas and grilled tomatoes can be cooked quickly while sauces are being made.

*Arrangement in the oven:* Chops, pudding and potatoes placed half way down the oven.
*Cooking Temperature:* Regulo 4 or 180°C (350°F).
*Cooking Time:* 1 hour.

When considering the cooking of meals in a time controlled oven, careful consideration should be given to the length of time food may be left sitting in a cold oven, often uncovered. Especially during hot weather it may be preferable to cook something quickly (e.g. a grill) on returning home, rather than risk any spoilage of food.

## POWER FOOD MIXERS

There are many types of food mixers available, from the large 'family size' domestic mixer to small hand mixers and separate liquidizers. Many attachments can be used on the large size mixers: basic attachments are used for mixing cakes, rubbing in pastry, whisking and making bread dough. Many additional attachments, however, can be added to some machines to mince, shred vegetables, squeeze juice from oranges and lemons, grind knives, open cans, and so on.

The 'liquidizer' consists of a large heavy glass or plastic jug in the bottom of which are fast rotating blades. A liquidizer may either be added as an attachment to a mixer, or may be a separate unit with its own motor. The main uses of a liquidizer are for pulping fruit and vegetables, making soups, making drinks, grinding coffee beans, making breadcrumbs, chopping herbs and nuts, preparing baby food, etc.

Many small 'hand mixers' will do most of the jobs which the basic large mixer will do. However, they are not able to cope with the same weight of ingredients as the larger mixer. Used sensibly though, they can take much of the hard work out of cooking. For example, in cake making use the mixer for creaming the fat and sugar, then beating in eggs, but stir in the dry ingredients by hand, if the mixture is too heavy for a small machine. Similarly, pastry can be 'rubbed in' with the mixer, but water added and mixed by hand. A mixer can do a great deal towards reducing the effort necessary in making many dishes.

# Index I

AGE, Food requirements 16–18
Almond macaroons 168
  Paste 171
Amino Acids 1
Anchovy Sauce 97
Apple, Baked 125
  Boiled Pudding 128
  Charlotte 126
  Dumplings 133
  Sauce 102
Au Gratin 28

BACON, Grilled 62
  and Egg, Fried 75
  and Egg Pie 117
Bacteria 194
Bake Blind, to 28
Baking 25
Baste, to 28
Batter, Coating 125
  Pudding 123
  Thin 123
Beans, Broad 83
  French 83
  Runner 83
Beef 57
  Olives 67
Beetroot 85
Beverages 183
Biscuits 165
  Cheese 110
  Creaming Method 166
  Ginger 167
  Jam Ring 166
  Lemon 165
  Melting Method 167
  Plain 166
  Rubbed-in Method 165
  Shortbread 165
  Shrewsbury 167
  Whisking Method 168
Blanch, to 28
Blancmange 134
Blended Sauces 100
Bloaters 48
Boiled Meat 64
  Accompaniments for 65
  Boiling 23

Bottling 195
  Fruit for 196
  Method for 197
  Syrup for 196–7
Bouquet Garni 28
Brains 72
Braising 24, 64
Brandy Butter 130
Bread, Brown 177
  and Butter Pudding 122
  and Cheese Pudding 107
  Rolls (Splits) 177
  Sauce 102
  'Shapes' 177
  White 176
Bread Making 174
  Quick Method 176
Breast of Lamb, Braised Stuffed 69
Broth, Chicken 38
  Scotch 38
Brown Stew 66
Brussels Sprouts 82
Bubble and Squeak 182
Buns, Chelsea 177
  Cherry 151
  Coconut 150
  Ginger 151
  Jam 149
  Rock 149
Butter Icing 169
Butterfly Cakes 151

CABBAGE 82
Cabinet Pudding 122
Cake, Cherry 155
  Christmas 157
  Christmas, Rich 156
  Date and Raisin 149
  Dundee 156
  Ginger 157
  Lardy 178
  Madeira 155
  Rich Chocolate 156
  Seed 156
  Simnel 157
  Sponge 159
  Sultana 155
  Walnut 156

Cakes, Butterfly  151
　Creaming Method  150
　Ingredients  147
　Large, Basic Recipe  155
　　Variations  155
　Made with Pastries  161
　Melting Method  157
　Queen  151
　Rubbed In  148
　Small Fancy  152
　Testing when cooked  148
　Types of Mixtures  147
　Whisking Method  159
Cake Tins, Preparation of  147
Carbohydrates  2
Carrots  85
Castle Pudding  127
Cauliflower  83
　au Gratin  109
Celery  88
　Soup  36
Cellulose  3
Cheese Biscuits  110
　Composition of  105
　d'Artois  111
　Digestibility  105
　Food Value  105
　for Cooking  105
　Macaroni  108
　and Onion Turnovers  111
　on Toast  107
　Pastry  140
　and Potato Pie  106
　Pudding  108
　Sauce  97
　Scones  145
　Soufflé  109
　Straws  109
　and Tomato Flan  110
　and Vegetable Flan  110
　Uses of  106
Chelsea Buns  177
Cherry Buns  151
　Cake  155
Chicken Broth  38
　Roast  77
Chocolate Cake, Rich  156
　Sandwich Cake  153
　Sauce  100
　Sponge Pudding  127
　Swiss Roll  160
Chops  62
Christmas Cake  157
　Cake, Rich  156
　Pudding  129

Chutney, Apple  203
　Tomato  203
Cocoa  185
Coconut Buns  150
Cod Steaks, Baked Stuffed  51
Coffee  183
Coffee Sandwich Cake  154
Cold Meat, Curry of  182
Cold Sweets  134
Conservative Method  84
Consommé  39
Convalescents, Food for  188
Convenience Foods  206
Cooked Egg Sauce  102
Cookery Terms  28
Cornflour Mould  121
Cornish Pasties  74
Crab  54
Cream Horns  163
　Slices  162
Croûtes  28
Croûtons  28, 40
Curry, Cold Meat  182
　Eggs  116
　Vegetable  192
　Prawn  55
　Sauce  103
Custard sauce  100, 102

Date and Raisin Cake  149
Dumplings for Stew  67
　Apple  133
Dundee Cake  156

Eclairs  164
Egg Custard, Baked  121
　Flan  132
Egg Cutlets  192
　Flip  186
　Sauce  97
Eggs Au Gratin  116
　Boiled  114
　Curried  116
　Digestibility of  113
　Fried  115
　Food Value  113
　Hard Boiled  114
　Poached  115
　Properties of  113
　Scotch  116
　Scrambled  115
　Stuffed  115
　Uses of  114
Enzyme Action  194
Eve's Pudding  130

# INDEX

FATS 2
Fillings for Cakes 169
Fish, Baked 48
  Buying 41
  Cakes 53
  Classification 41
  to Clean 44
  Composition 41
  Cooking 44
  Digestibility 41
  to Fillet 43
  Food Value 41
  Fried 46
  Grilled 45
  Pie, Russian 52
  Poached 44
  Preparation of 42
  Quantity to Buy 42
  Steamed 45
  Stuffed 49
Flaky Pastry 143
Flan Pastry 140
Food, Hygiene 21
  Requirements (Age and Occupation) 16–18
  Storage of 20
  Values 1
Forcemeat, Veal 78
French Dressing 95
Fruit, Bottled 196–198
  Crumble 130
  Flan (Pastry) 136
  Flan (Sponge) 137
  Fritters 125
  Gingerbread 158
  Layer Pudding 128
  Loaf 149
  Pie 132
  Preserving 194
  Salad, Fresh 135
  Sauces 101
  Scones 145
  Stewed 126
  Tart 133
Frying, Care with 27
  Deep Fat 26
  Dry 26
  Fats for 25
  Shallow Fat 26

GAMMON, Grilled 62
Gingerbread 158
  Fruit 158
Ginger Biscuits 167
  Buns 151

Ginger (*contd.*)—
  Parkin 158
  Sponge Pudding 128
Glacé Icing 170
Glaze, to 28
Gooseberry Fool 136
Grapefruit 31
Gravy 61
Grilled Meat 62
  Accompaniments for 63
Grilling 25

HADDOCK, Poached 50
  Steamed 49
Halibut, Grilled 50
Handy Measures 30
Heart, Pot Roast 73
  Preparation of 71
Herrings, Roes on Toast 53
  Soused 52
Hors d'Oeuvres 31
  Mixed 31
Hot Pot 68

ICING, Butter 169
  Glacé 170
  Flavoured 170
  Methods of 172
  Royal 172
Invalid Cookery 187
  Food Requirement 187
  Diet 187
Irish Stew 68

JAM, Apricot 201
  Blackberry 201
  Blackberry and Apple 201
  Blackcurrant 201
  Buns 149
  Cap Pudding 127
  Damson 202
  Gooseberry 202
  Making 198
  Making, Fruit for 198
  Method of Making 200
  Plum 202
  Puffs 162
  Raspberry 202
  Ring Biscuits 166
  Sauce 101
  Strawberry 202
  Tarts 161
  Tart, Plate Jam 131
  Turnovers 132

Jelly, Fresh Fruit   135
   Fruit in   134
   Milk   134
Junket   134

KEDGEREE   54
Kidney, Preparation of   62
   Soup   35
Kippers   48

LABOUR Saving Devices   208
Lamb, Breast of, Braised Stuffed   69
Lardy Cake   178
Leeks   86
Left-over Foods, Use of   181
Lemonade   185
Lemon Curd   205
   Meringue Pie   137
   Sandwich Cake   154
   Sauce   101
   Sponge Pudding   128
Light Diet   188
Liquid Diet   187
Liver   71
   Stuffed   72
   and Bacon, Fried   73
   Casserole   72
   Preparation of   62

MACARONI Cheese   108
Macaroons, Almond   168
Mackerel, Grilled   50
Madeira Cake   155
Madelenes   152
Maitre d'Hotel Butter   103
Marketing   19
Marmalade, Mixed Fruit   203
   Sauce   101
   Seville Orange   202
Marrow   88
   Stuffed   89
Marzipan   171
Meal Planning   10–13
Measures   30
Meat, Braising   24
   Boiling   64
   Buying   60
   Cuts of   56
   Food Value   56
   Frying   25, 63
   Grilling   62
   Methods of Cooking   60
   Preparation of   61
   Roasting   60
   Steaming   65

Meat (*contd.*)—
   Stewing   63
   Structure of   56
Melon   31
Meringues   163
Methods of Cooking   23
Mince   74
Mincemeat   205
Mince Pies   161
Mint Sauce   103
Mineral Elements   7
Mirepoix   28
Mixed Grill   65
Mixers   210
Mock Cream   169
Moulds   194
Mushrooms, in Sauce   88
   Fried   88
   Grilled   88
   to Prepare   88
   Soup   36, 37
Mutton, *see also* Lamb   60

NICOTINIC Acid   6
Nut Cutlets   193
Nutritive Value of Foods   1

OATCAKE   167
Oatmeal Pastry   140
Offal, Uses of   71
Omelets, Fillings for   118, 119
   Pan to Prove   117
   Plain   118
   Soufflé   119
Onions   85
   Pickled   204
   Rings, Fried   66
   Sauce   98
   Soup   37
Orangeade   186
Orange Sandwich Cake   155
   Sauce   101
   Sponge Pudding   128

PANADA   28
Pancakes   124
Parsley Butter   103
   Sauce   98
Parsnips   85
Pasties, Cornish   74
Pastry, Cheese   140
   Fat for   139
   Flaky   143
   Flan   140
   General Rules   139

## INDEX

Pastry (contd.)—
  Oatmeal 140
  Rough Puff 141
  Shortcrust 139
  Suet Crust 141
Patties, Shrimp 54
Patty Cases 162
Peas 83
Pectin 198
Piccalilli 204
Pickled Onions 204
Plaice, Fried 51
Potato Cakes 182
  Soup 37
Potatoes, Baked (jacket) 87
  Boiled 86
  Chipped 87
  Creamed 86
  Duchesse 87
  Fried 87
  Roast 87
  Stuffed 106
  to Prepare 86
Poultry, Accompaniments to Roast 77
  Buying 77
Prawn Curry 55
Preparation of Meals 13
Presentation of Meals 13
Preserving, Aims in 195
  Methods 195
  Principles 194
Protein 1
Prunes, Stewed 126
Puddings, Hot 120
  Apple Charlotte 126
  Boiled Apple 128
  Baked Sponge 130
  Batter 123
  Bread and Butter 122
  Cabinet 122
  Castle 127
  Chocolate Sponge 127
  Christmas 129
  Eve's 130
  Fruit in Batter 124
  Fruit Layer 128
  Ginger Sponge 128
  Jam Cap 127
  Lemon Sponge 128
  Milk 120
  Orange 128
  Queen of 122
  Rice 120
  Roly Poly, Baked 131

Puddings (contd.)—
  Roly Poly, Steamed 129
  Semolina 120
  Spotted Dick 127
  Steamed Sponge (Basic Recipe) 127
  Steamed Suet 128
  Syrup 127
  Yorkshire 124
  Purée 28

QUEEN Cakes 151
  of Puddings 122

RASPINGS 28, 182
Reheated Dishes 180
  Rules for Making 180
Rice, Boiled 89
  Pudding 120
Rissoles 181
Roast Chicken 77
Roast Meats—Accompaniments 61
Roasting 25
Rock Buns 149
Roes on Toast, Herring 53
Roughage 9
Rough Puff Pastry 141
Roux 28
Royal Icing 172
Russian Fish Pie 52

SAGE and Onion Stuffing 78
Salad, Celery and Apple 94
  Dressing 95
  Fresh Fruit 135
  Green 93
  Ingredients for 91
  Orange 94
  Preparation of 91
  Potato 94
  Rules for Making 92
  Summer 93
  Tomato 94
  Winter 93
Sandwich Cakes
  Chocolate 153
  Coffee 154
  Lemon 154
  Orange 155
  Sponge 159
  Victoria 153
Sauces, Anchovy 97
  Apple 102

Sauces (contd.)—
  Béchamel  99
  Blended  100
  Bread  102
  Brown  99
  Cheese  97
  Chocolate  100
  Custard  100, 102
  Curry  103
  Egg  97
  Gravy  61
  Jam  101
  Lemon  101
  Marmalade  101
  Mint  103
  Mock Tartare  98
  Mushroom  98
  Mustard  98
  Onion  98
  Orange  101
  Parsley  98
  Roux  96
  Shrimp  99
  Syrup  102
  Tomato  103
  Types of  96
  White  96
  White Cornflour  100
Sausage and Mash  76
  Rolls  76
Scones, Cheese  145
  Drop  146
  Fruit  145
  Girdle  145
  Plain Oven  144
  Wholemeal  145
Scotch Broth  38
  Eggs  116
  Pancakes  146
Seed Cake  156
Semolina Pudding  120
Shell Fish  54
Shepherd's Pie  181
Shortbread  165
  Biscuits  165
Shortcrust Pastry  139
  Variations on  140
Shrimp Patties  54
  Sauce  99
Simmer, to  28
Simnel Cake  157
Simple Hors d'Oeuvres  31
Soup, Celery  36
  Chicken Broth  38
  Chicken and Mushroom  39

Soup (contd.)—
  Consommé à la Jardinière  39
  Kidney  35
  Mixed Vegetable  37
  Mushroom  36
  Purée method  36
  Onion  37
  Potato  37
  Scotch Broth  38
  Tomato  38
  White Vegetable  35
Soups, Amount to Serve  34
  Broths  38
  Clear  39
  Food Value  34
  Purée  36
  Thickened  34
  Types of  34
Spaghetti alla Bolognese  75
Spinach  83
Splits  177
Sponge Cake  159
Spotted Dick  127
Spring Greens  83
Starches  3
Steak, Grilled  62
  and Kidney Pudding  70
  and Onions, Fried  66
  Pie  70
Steaming  23, 65
Stew, Brown  66
  Irish  68
  Types of  63
Stewing  24, 63
Stock Cubes  34
Stock  33
  To Make  33
  Types of  34
Stuffings, for Fish  49
Suet Crust Pastry  141
Sugars  2
Sultana Cake  155
Sweat, to  29
Swedes  85
Sweetbreads  71
Swiss Roll  160
  Chocolate  160
Syrup Pudding  127
  Sauce  102
  Tart  131

TABLE laying  13
Tart, Fruit  133
  Jam  131
  Syrup  131

## INDEX

Tea  183
Teacakes, Quick  178
Time Controlled Ovens  208
Toad in the Hole  77
Tomato Juice  31
  Sauce  103
  Soup  38
Tomatoes, Baked  89
  Bottled  198
  Fried  89
  Grilled  89
  Stuffed  90
Trifle  136
Tripe  72
Turnips  85

VEAL Forcemeat  78
Vegetable Curry  192
Vegetables, Buying and Storing  80
  Cooking  82, 84
  Food Value  80
  Frozen  81
  Green  82

Vegetables (*contd.*)—
  In Season  81
  Preparation  82
  Preserving  194
  Root  83
  Types of  80
Vegetarian Cookery  190
  Pie  191
Vegetarianism  190
Victoria Sandwich  153, 164
Vitamins  3

WALNUT Cake  156
Water  9
Welsh Cheese Cakes  161
Welsh Rarebit  107
Whisking Method  159

YEAST, in Bread Making  174
  Mixtures  176
Yeasts  174, 194
Yorkshire Pudding  124

ZEST  29

# Index II

**BREAKFAST**
Grapefruit  31
Stewed Apple  126
Stewed Prunes  126

Bacon and Eggs, Fried  75
Eggs, Boiled  114
  Poached, on Toast  115
  Scrambled, on Toast  115
Kedgeree  54
Mushrooms, Fried  88
  Grilled  88
  in Sauce, on Toast  88
Sausages, Fried  63
  Grilled  62
Smoked Haddock  44
Tomatoes, Fried  89
  Grilled  89

Coffee  183
Tea  183
Cocoa  185

**MID-MORNING SNACK**
Biscuits  165
Cakes  147
Scones  144

Chelsea Buns  177

Coffee  183
Lemonade  185
Orangeade  186

**LUNCH OR DINNER**
Hors d'Oeuvres  31

Soups  34

**Main Course**
*Meat Dishes:*
  Beef Olives  67
  Boiled Meat  64
  Braised Stuffed Breast of Lamb  69
  Brown Stew and Dumplings  66
  Chicken, Roast  77

Meat Dishes *(contd.)*—
  Cornish Pasties  74
  Curried Meat  182
  Fried Liver and Bacon  73
  Fried Steak and Onions  66
  Grilled Chops  62–63
  Hot Pot  68
  Irish Stew  68
  Liver Casserole  72
  Mince  74
  Mixed Grill  65
  Rissoles  181
  Sausage and Mash  76
  Shepherd's Pie  181
  Spaghetti alla Bolognese  75
  Steak and Kidney Pudding  70
  Steak Pie  70
  Stuffed Liver  72
  Stuffed Marrow  89
  Sweetbreads  71
  Toad in the Hole  77
*Fish Dishes:*
  Baked Stuffed Cod Steaks  51
  Prawn Curry  55
  Fish Cakes  53
  Fried Fish  46, 51
  Grilled Fish  45
  Poached Haddock  50
  Russian Fish Pie  52
  Soused Herrings  52
  Steamed Fish  45
*Additional Dishes:*
  Egg Cutlets  192
  Nut Cutlets  193
  Omelets  118
  Salads  91
  Vegetable Curry  192
  Vegetarian Pie  191
  Egg and Cheese Dishes, as for High Tea and Supper

Vegetables  80

Sauces  96

Puddings  120
Cold Sweets  134

Lemonade 185
Coffee 183
Tea 183

## AFTERNOON TEA
Biscuits 165
Bread, Brown 177
  Rolls 177
  White 176
Cakes, Creaming Method 150
  Melting Method 157
  Rubbing-in Method 148
  Whisking Method 159
Jams 198
Lemon Curd 204
Scones 144
Yeast Cakes and Buns 177

Tea 183

## HIGH TEA AND SUPPER
Bacon and Egg 75
Bacon and Egg Pie 117
Bread and Cheese Pudding 107
Cheese and Onion Turnovers 111
  and Potato Pie 106
  Pudding 108
  Soufflé 109
  and Tomato Flan 110
  and Vegetable Flan 110
Cornish Pasties 74
Curried Eggs 116
  Meat 182
  Prawns 55
Eggs au Gratin 116
Fish Cakes 53
Fried Fish 46
Grilled Fish 45
Kedgeree 54
Macaroni Cheese 108
Mixed Grill 65
Omelets 118

Poached Fish 44
Rissoles 181
Salads 91
Sausage and Mash 76
Scotch Eggs and Salad 116
Shepherd's Pie 181
Soused Herrings and Salad 52
Spaghetti alla Bolognese 75
Stuffed Eggs and Salad 115
Stuffed Tomatoes 90
Toad in the Hole 77

*On Toast:*
  Cheese 107
  Herring Roes 53
  Mushrooms, Fried 88
    Grilled 88
    in Sauce 88
  Poached Egg 115
  Scrambled Egg 115
  Tomatoes, Grilled 89
  Welsh Rarebit 107

Cold Sweets 134

Bread 176

Cakes 148

Yeast Buns 177

Jams 198

Tea 183
Coffee (for Supper) 183

## SAVOURIES
Cheese D'Artois 111
  Biscuits 110
  Scones 145
  Straws 109
Sausage Rolls 76
Shrimp Patties 54